Rathjen ● Irish Company

Friedhelm Rathjen

# Irish Company

## Joyce & Beckett
## and more

2021

Versions of parts of this book have previously appeared in the following publications: *Beckett's Literary Legacies* (Newcastle: Cambridge Scholars Publishing), *A Collideorscape of Joyce: Festschrift for Fritz Senn* (Dublin: Lilliput), *In Principle, Beckett is Joyce* (Edinburgh: Split Pea), *Inside Ireland* (Dublin), *Ireland of the Welcomes* (Dublin), *James Joyce Quarterly* (Tulsa, Oklahoma), *Joyce Studies Annual* (Austin, Texas), *Papers on Joyce* (Sevilla), *An Occasional* (Zurich), *od Joyce'a do literatury* (Kraków: Universitas), *Samuel Beckett Today / Aujourd'hui* (Amsterdam).

## ƎDITION ReJOYCE

Vols. 31-32

2nd printing (first paperback edition)

**Bibliografische Information Der Deutschen Bibliothek:**

Die Deutsche Bibliothek verzeichnet diese Publikation in der Deutschen Nationalbibliografie; detaillierte bibliografische Daten sind im Internet über <www.dnb.de> abrufbar.

© Alle Rechte liegen beim Autor
EDITION ReJOYCE Scheeßel 2010, Südwesthörn 2021
rejoyce@gmx.de
Satz, Titelfoto und Umschlaggestaltung: Friedhelm Rathjen
Herstellung: Books on Demand GmbH, Norderstedt
ISBN 978-3-00-031353-0 (Hardback)
ISBN 978-3-947261-51-2 (Paperback)

# Contents

## III: Getting back

# Prefatory Note

*This Book?!:* is not a continuum! (not simply fractured into white and black and grey pieces by author! For any of them, be it Joyce or Beckett or company, is always someone else, and the same for me: the fellow who talks of the rain; rides on a bicycle; book-worms; stalks through textual groves; annotates; small-talks; writes; man of a thousand thoughts; of fragmenting categories; who sums up; translates; paraphrases; tries to explain; says "In Principle, this is that": that's me and my book!): a tray full of glistening snapshots.

F.R.

# I: Getting there

# Singing Wheels&#42;
## Cycling the Irish Border in 1999

On Boa Island in Lower Lough Erne, only a stone's throw from the Donegal border, a mysterious little statue from pre-Christian times can be spotted on an old cemetery. So far, nobody has yet found out who made this artefact, or for what reason. All the more tempting it is to take this statue as a symbol of the present state of Ireland: it is a janus-faced statue. Both sides are inseparately united, but the two faces stare in quite opposite directions. Could this be the fate of Ireland? On a cycling tour I wanted to find out what, if anything, the border which separates the Irish Republic from Northern Ireland really means today.

Starting point for my trip was Dundalk in the Republic, and my final destination had to be Derry, the northern city which is still called Londonderry by many, although the name has been officially changed back to the shorter version some years ago. The route in between was not really my own decision but rather dictated by political geography: I wanted to cross the border at each of the twenty official check-points identified on my slightly out-of-date touring map, and at a number of unofficial crossing points in between; I wanted to always stay as close to the border as possible, and I wanted to spend more or less equal time on both sides of the border. Including just a few detours caused by insufficient signposting, this all summed up to about 500 kilometres (a bit more than 300 miles), which I managed to cycle in four days. You think this is quite fast? May-be it is, but luckily there was a strong wind blowing from southerly directions. Mind you, I'm speaking of real winds, not of any metaphorical wind of change: hereabouts during the last few centuries people have done so much harm by using metaphorical language that we should really prefer precise and practical speech. The new overriding motto is: pragmatism.

Yes, pragmatism – but how, in sheer practice, do you find out where to use Irish punts and where payment should be in sterling? During my trip, more than once I found myself wondering on which side of the border I was. How do you distinguish both parts of Ireland from each other? On both sides of the border, a daily mix of sun, wind and sometimes rain makes ditches and fields radiate with bright colours of green; on both sides the small country lanes that every cyclist loves meander through hills and country-sides of a charming gentleness; and on both sides of the border, the lone cyclist finds the people young and old to be extremely cordial and friendly. So, should we care at all on which territory we are?

---

&#42;    First published as the article "What Border? A Cycling Exploration," by Friedhelm Rathjen, in *Inside Ireland* No. 96, Spring 2002, pp. 22 f. A much fuller description in German language has been published in book form as *Singende Fahrradreifen in Ulster: Eine irische Grenzerfahrung* (Scheeßel: Edition ReJoyce, 2004).

I had to care, of course, because this was the point of my trip, after all. So I was always eager to find out where exactly I crossed the border – not always an easy feat. I knew even before I started my journey that there were no border controls any more, but I had prepared myself to take photographs of check-points and smiling border police-men, may-be even of IRA slogans on the walls. Reality, however, looked much better than I had dared to dream of. The border had simply disappeared. When on the shores of Carlingford Lough, somewhere between Omeath and Newry, I crossed from the Republic into Northern Ireland, this was the first but by no means the last instance where my crossing the border went completely unnoticed. Not before I noticed that the signposts looked different did I realize that I actually was on new territory.

During the next few days, this happened again and again. Okay, if I spotted red telephone boxes I knew I was in the north, and if all signposts gave distances in kilo-metres I knew I was back in the south. Sometimes the tarmac somehow changed when I was crossing the border (and contrary to public belief, the better tarmac is not always found in the north), but a number of new roads have even been tarred with complete disregard to state boundaries. The best border indications nowadays are the petrol stations which profit from the price gap between north and south. A few years ago, when both currencies where nearly equal, petrol was cheaper north of the border, but meanwhile things have changed a lot: only a millionaire or a philanthropist would patronize a northern filling station, given the fact that just a few steps down the road petrol is much cheaper. Some clever station owners even run a filling station each on both sides of the border so that they can respond to any fluctuation of currencies at short notice. On the main road from Monaghan (Irish Republic) into Armagh (Northern Ireland) I spotted a *Border Filling Station* located virtually on the bridge spanning River Blackwater which forms the border here.

"Fermanagh welcomes you, ... naturally": I saw a lot of signposts like this one, but never did they welcome me into a new state, always into a new county only, and it was my task to know or find out which county belonged to which territory. Oddest of all were the only official greetings that welcomed me every time I cycled into county Donegal: the fact that I entered new territory was not even mentioned, but in three languages I was told to drive on the left side of the road! Surely no car driver will be able to make his or her way through Northern Ireland without driving on the left already. Yes, and near Belturbet in Cavan, where the bridge into county Fermanagh had been blown up decades ago, I could not only profit from a brand new bridge but also take a rest in the close vicinity of a nice bronze monument declaring "Peace for all." This monument depicts a couple exchanging kisses (and may-be more) in a way that should be a model for things to come.

In Belturbet, people are eagerly waiting for the tourists that could help to set a region on its feet that suffers from major economical problems. "Please mention in your report that everybody is welcome here," a woman in a shop tells me, "and that there's nothing here that has anything to do with troubles." The Fermanagh / Cavan border area, however, although still waiting for more people to come, has always at least had

*Boa Island*

*Station Island, Lough Derg, near Pettigo*

*Dunnamanagh*

*Corranny Lough on the Clones-Fivemiletown Road*

*Border bridge near Clady*

*Kingfisher Trail*

the advantage that this is the Irish lakelands region where even during the worst years of the troubles anglers and skippers went. The number of tourists has slightly increased since just a few years ago the Shannon-Erne waterway (connecting both rivers and providing a gigantic water system exclusively for recreational activities) has been reopened.

During the troubles, things were much worse in more northerly border towns. In the summer of 1986, when Irish writer Colm Tóibín undertook a walk along the whole Irish border, he found Garrison to be a real "ghost town"[1]. Nothing could be farther from reality today: the ugly duckling has grown into a swan, gaining a lot from its fine situation on the shores of huge Lough Melvin and offering visitors a rich variety of accommodation, plus a holiday centre where you can do everything conceivable from water-skiing to mountain-biking. And even in Pettigo, a small town separated into two parts by the border, there is much change for the better. In the early 1990s, Pettigo looked rather shabby and suffered from a high amount of unemployment, but today it has grown quite pretty. Everywhere on the outskirts, there are new bungalows (quite a number of these offering bed & breakfast), and a community employment scheme is trying its best to qualify unemployed on such fields as craftwork, fine food production or tourist guidance. An elderly gentleman on the road whom I confront with old photographs shows quite a lot of enthusiasm: "Oh yes, there's been a lot of change! No problems with the border any more – because it doesn't really exist any longer. Only the weather could be better now!" Well, but the weather could also be a lot worse ...

"There's no border any more": this is the sentence I hear everywhere, on both sides, and it's always a sentence that sounds full of hope. Most people, however, very well realize that things need time to improve. "There's no border any more," my host in Castleblaney tells me, too. "The only border there is is the border between those who have money and those who haven't. There's a lot of money made out of the border" – not by this brave man, apparently.

Castleblaney is situated near the Armagh border, and perhaps this is a problem: for decades, south Armagh had been known as a "bandit country" where British troops were never safe. Until this very day, the people here seem to sympathize with the IRA: I spot some such slogans as "free all POWs" or "disarm the RUC." Even here, however, there are numerous indications of a peaceful change. Slogans of hatred or revenge are virtually non-existent, even in highly-republican areas, and everywhere people are building new houses and new roads. This clearly shows that people here feel at home – normality has returned. "Of course you can't simply forget what happened," people keep telling me, "but we do sincerely hope that our children will grow up into a peaceful world where the old stories don't matter." There's scarcely anyone who does not express hope for the children.

And who could be without hope amid the unbelievably beautiful landscape through which I am cycling, shielded by a clear blue sky? "I used to cycle a lot when I was younger," a filling-station-cum-post-office-attendant had told me earlier in the day,

---

[1]    Colm Tóibín, *Bad Blood: A Walk Along the Irish Border* (London: Vintage, 1994), p. 69.

"and on a fine morning like this one I thought the wheels would sing to me." I nearly start to sing myself, given the fact that the green scenery all around looks like sheer idyll and most people even exceed their usual friendliness as soon as they spot me, the lone cyclist from abroad. Sure, a few heads are shaken, for cycling is not fashionable in Ireland as it used to be in the older days, and even in larger towns it's not always easy to find a cycle shop – but along the border things appear to be a bit better. In Ulster, there's a whole network of excellent long-distance cycling routes, all very well signposted, and always using quiet country lanes. The longest of these, the Kingfisher Trail (370 KM), brilliantly ignores all borders and connects Fermanagh with the southern counties Monaghan, Cavan, Leitrim and Donegal.

In the southern parts of county Tyrone, between Aughnacloy and Fivemiletown, I criss-cross another signposted cycling route, named after novelist William Carleton. Yes, of course I always keep the phalanx of Irish writers in my head while cycling, for literature has always been part of my Irish experience, and the rhythm of my pedalling ideally harmonizes with the metrical foot of well-remembered poetry. Verse written by catholic poets Patrick Kavanagh ("The bicycles go by in twos and threes"[2]) and Seamus Heaney ("And the bicycle ticked, ticked, ticked"[3]) keep me in steady pace while I pass fluttering Union Jacks. Oh yes, this is protestant terrain, but of course it makes no difference any more, all the more so for me as a tourist. There's nothing to scare me away from using the old smugglers' road from Fivemiletown over steep Carn Rock to Clones – and although I have to admit that I was dripping with sweat while climbing up the road, the reason has certainly nothing to do with the fact that Colm Tóibín, when walking along the border in the mid-eighties, was warned about taking this route because he would be likely to run into paramilitary patrols. Gone are the days, and luckily so!

A few kilometres outside Clones, just on the border, I'm looking for the homestead of farmer and writer Eugene McCabe, with whom I have made an appointment. McCabe's novels and stories are set in these borderlands and describe the beauties of the landscape, but also the excesses of violence. What I'm particularly interested in (under the impression of my cycling tour) is the essay "Borderlands," in which Eugene McCabe gives us his personal view: "The haggard field behind our house looks down on Lackey Bridge, a focus for over a decade. American senators have come to take a look, along with taoisigh, tánaistí, prayer groups, Sinn Féin jazz festivals, a persistent road-opening committee and TV crews from all over Europe."[4] After having read these lines, I had imagined to find a huge bridge, spanning a mighty river, but what I really find is only a streamlet with a tiny new construction leading across. Why all this fuss about such a far-from-spectacular bridge? "Well, this has always been just another symbolic

2    Patrick Kavanagh, "Inniskeen Road: July Evening," Frank O'Connor (ed.), *A Book of Ireland* (London and Glasgow: Collins, 1959), p. 59.

3    Seamus Heaney, "A Constabler Calls," *North* (London: Faber, 1971), pp. 66 f., p. 67.

4    Eugene McCabe, "Borderlands," Malcolm Anderson and Eberhard Bort (eds.), *The Irish Border: History, Politics, Culture* (Liverpool: Liverpool University Press, 1999), pp. 1-5, p. 3.

affair," Eugene tells me. And symbolism, this becomes clearer and clearer to me while cycling along the border, is something that we should finally get rid of, at least in these parts of Ireland. So I ceremoniously revoke all my attempts to find the Irish border situation depicted in the janus-headed statue on Boa Island. In fact, the people on both sides of the border do *not* look into opposite directions any more – they all look to where the hope is, they all look ahead.

In his "Borderlands" essay, Eugene McCabe also tells us the true story of a bearded Ukrainian blacksmith, who came to Fermanagh a few years ago, wearing American army surplus combat jacket, duds and cap. When he was told it was unwise to wear such a uniform in this area, the man roared laughing: "I have nothing else to wear … they will have to shoot me."[5] And for six weeks, the Ukrainian crossed the border each day, on foot or bike, and never saw another uniform. "He often said that he found this Border area the loveliest and most peaceful place he had been since leaving Kiev. [...] And the point of this story? If a young stranger can fall in love with our Border country and its people in bad, sad times, how many thousands might come here in the future if the bombs were put away for good and agreement reached?"[6] Meanwhile, this future has come – and the borderlands' rural idyll with its special old-world charm can be witnessed, travelled and enjoyed by lovers of quietude without running any kind of risk, apart from the risk to fall in love with this country, too.

From Eugene McCabe's farm, country lanes run into four different directions – and so criss-crossy is the borderline hereabouts, that it's virtually impossible to reach another human dwelling on any of these roads without crossing the border at least once. Meanwhile, however, this has lost all significance for me, and I don't mind any more on which territory I am. The border between both parts of Ireland is not even an open border any more – it's a non-existent border. This, by the way, also means that there are no unofficial border crossings any more: everyone may go where he or she wants to. At the end of my 500 kilometres, I have crossed the border 35 times, never having been more than 8 KM away from the borderline. But I have not met a single border police-man, soldier or customs officer, let alone paramilitaries. And the wheels of my bike simply don't stop to sing to me.

---

[5]     Ibid.
[6]     Ibid., p. 4

# Walking Donegal with Dylan Thomas*

Fame came early in the short life of Welsh poet Dylan Thomas (1914-53). When he was 20 years of age, he already played his part in London's literary scene of the day. And he already had to pay tribute to the excesses of his rather Bohemian life-style, including heavy drinking on a more or less daily basis. Geoffrey Grigson, a friend of the poet, at last urged Thomas to leave London for a while and made arrangements for a place of retreat. As a result, Dylan Thomas spent the summer of 1935 in Ireland – in a small cottage in Co. Donegal.

"Here in Ireland I'm further away than ever from the permanent world," Thomas tells a friend in a letter written in August 1935. "I'm writing by candle-light all alone in a cottage facing the Atlantic [...] Soon I'm going out for a walk in the dark by myself; that'll make me happy as hell."[1] Still today Donegal seems to be the ideal region to be all by oneself and feel "happy as hell," provided one shares the poet's sense for solitude and a "terribly out-of-the-way and lonely place." Donegal, after all, is the remotest and wildest of all Irish counties, facing the Atlantic to the south, west, and north, and bordering Northern Ireland to the east. Tourists tend to ignore this austere but beautiful part of Ireland and thus miss an overwhelming landscape and seascape which is incomparable to almost any other.

There may seem to be a certain irony in the fact that Grigson chose Ireland, of all places, in his attempts to withdraw alcoholic beverages from Dylan Thomas, but the holiday refuge he found him was so secluded from the world that chances for success were not too bad. "I am," Thomas explains in a letter to still another friend, "ten miles from the nearest human being, with the exception of the deaf farmer who gives me food. And in spite of the sea and the lakes and my papers and my books and my cigarettes (though they're darned hard to get and I've few left of them) and my increasing obsession with the things under the skin, I'm lonely as Christ sometimes and can't even speak to my father on an ethereal wavelength."[2] During the "wild Irish nights," Thomas is thrilled by the fancies and shivers which nourish his writings.

Only once a week Thomas brings himself to walk the ten miles to the next pub, more often than not in tough weather. "It rains and it rains. All the damned seagulls are fallen angels. Frogs and storms and squids and clegs and midges and killing beetles. Dead sheep in the bracken."[3]

---

\* First published as the article "Walking Donegal with Dylan Thomas," by Friedhelm Rathjen, in *Ireland of the Welcomes* Volume 50 No. 3, May – June 2002, pp. 20-27.

[1] Dylan Thomas, The Collected Letters, ed. Paul Ferris (London: Paladin / Grafton, 1987), p. 198.

[2] Ibid., p. 190.

[3] Ibid., p. 191.

The address given by Dylan Thomas for his holiday resort is "Glen Lough Co. Donegal Meenacross Lifford," which makes it not quite easy to find the exact location where he stayed. Lifford merely names the postal district of Donegal and does not give a clue. If you're lucky and own a good map, you'll be able to find a place called Meenacross on the shore of Trawenagh Bay, about 13 miles to the north of Ardara – but beware! This is the wrong Meenacross! Another, even smaller place of the same name is to be found ten miles southwest from Ardara, on the road to Glencolumbkille, and this is where we finally are on the right track. A few miles northwest again, there is a townland called Glenlough, where the Glenlough River comes running down from mountain lakes through a steep and rocky glen into the Atlantic ocean, and on the banks of this small river, sheet no. 10 of the new *Discovery Series* map shows two buildings, far away from any track or road. This, finally, is exactly the place where Dylan Thomas stayed in the summer of 1935.

Originally, this place at the end of the world had been discovered by American artist Rockwell Kent in the 1920s. Kent had converted an old donkey-sty into a makeshift studio, but finally abandoned it again when he got weary of too much solitude. This former studio is the cottage which Dylan Thomas rented in 1935. The cottage nearby was occupied by the "deaf farmer" Dan Ward and his Irish-speaking wife Rose, who provided meals and sometimes a bit of poitín (illicit whiskey – Dylan Thomas was not completely abstemious, after all) for the poet. Dylan Thomas went fishing up in the mountain lakes or enjoyed himself down at the seashore, and late at night he joined farmer Dan for a chat in front of the peatfire and listened to the farmer's fairy-tales.

The shortest way to Glenlough (and presumably the one taken by Thomas) is from the village of Straboy over the steep mountains, more or less as the crow flies, but such a footmarch over rough terrain can not be recommended to anyone lacking a superb sense of direction and a good map. It seems preferable instead to start the walk from Port, an abandoned fishing village on the seashore at the end of a small road. If you walk northwards from Port and follow the rugged and breathtakingly beautiful coast, after about an hour's walking you'll reach the mouth of Glenlough River, following which for another twenty minutes will take you to what remains of Dylan Thomas's place of retreat from the summer of 1935.

Or if you prefer, just stay at the seashore and try to imagine Dylan Thomas and his friend Grigson (who stayed with Thomas for the first week) singing out the "Ram of Derbyshire" aloud to the seals, and throwing stones at pebbles onto which they had doodled the features of colleagues and literati they disliked! If you've got personal enemies, maybe this is the place and the way to take revenge! But beware: in the poems Thomas wrote during his Donegal holidays and afterwards, there are mentionings of castaways "riding the sea light on a sunken path,"[4] of "invalid rivals" who "sail on the

---

4  Dylan Thomas, "Grief Thief of Time," *The Poems of Dylan Thomas*, ed. with an introduction and notes by David Jones (New York: New Directions, 2003), p. 127.

level, the departing adventure, to the sea-blown arrival,"[5] and of "the undead water" where "a double angel" spouts "from the stony lockers like a tree on Aran."[6]

If you happen to be a dedicated hill-walker, you may feel tempted to follow the coastline all the way to Maghera on Loughros Beg Bay, where there is a vast stretch of beach and sanddunes that seems ideal for taking a rest after a long and exhausting walk. And exhausting this cliffside walk really is, for you have to climb over the slopes of Slievetooey Mountain, dropping from a height of about 1300 feet directly into the sea.

The coastline from Port to Maghera is part of a 25 miles stretch of jagged rocks, cliffs, stacks, bays and promontories running around the whole Glencolumbkille peninsula from Teelin and Slieve League on its southern to Maghera on its northern shore. It is exactly this coastline of which Murray's 1912 *Guide to Ireland* states that it "can hardly be excelled by any locality in the British Isles."[7] Luckily, little or nothing has changed along this coastline since 1912, so we can still rely on Murray's well-considered judgement. For the experienced and daring walker, there can scarcely be a more rewarding task than a two days' march from Teelin along the sea-shore via Slieve League, Glencolumbkille and Port to Maghera. This is nothing for beginners, though: Slieve League, the highest sea-cliffs in all Europe, includes two 'One Man's Passes' 1800 feet above the roaring ocean, which should be attempted only by walkers who are absolutely vertigo-proof, and a forced march of 15 hours or more surely is not suitable for the lazy, lame or inexperienced, even if divided into two day's walks.

The best place for breaking such a strenuous undertaking is the lovely little seaside town of Glencolumbkille, which offers all types of accommodation. In addition, Glencolumbkille is an early centre of Christianity where prehistoric as well as monastic monuments are to be found in abundance. This is the home of Saint Colmcille; in his honour, a pilgrimage is still performed every year by way of a walk covering 15 stations.

In all frankness it should be said that Dylan Thomas cannot have been delighted to find himself in the vicinity of religious faith and devoutness. It seems that Thomas preferred a pantheistic sense of druidism to Christianity. In one of his letters he bizarrely reflects on the "spiritual anatomy of the worms in Donegal"[8] and mocks the piety of his hosts, saying that he constantly expects to find a crucifix in his soup or a crucified broiler on the tray!

The Glencolumbkille district where Dylan Thomas spent his holidays is only one of at least three parts of Donegal that are suitable for hill-walking. The range of the Derryveagh Mountains up in the north includes Glenveagh National Park (open daily from April to October) and 'the Irish Fujiyama', Mount Errigal, a graceful quartzite cone. Errigal is the highest mountain in Donegal and at the same time one of the best accessible – up to the summit and down again takes less than three hours, and from

---

5   Dylan Thomas, "I, In My Intricate Image," ibid., pp. 128-31, p. 129.
6   Ibid., p. 130.
7   *Murray's Handbook for Ireland*, 1912, as quoted by Tony Whilde & Patrick Simms, *Walk Guide West of Ireland* (Dublin: Gill & Macmillan, 1994), p. 124.
8   Thomas, *The Collected Letters*, p. 192.

Errigal's two tiny peaks almost all of Donegal and much of neighbouring Northern Ireland is within view. Quite contrary to Errigal, the Blue Stacks in southern Donegal are a remote, wet and rocky range lacking all spectacular features but offering a lot of atmosphere to the seekers of loneliness and quietude. Visitors should be warned, however: there is not a single human dwelling and scarcely a road or even track in this rugged upland, navigation is always difficult, and in order not to get lost right away, a good map and a walking guide are absolutely indispensable. (A recommendable guide is David Herman's *Hill Walkers Donegal: 34 Sea-cliff and Hill Routes for the Stroller and Mountaineer*, issued by Shanksmare Publications, Dublin.)

What distinguishes the Glencolumbkille region from the Derryveaghs and the Blue Stacks is that only here high and precipitous mountains rise directly from the sea. The combination of mountain and sea-cliff scenery provides much of the special charm of Dylan Thomas's 1935 holiday resort, and still another note is added by the lakes that nestle high up in the hills. One of these is Lough Anaffrin, a 3000 feet stretch of clear mountain water surrounded by steep walls of solid rock. Strangely enough, the name of this lake when read backwards sounds nearly like Nirvana, and Dylan Thomas indeed made his brave attempts to enter into nothingness. After nightfall, he and his friend Grigson used to struggle uphill to Lough Anaffrin, shout "We are the dead" and wait for the echoes to repeat: "We are the dead, are the dead, the dead!" One night, they did this until they themselves were so frightened by the echoes that they came stumbling down all shivering to find human company again by the fireside in Dan Ward "the deaf farmer's" cottage.[9]

When finally the time came for Thomas to leave, he did something we surely should not repeat if we want the Donegal people to stay the hospitable and friendly hosts they are: he walked away over the mountains and caught the bus without paying for his food and lodging. Never did he return to Donegal – but he came back to Ireland at least once, in August 1946, this time with his wife Caitlin who was of Irish stock. Thomas was supposed to write about the Puck Fair in Killorglin, Co. Kerry, but he never did. He spent "a day on the Blasket: a very calm day, they say: the wind blew me about like a tissue-paper man, and dashed us against the donkeys."[10] Two years before, Thomas had unsuccessfully tried to write a film script version of Maurice O'Sullivan's Blasket Island autobiography *Twenty Years A-Growing*[11] – but that is quite another story and a far way to go from the Donegal experience.

---

[9]  See Paul Ferris, *Dylan Thomas* (Harmondsworth: Penguin, 1978), p. 131.
[10]  Thomas, *The Collected Letters*, p. 603.
[11]  See ibid., pp. 526, 529 f.

# The Joys of Cycling with Beckett*

In 1998, the world's most famous cycling race, the *Tour de France*, started in Dublin and stayed in Ireland for three days before continuing through France and, as always, finishing in Paris. This means that the *Tour* took a course that was similar to Nobel Prize winner Samuel Beckett's course of life: Beckett, who was born in Dublin in 1906, lived most of his life in France and died in Paris in 1989. Moreover, in his earlier years Beckett was a keen cyclist, and bicycles figure prominently in his works. One of the key phrases of the novel *Mercier and Camier* states: "The bicycle is a great good. But it can turn nasty, if ill employed."[1]

Mercier and Camier are trying to leave a city that can be identified as Dublin. After a while, they succeed to get into the mountains, where they part company; in the end, they are both in the city again. Samuel Beckett was born in Foxrock, one of Dublin's suburbs at the foot at the Wicklow Mountains. This means that for him, both the city centre and the mountains were easily accessible on bike. Twenty years ago, before I knew any of Beckett's works, I myself toured Ireland on a bicycle, and on the first day of my tour I crossed the Wicklow Mountains via the old military road, a description of which I later found in Beckett's *Mercier and Camier*:

> A road still carriageable climbs over the high moorland. It cuts across vast turf-bogs, a thousand feet above sea-level, two thousand if you prefer. It leads to nothing any more. [...] None ever pass this way but beauty-spot hogs and fanatical trampers. Under its heather mask the quag allures, with an allurement not all mortals can resist. Then it swallows them up or the mist comes down.[2]

This landscape, Beckett's favourite landscape in all Ireland, surfaces frequently in his writings, and even in his last years Beckett when closing his eyes was transported here: "the old haunts were never more present [...] I walk those backroads with closed eyes"[3]. Walking the mountains was a habit young Beckett adopted from his father, but as an adolescent he preferably used a motorcycle, as Deirdre Bair, his first biographer, reports:

> He was a reckless driver and had been involved in several serious accidents before enrolling at Trinity, but had ruined the machines without harming himself. In helmet and goggles, he flew over the narrow roads and ditches, stony-faced and grim, impervious to the dangers that lay around every curve in the landscape.[3]

* First published as the article "The Joys of Cycling with Beckett," by Friedhelm Rathjen, in *Ireland of the Welcomes* Volume 47 No. 5, September – October 1998, pp. 16-21.

[1] Samuel Beckett, *Mercier and Camier* (London: Calder & Boyars, 1974), p. 72.
[2] Ibid., p. 79.
[3] Samuel Beckett in 1985, as quoted by Eoin O'Brien, *The Beckett Country: Samuel Beckett's Ireland* (Monkstown: Black Cat Press, 1986), p. xxvi.
[3] Deirdre Bair, *Samuel Beckett: A Biography* (London: Pan / Picador, 1980), p. 45.

22

There lay not only dangers, however, but also chances for success: in March 1925, Beckett on his 2.75 h.p. A.J.S. took part in a motorcycling race through the Wicklow Mountains.

When his father Bill bought an automobile, Beckett again changed his vehicle but was less successful. Bair explains:

> several times he lost the use of the car for legal infractions and several times Bill simply forbade him to drive it, which reduced him to the motorcycle when he had one in running condition or, most humiliating of all, to an ordinary bicycle.[4]

This humiliation, needless to say, could have easily put an end to the high esteem in which Beckett held the bicycle, were it not for Beckett's own first *Tour de France*.

Just like I did half a century later, Beckett discovered and explored his land of heart's desire on a cycling tour. In June 1926, he went to France and for a few weeks pedalled through the Loire valley. Right at the beginning he got acquainted with a young American named Charles C. Clarke, and when Clarke returned to Europe the following year, he joined Beckett for some time in Foxrock, from where both friends made several cycling trips into Co. Wicklow. From this time on, the bicycle had regained its place in Beckett's heart and subsequently found its way into the world of his literary works.

Beckett's oeuvre is well known to be marked by bleakness and despair. If a bicycle comes into play, however, there is always a light of hope, joy and even love in these texts. Indeed, Beckett develops a mode of eroticism that is closely linked to the bicycle. In one of the stories of the early volume *More Pricks than Kicks*, the main character Belacqua Shuah on his walk through the Fingal district to the north of Dublin is accompanied by a girl named Winnie. She is trying to seduce Belacqua, but her game is lost after the young man, "who could on no account resist a bicycle"[5], has spotted a bike hidden by its owner in the grass. Belacqua seizes the first opportunity to get rid of Winnie and instead steal the desired vehicle:

> He changed his course and came to where the bicycle lay in the grass. It was a fine light machine, with red tyres and wooden rims. [...] The machine was a treat to ride, on his right hand the sea was foaming among the rocks, the sands ahead were another yellow again, beyond them in the distance the cottages of Rush were bright white. Belacqua's sadness fell from him like a shift. He carried the bicycle into the field and laid it down on the grass.[6]

For Belacqua, it seems, the bicycle is a dearer love companion than a girl, and the same is true of a later one of Beckett's heroes, the narrator of the novel *Molloy*, who affectionately remembers his bicycle and its horn and says:

---

[4]    Ibid., p. 53.

[5]    Samuel Beckett, "Fingal," *More Pricks than Kicks* (London: Pan / Picador, 1974), pp. 21-32, p. 26.

[6]    Ibid., p 29.

What a rest to speak of bicycles and horns. Unfortunately it is not of them I have to speak, but of her who brought me into the world, through the hole in her arse if my memory is correct. First taste of shit.[7]

Molloy, an old tramp who can scarcely move, is unable to love his mother, but his love for the truly Beckettian vehicle can never be shattered:

Dear bicycle, I shall not call you bike, you were green, like so many of your generation. I don't know why. It is a pleasure to meet it again. To describe it at length would be a pleasure. It had a little red horn instead of the bell fashionable in your days. To blow this horn was for me a real pleasure, almost a vice.[8]

Beckett's despairing characters time and again derive pleasure from their bicycles. Moran, the second hero of *Molloy*, muses on the question of what vehicle to use and calls this "the fatal pleasure principle"[9]. After having acquired a bike, he states that he "would gladly write four thousand words on it alone."[10] When he and his son succeed in mounting the bike, Moran is getting really enthusiastic:

Go easy, I said. The wheels began to turn. I followed, half dragged, half hopping. I trembled for my testicles which swung a little low. Faster! I cried. [...] Happily it was downhill. Happily I had mended my hat, or the wind would have blown it away. Happily the weather was fine and I no longer alone. Happily, happily.[11]

This incident of happiness, although not without dangers for Moran's erotic drive (see his fear for his "testicles"), is quite a rare moment in Beckett's work, and it would never have existed without the bike.

Dealing with his bike and horn is "a real pleasure, almost a vice," says Molloy, but unfortunately bicycles disappear from Beckett's work after this. Malone, Molloy's successor in the trilogy of Beckett's novels, resumes that he would have like to talk about his bicycle bell, one of his last possessions, but is unable to do so any more. In Beckett's work, the bicycle has to vanish because Beckett's characters lose any capability to move.

A bike means joy, pleasure and hope – but only as long as Beckett's characters are able to ride it. There are a few instances where bicycles are used dysfunctionally. Mercier and Camier for some time own a bike but never ride on it; after they lose it, their friend-ship disintegrates. In the novel *Watt*, there is a man carrying his bike up and down the stairs in a railway station, instead of being carried by it. At the end of the same novel, another bike is transported by train and owned by a person named Miss Walker. All this,

---

[7]  Samuel Beckett, *Molloy*, *The Beckett Trilogy* (London: Pan / Picador, 1979), pp. 7-162, p. 17. (Later in the novel, when stuck in a place called Shit, Moran sends his son into a town called Hole in order to acquire a bicycle.)

[8]  Ibid.

[9]  Ibid., p. 91.

[10]  Ibid., p. 143.

[11]  Ibid., p. 145.

of course, means that the bicycle's main function is perverted and therefore the joys of cycling are beyond reach.

Another kind of cycling connection can be reported for Beckett's most famous play, *Waiting for Godot*. No bicycle appears in this play, but Hugh Kenner in his essay "The Cartesian Centaur" reports that Beckett once, when asked about the meaning of Godot, mentioned

> a veteran racing cyclist, bald, a 'stayer,' recurrent placeman in town-to-town and national championships, Christian name elusive, surname Godeau, pronounced, of course, no differently from Godot.[12]

*Waiting for Godot* surely is not about cycling races, but maybe the play has something to do with what can be called the bicycle principle.

The main point in *Waiting for Godot*, as well as in most of Beckett's works, is that nothing seems to change and something is repeated more or less eternally. These are exercises in repetition and variation – and the same can be said of the motions of the bicycle: its rider is moved through the landscape but does not move in relation to the vehicle. The bicycle's chain and wheels are continuously moving forward but never escape their cyclic nature and always return to where their motion starts. The bicycle for Beckett seems to have been an infinity machine. Cycling enthusiasts know that of all moving animals and machines, the bicycle has been scientifically proven to be the most efficient. Mankind never came closer to the old dream of a *perpetuum mobile* than with this fascinating two-wheel machine. Weather and terrain permitting, a bicycle and its rider can stay in motion for hours on end without exhausting all energies.

Interestingly enough, the mathematical symbol of infinity, the figure 8 turned on its side, looks more or less like a stylized bicycle. Both the bicycle and the infinity symbol comprise of a pair of cycles (or wheels). Beckett aficionados know all too well that the infinity symbol was as dear to Beckett as was the bicycle, and so it seems that both are interconnected. Flann O'Brien's cyclists' novel *The Third Policeman* is not the only Irish work of literature where a bicycle is used as a means for transforming an action into eternity by way of constant repetition – and even Beckett's and O'Brien's German colleague Arno Schmidt, another man of letters who shares an interest both in bicycles and the infinity symbol, knows how to unobtrusively combine a bike with the figure 8. In his novella *Dark Mirrors*, the last of mankind is still cycling in a depopulated world and paying his tribute to Moran's "fatal pleasure principle," to "the great good" that "can turn nasty":

> *The wild May sun was seething so,* I sat down on the pavement beneath it, in the middle of the asphalt, and stretched out my feet (bike in the shade, right? – Why, really?) But I was just too restless after all and pulled myself up again: operating a bike is

---

12    Hugh Kenner, "The Cartesian Centaur," Martin Esslin (ed.), *Samuel Beckett: A Collection of Critical Essays* (Englewood Cliffs: Prentice-Hall, 1965), pp. 52-61, p. 56.

wonderful! And these empty towns lovelier still; I made eight circles at the intersection; when I backpedaled, I stood like a wall.[13]

Why does Schmidt's lonely hero make exactly *eight* circles? It seems that this is his way to enact infinity in a world that has lost all hopes that something like eternity could exist. Although in the succession of Arno Schmidt's works, the bicycle tends to become more of a sex machine and less of an infinity machine[14], the bi-cyclical nature of both the infinity symbol and the bike is always clear to Schmidt, too.

In 1981 Samuel Beckett wrote a short prose piece entitled "The Way" which he never consented to publish. In this text, Beckett twice describes a way running up and down a hill, a footpath shaping the figure 8: "The way wound up from foot to top and thence on down another way."[15] The first part of this text bears the figure 8 as its title; the second and final part's title is the infinity symbol. There is no bicycle in this text, but the shape of the infinite way up and down a barren hill is the shape of Beckett's favourite vehicle. Beckett has finally managed to translate the bicycle principle into landscape itself, into his favourite landscape of Irish hills through which he steers a never-ending course: "In unending ending or beginning light. Redrock underfoot. So no sign of remains a sign that none before. No one ever before so —"[16]

This may sound a little bit too abstract, but the reader may forgive me if I close on a personal note. Beckett's never-ending way through the hills of Irish counties Dublin and Wicklow is exactly the course which I took up when I started my cycling tour around Ireland twenty years ago. I'm still cycling. For me, Ireland is the ideal terrain for pedalling, and reading Beckett has deepened my understanding of what this means. It does not seem likely that the heroes of *Tour de France* will come back to Ireland, but I always will yes I will Yes.

---

[13]     Arno Schmidt, *Dark Mirrors, Nobodaddy's Children*, trans. John E. Woods (Normal, IL: Dalkey Archive Press, 1995), pp. 177-236, p. 185.

[14]     See my article "'Fahrräder: die schönsten Maschinen!' Zum Radfahren bei Arno Schmidt," Frank Legl (ed.), *Zettelkasten 17: Aufsätze und Arbeiten zum Werk Arno Schmidts: Jahrbuch der Gesellschaft der Arno-Schmidt-Leser 1988* (Wiesenbach: Bangert & Metzler, 1988), pp. 123-52, rpt. in Friedhelm Rathjen, *Der Ernst des Lesens: Beinharte Forschung zu Arno Schmidt & Consorten* (Scheeßel: Edition ReJoyce, 2006), pp. 41-60.

[15]     Samuel Beckett, typescript of unpublished text "The Way," facsimile in Carlton Lake (ed.), *No Symbols Where None Intended: A Catalogue of Books, Manuscripts, and Other Material Relating to Samuel Beckett in the Collection of the Humanities Research Center* (Austin: Humanities Research Center, 1984), p. 193; also included in my booklet *Samuel Beckett & seine Fahrräder: Ein treffliches, leichtes Gerät mit Holzfelgen und roten Reifen* (Darmstadt: Häusser, 1996), p. 44.

[16]     Ibid.

# What Happened to Joyce in Galway and Connemara?*
## An Attempt to Baedekerize James Joyce

Joyce Country is the name traditionally used for designating the north-eastern part of Connemara, a region bordering the Maumturk Mountains to the south-west, the Partry Mountains to the north and the narrow spit of land between Lough Corrib and Lough Conn to the east. Rarely is this peaceful and lovely region mentioned in travellers' guides, but if it is, sometimes you can find the absurd remark that the Joyce Country was "made famous by the renowned Irish writer, James Joyce."[1] Nothing could be less true.

In a way, James Joyce was not even an Irish writer at all – he always was and remained a Dublin writer. When Joyce left Dublin in 1904 to live on the continent for the rest of his life, he had scarcely ever seen anything of the rural Ireland 'beyond the pale'. His one and only connection with 'real Ireland' was his beloved and future wife Nora Barnacle who accompanied him to the continent: Nora came from the west, from Galway. It seems that Joyce indeed had to leave his home country in order to take some interest in its western parts. In Trieste on the shores of the Adriatic Sea he began to listen to Nora's songs and stories. Also in Trieste, he earned some irregular money by writing articles for the local *Piccola della Sera* on the so-called 'Irish question' – articles in which Joyce pretended to have the expertise that in reality he quite obviously lacked.

Only twice, in 1909 and again in 1912, did Joyce make an attempt to see the west of Ireland himself. In 1909, he stayed in Dublin for some time in order to establish the very first Irish cinema, being paid for by Triestine businessmen. At the end of August, Joyce and his son Giorgio undertook a trip to Nora's home in Galway. Before going, Joyce told Nora in a letter (dated 21 August) how concerned he was about not being able to afford the trip:

> I wrote today to your mother but really I don't want to go. They will speak of you and the things unknown to me. I dread to be shown even a picture of you as a girl for I shall think 'I did not know her then nor she me. When she sauntered to mass in the morning she gave her long glances sometimes to some boy along the road. To others but not to me.' [...] I am absurdly jealous of the past.[2]

---

\* First published as the article "What Happened to Joyce in Galway and Connemara? An Attempt to Baedekerize James Joyce," by Friedhelm Rathjen, in *Papers on Joyce* No. 6, 2000, pp. 59-65.

[1] *Irland* (Bindlach: Gondrom, 1987), p. 54; my translation from German.

[2] James Joyce, *Letters of James Joyce*, vol. II, ed. Richard Ellmann (New York: Viking Press, 1966), p. 237. – James Joyce, *Selected Letters of James Joyce*, ed. Richard Ellmann (New York: Viking Press, 1975), p. 160.

If Joyce did not overcome his jealousy of the past, he at least overcame the financial difficulties by means of a quite typical Joycean artifice. He had a pack of visiting-cards printed for himself, identifying him as a staff member of the *Piccolo della Sera*, produced one of the cards at the Midland Railways' counter and scrounged a complimentary ticket to Galway by pretending to work on a series of articles about Ireland and promising to write at least one piece about Galway (which, of course, he never intended to do).

Having arrived in Galway, coward Joyce was not so sure if Nora's relatives would really like to see him, so he sent four year old Giorgio ahead of himself and waited across the street until it was clear that he was welcome. Joyce's trip to Galway proved a great success. The young writer was called "Shames Showe" and "The Man with the X-ray Eyes"[3] by everybody and proudly walked along Galway Bay with Nora's sister Kathleen. He was put up for the night by Nora's uncle Michael Healy in Dominick Street, from where on 26 August he wrote a letter card to Nora musing about the strangeness of life, telling her that he intended next day to see the house where Nora had lived with her grandmother and to have a look into Nora's old room on the pretext of wanting to buy the property. Perhaps, he told Nora, they might both return to Galway together the next year: "You will take me from place to place and the image of your girlhood will purify again my life."[4]

Galway, which at that time was a town of no more than 15,000 inhabitants, opened up a completely new world for Joyce, who plunged right into it and even forgot about his chronic health problems. Here at last he had found a key not only to the unknown west of Ireland but also to Nora's hidden past. Back in Dublin, he wrote to his "little Galway bride" Nora telling her of the tears in his eyes after having heard Nora's mother sing out "The Lass of Aughrim" to him.[5]

Annie Barnacle's home in Galway in which this happened can still be seen today, nearly unchanged, in no. 8 Bowling Green. Two enthusiastic Galway ladies have turned the house into a small museum, the Nora Barnacle House, open daily in the summer season. This is the ideal place to commemorate Nora Barnacle Joyce, great lifetime companion to a great writer.

Joyce's being so moved by hearing "The Lass of Aughrim" results from his having known part of the song from Nora already and having used it before in his masterly story, "The Dead." This story, based on Nora's Galway memories, centres on the main character Gabriel Conroy's being jealous of Michael Furey, a boy loved by Gabriel's wife Gretta years ago and subsequently having died because of her – a really heart-rending Irish wild-west story. In the story, Gabriel refuses to make the journey west and instead turns his eyes towards Europe; Joyce himself, however, seems to have discovered through his trip to Galway that his despising rural Ireland was to harsh an

---

3    John Garvin, *James Joyce's Disunited Kingdom and the Irish Dimension* (Dublin: Gill and Macmillan, 1976), p. 108.

4    Ibid., p. 164.

5    Ibid., p. 165. – *Letters of James Joyce*, vol. II, p. 242.

attitude and there was something he had to make up for. Apparently he planned to spend a belated honeymoon with Nora in County Galway.

Three years passed, however, before the next Joycean trip to Galway occured – and this time the trip was made by Nora and daughter Lucia. Joyce stayed in Trieste, boasted his independence and newly gained bachelorhood for a few days – but then his loneliness made him collapse. Soon he had scrounged the fare for the trip, and the whole family was united for four full weeks in the west of Ireland. Proudly Nora told her sister-in-law Eileen in a letter (dated 14 August 1912) that "all the people here were talking about him for running after me"[6].

Joyce and Nora went to the Galway Races and enjoyed themselves, although the weather could have been better, as Nora noted:

> we would enjoy it more if we had not such bad weather every second day rainy when its not rainy we usually go to the beach in the morning. the air is splendid here and the food Jim Georgie and myself are sleeping in my Uncle's Lucia sleeps with mother you'd be surprised at how homely she has got [...] the two children love the place they are all out all day they dont give themselves time to eat Jim is also very much improved and myself [...].[7]

On dry days, Joyce, although not quite sportsmanlike, even exercised himself by rowing on the River Corrib. When it rained, he took to writing, the first result being an article entitled "The City of the Tribes" which Joyce soon after submitted to the *Piccolo della Sera*, thus belatedly keeping his old promise to Midland Railways, after all.

It should be noted, however, that Joyce's article is a rather superficial account of Galway's great past. The first sentence reflects the prejudice that Joyce himself had overcome only recently:

> The lazy Dubliner, who travels little and knows his country only by hearsay, believes that the inhabitants of Galway are descendants of Spanish stock, and that you can't go four steps in the dark streets of the City of the Tribes without meeting the true Spanish type, with olive complexion and raven hair.[8]

Perhaps the best part of the article is the impressionistic last paragraph: "The evening is quiet and grey. From the distance, beyond the waterfall, comes a murmur. It sounds like the hum of bees around a hive. It comes closer." This murmur is produced by distant bagpipes, "playing a vague and strange music."[9]

Joyce and Nora also undertook a day trip to the Aran Islands, and although a day is scarcely enough time to get a full impression of these isles, again Joyce scribbled down an article for his Triestine paper: "The Mirage of the Fisherman of Aran." Not

---

[6]    Ibid., p. 302.
[7]    Ibid.
[8]    James Joyce, "The City of the Tribes: Italian Echoes in an Irish Port," *The Critical Writings of James Joyce*, ed. Ellsworth Mason and Richard Ellmann (New York: Viking Press, 1959), pp. 229-33, p. 229.
[9]    Ibid., p. 233.

surprisingly, this article does not show the depth and understanding that can be found in John Millington Synge's famous book *The Aran Islands*, written a few years earlier. It seems that Joyce tried to imitate Synge's characteristic tone, but of course Synge had spent several months on the islands before being able to write his book. Small wonder, then, that what is most impressive in Joyce's article is his description of the journey out:

> The little ship carrying a small load of travellers [...] leaves the little port of Galway and enters open water, leaving behind on its right the village of Claddagh, a cluster of huts outside the wall of the city. A cluster of huts, and yet a kingdom. Up until a few years ago the village elected its own king, had its own mode of dress, passed its own laws, and lived to itself. The wedding rings of the inhabitants are still decorated with the king's crest: two joined hands supporting a crowned heart.[10]

Apparently Joyce did not know that the Claddagh ring had been designed by a Galway goldsmith named William Joyce – had he known it, he would surely not have failed to mention this.

The huts of Claddagh village have been demolished in 1932 in favour of a new housing-estate, but this is not the only reason why it's so hard today to imagine the atmosphere which Joyce encountered in Galway. In 1912, Galway had been in decline for about a century already, whereas today Galway is Ireland's boomtown. If we want to find traces of what Joyce saw nearly 80 years ago, we have to turn to Galway's more unspectacular corners. One of these is Rahoon cemetery, about 1.5 miles west of the city centre. If you enter the cemetery through the old gate and turn your attention to the third grave on the left-hand side, a huge vault-like structure, you will be able to decipher the name of Michael Maria Bodkin, died in the year 1900, aged 20 years. This Michael Bodkin was Nora Barnacle's early admirer, the real-life model for Michael Furey in Joyce's story "The Dead." In 1912, Joyce and Nora visited the grave. Nora had tears in her eyes, and Joyce later wrote about this in his poem "She weeps over Rahoon":

> Rain on Rahoon falls softly, softly falling,
> Where my dark lover lies.
> Sad is his voice that calls me, sadly calling,
> At grey moonrise.[11]

In the story "The Dead," written long before, the dead boy's grave is transferred to the cemetery of Oughterard, a small village about which *Murray's Handbook for Ireland* in 1906 said: "With the exception of the enormous Union Workhouse, it does not contain anything worth notice."[12] For Joyce, of course, there was another exception, and

---

[10]   James Joyce, "The Mirage of the Fisherman of Aran: England's Safety Valve in Case of War," *The Critical Writings of James Joyce*, pp. 229-33, p. 229.

[11]   James Joyce, "She weeps over Rahoon," *Pomes Penyeach and other verses* (London: Faber 1966), p. 16.

[12]   *Murray's Handbook for Ireland*, 1906, as quoted by Nathan Halper, "The Grave of Michael Bodkin," *James Joyce Quarterly* 12.3 (Spring 1975), p. 278.

so on Sunday, 4 August 1912, he pedalled 35 miles by bike to see the cemetery. Afterwards he told his brother Stanislaus that the cemetery looked exactly like he had described it in his story – and he added delightedly that he had discovered the grave of one J. Joyce. This, however, seems hardly a miracle in a region where Joyce is one of the most frequent surnames.

The day after he had been to Oughterard, Joyce made another trip into rural Connemara, this time to the tiny village of Clifden far in the west, in order to visit the famous Marconi wireless station and interview Marconi himself for the *Piccolo della Sera*. Guglielmo Marconi had founded the station in 1907 and from here telegraphed the first transatlantic wireless messages to Cap Breton, Canada. The station consisted of about twenty buildings and a narrow-gauge railway which transported everything that was needed from Clifden to the station's site in the bog of Derrigimlagh. Unfortunately only ruins remain today. The Marconi station was burnt down by IRA activists in 1922.

Joyce did not succeed in 1912 to interview Marconi – maybe he did not even find the station. So he could not write another article for his newspaper in Trieste. In Joyce's enigmatic last novel *Finnegans Wake*, however, we can spot a few references to the "mightif beam maircanny"[13] (combining 'mighty beam' and 'might have been, Marconi'): "as softly as the loftly marconimasts from Clifden sough open tireless secrets [...] to Nova Scotia's listing sisterwands. Tubetube!"[13]

Clifden is about fifty miles away from Galway, so it seems clear that James Joyce did not cycle all the way through Connemara. He was lucky enough to be able to rely on the service of the Galway to Clifden railway line, opened in 1895 and closed down in 1935. Joyce must have made the trip via Maam Cross, Recess and the small station at Ballynahinch. Ballynahinch castle, which today houses a four-star hotel, in 1912 still was the homestead of the Martin family, one of the 'fourteen tribes' of Galway.

It is a pity that Joyce did not report on his trip into rural Connemara, even if it seems clear that a report from Joyce would not have been as well-informed as the reports written by John Millington Synge seven years before. Synge travelled through Connemara and Mayo in 1905, accompanied by painter Jack B. Yeats. Maybe Joyce's attempts at travel-writing for the *Piccolo della Sera* were half-hearted attempts to emulate Synge's reports for a British newspaper. On the other hand Joyce would not have been able to see Connemara with other eyes than that of a stranger – his one and only key to the Ireland 'beyond the pale' was Nora, his "little Galway bride": her roots he discovered in Galway.

But what about Joyce's own family roots? What about the Joyce Country? Joyce's father, after all, all his lifetime stuck to the notion that he was a descendant of the Joyces of Galway, one of the fourteen tribes. James Joyce, however, made no attempt to take up this history when the railway carried him through Maam Cross, only a stone's throw from the Joyce Country.

---

[13]    James Joyce, *Finnegans Wake* (London: Faber, 1975), 408.16.
[13]    Ibid., 407.20.

*Bowling Green, where Nora Barncacle grew up, and the River Corrib in Galway*

*Lough Nafooey in the Maamtrasna region of Connemare, the heart of the Joyce country*

Let us nevertheless pay a visit to the Joyce River's green valley and contemplate the magic hidden in the name of Joyce – there is still a chance to bring the story full circle. Halfway between Maam and Leenane, there is a small road to the right-hand side leading past Lough Nafooey, until we reach Maamtrasna. Just here, on the border of counties Galway and Mayo, a Welsh Norman settled at the end of the 13th century: Thomas de Joise, progenitor of the Joyce tribe. And just here, in Maamtrasna, a bloody crime occured in 1882, the year James Joyce was born.[14]

During a night in August, 1882, a family called Joyce was murdered – only 9 year old Patsy survived, severely wounded. There were three informers, also called Joyce, and within a few days, ten men were arrested. Two of these acted as Queen's evidences and were released; five men made a confession in order to save their lives. The remaining three kept protesting their innocence and were finally sentenced to death: Patrick Joyce, Patrick Casey and, above all, Myles Joyce, who subsequently became something of a martyr in local folklore, since the trial was pushed through rather scandalously.

James Joyce must have heard a popular version of this murder case rather early from Nora, for in 1907 already – i.e., before he himself travelled to the west of Ireland – he wrote an article about the case for the *Piccolo della Sera*, entitled "Ireland at the Bar." In this article, Joyce uses Myles Joyce as the prototype of the Irish backwoodsman falling victim to the English occupants' injustice. James Joyce, either being misinformed of deliberately distorting facts, clearly overshoots the mark in his attempt to stand up for his namesake Myles Joyce[15], but his overall message becomes clear at the end of the article: "There is less crime in Ireland than in any other country in Europe."[16]

This, at least, is the overall impression that we get when we today travel Connemara in general and the Joyce Country in particular: this is sheer idyll, peaceful and quiet. We cannot resist the temptation to climb one of the mountains alongside the Joyce River valley, lay down in moss and heather, peep up into the sky and imagine James Joyce finding himself a resting-place in Connemara like his old crony Oliver St John Gogarty, who settled in nearby Renvyle House.

Unimaginable? Well, maybe. The Joycean holidays in Galway ended unpleasantly. There was news from Trieste saying that Joyce's Irish teacher's certificate was not accepted and that his landlady had evicted him. In Dublin his attempts to get his collection of short stories, *Dubliners*, published failed. Frustrated, Joyce turned his back to his native Ireland, never to come back.

And even the goodwill he had shown in the case of poor Myles Joyce was gone, and James Joyce again tended to associate the west of Ireland with poteen (illicit whiskey), violence, dirt and peatsmoke. In *Finnegans Wake*, we can find details of the Maamtrasna murders in the episode dealing with a certain Festy King (Irish Joycean

---

[14] For a detailed account of the case, see Jarlath Waldron, *Maamtrasna: The Murders and the Mystery* (Dublin: Edmund Burke, 1992).

[15] Details of Joyce's misconception are listed by Christine O'Neill-Bernhard, "Symbol of the Irish Nation, or of a Foulfamed Potheen District: James Joyce on Myles Joyce," *James Joyce Quarterly* 32.3/4 (Spring / Summer 1995), pp. 712-21.

[16] James Joyce, "Ireland at the Bar," *The Critical Writings of James Joyce*, pp. 197-200, p. 200.

John Garvin holds that Joyce might have read the name Festus King on a shop front in Clifden while looking for the Marconi station in 1912[17]). The "wasnottobe crime conundrum" now is acted out as follows:

> a child of Maam, Festy King, of a family long and honourable associated with the tar and feather industries, [...] gave an address in old plomansch Mayo of the Saxons in the heart of a foulfamed potheen district [...].[18]

Just before this, Joyce mentions "blackfaced connemaras"[19], which is a breed of sheep popular in the west of Ireland. Well, James Joyce indeed never managed to get into the Joyce Country. He will never know what he has missed.

---

[17]   See Garvin, p. 161.
[18]   Joyce, *Finnegans Wake*, 85.22-26.
[19]   Ibid., 76.1.

# James Joyce as a Cyclist*

In the "Ithaca" episode of *Ulysses*, "cycling on level macadamised causeways" is subsumed under "lighter recreations"[1], but cycling is not only a recreation, it is a facility of transit, too. "What facilities of transit were desirable?"[2] The answer is twofold: "When citybound frequent connection by train [...]. When countrybound velocipeds, a chainless freewheel roadster cycle with side basketcar attached"[3].

In the summer of 1912, James Joyce journeyed "countrybound": from Galway, the home-town of his companion Nora Barnacle, he made two trips into rural Connemara, the first one (on Sunday, 4 August) to Oughterard, 17 miles from Galway, in order to see the graveyard playing a prominent role in "The Dead," and the second one (on Monday, 5 August) to Clifden, no less than 49 miles from Galway, in order to visit the transatlantic wireless station in the bog of Derrygimlagh and conduct an interview with its founder, the famous Italian Guglielmo Marconi.[4] What "facilities of transit" could have been "desirable" for Joyce for these two trips? For the first one, the 34 miles' journey to Oughterard and back on a sunny Sunday, a "velocipede" seems to be quite adequate, but can anyone who is familiar with Joyce's bodily shape imagine the thirty year old writer do the second trip on a bicycle, too? This would have meant a return journey of nearly one hundred miles all in all, quite a feat for non-practised riders even on good tarmac[5], and in 1912 the road from Galway to Clifden did not everywhere really resemble a "level macadamised causeway" but rather consisted mainly of potholes and gravel.

---

*    First published as the article "James Joyce as a Cyclist," by Friedhelm Rathjen, in *Joyce Studies Annual* Volume 2003, pp. 175-82. Copyright © 2003 by the University of Texas Press. All rights reserved.

[1]  James Joyce, *Ulysses: The Corrected Text*, ed. Hans Walter Gabler (Harmondsworth: Penguin, 1986 [Student's Edition], 17.1592-3.

[2]  Ibid., 17.1573.

[3]  Ibid., 17.1574-6.

[4]  Guglielmo Marconi (1874-1937), who had installed the radio station (the first one to transmit wireless messages from Europe to America) just five years before, was a real celebrity at that time, having received a Nobel prize in 1909. It is a nice coincidence that the Public Gardens in Trieste, where there is a bust of Joyce today, are bordered by a street bearing the name "Via Guglielmo Marconi."

[5]  I am speaking from experience. I have undertaken quite a few cycling trips through all parts of Ireland since 1978, but the longest distance I ever managed to cycle in one day was a strenuous ride of ninety miles into Derry on the last day of zigzagging the Irish border in early October 1999 – the next day I was suffering from a severe tendinitis. See Friedhelm Rathjen, "Die Grenzerfahrung: Von Dundalk nach Derry an der 'Border' entlang," *irland journal* 10.6 (November 1999), pp. 24-39; Friedhelm Rathjen, "What Border?: A Cycling Exploration," *Inside Ireland* 96 (Spring 2002), pp. 22 f., rpt. as "Singing Wheels: Cycling the Irish Border in 1999" in the present collection, pp. 11-16.

One hundred miles by bike: Tour de France champion Lance Armstrong will manage to ride this distance in just four hours, but non-racing cyclists on holiday trips usually need twice as long, plus some extra time for pausing, eating, drinking, and sightseeing. James Joyce, who quite in contrast to his subsequent friend and disciple Samuel Beckett (who was a keen cyclist in his younger years[6]) never excelled as a sportsman, clearly cannot have cycled from Galway to Clifden and back on that August day in 1912. Why, then, do almost all his biographers tell us that he did?

The first one to have dealt with this matter is Herbert Gorman. In *James Joyce* (first published in 1939), he writes about Joyce's summer of 1912:

> Joyce enjoyed life very much in Galway. He rowed and cycled and drove about the countryside, observing with pleasure the freshness of the fields and the simplicity of the natives. At Oughterard he visited the little graveyard he had pictured in his long short story, "The Dead," and discovered there a headstone with the name "J. Joyce" engraved upon it. [...] The only writing he did was two articles on the Aran Islands for the *Piccolo della Sera*. An idea that he conceived of interviewing Marconi for the Triestine journal came to nothing, it being impossible to get into direct touch with the great Italian inventor of wireless telegraphy. This was his one and only visit to the so-called Joyce country in Connemara.[7]

As we see here, Gorman mentions Joyce's rowing and cycling exercises, but does not pretend to know how Joyce managed to get to Clifden. Judging from a few details (especially the "J. Joyce" anecdote), it seems that Gorman had access already to Joyce's correspondence with his brother Stanislaus. On 7 August 1912, Joyce wrote a letter to Stannie which seems to be the one and only source for all the cycling details to be found in later commentaries. In this letter James Joyce writes:

> I went to Clifden on Monday to interview Marconi or see station. Could do neither and am waiting reply from Marconi House London. [...] I cycled to Oughterard on Sunday and visited the graveyard of *The Dead*. It is exactly as I imagined it and one of the headstones was to J. Joyce.[8]

---

[6]  See Friedhelm Rathjen, *Samuel Beckett & seine Fahrräder: Ein treffliches leichtes Gerät mit Holzfelgen und roten Reifen* (Darmstadt: Häusser, 1996), rpt. as "Becketts Fahrräder: Von Last und Lust zwischen Lenker und Tretlager" in Friedhelm Rathjen, *weder noch: Aufsätze zu Samuel Beckett* (Scheeßel: Edition ReJoyce, 2005), pp. 19-43; for an abbreviated and simplified English version, see Friedhelm Rathjen, "The Joys of Cycling with Beckett," *Ireland of the Welcomes* 47.5 (September – October 1998), pp. 16-21, rpt. in the present collection, pp. 21-26.

[7]  Herbert Gorman, *James Joyce* (New York: Rinehart & Company, 1948), 210. Of course Gorman is wrong in what he says about the two articles Joyce wrote for the *Piccolo della Sera*: only one of these is about the Aran Islands ("The Miracle of the Fisherman of Aran"), the other one deals with Galway ("The City of the Tribes").

[8]  James Joyce, *Letters of James Joyce*, vol. II, ed. Richard Ellmann (New York: Viking Press, 1966), pp. 299 f.

Here Joyce mentions *both* his trips into Connemara, but only for one of these, the (much shorter) one to Oughterard, the bicycle is identified as being his means of transport.

If things seem to be quite clear so far, the mixing-up of details starts with Richard Ellmann's Joyce biography, first published in 1959. Ellmann does not mention Marconi and the trip to Clifden at all, but he extracts the following information from the letter quoted above:

> Joyce took up rural sports; he rowed and one Sunday bicycled forty miles. The pain in his side did not trouble him. He and Nora went together to Galway Races and, more lugubriously, he paid a visit by bicycle to the graveyard at Oughterard, seventeen miles away [...].[9]

Ellmann here suggests that there were at least two cycling trips: one on a Sunday over the distance of forty miles, and another one to Oughterard, "seventeen miles away." The truth is, as we have seen in Joyce's letter, that the Oughterard trip was the only cycling trip, so Ellmann makes a dubious (and perhaps even conscious) double mistake by (1) exaggerating the length of the trip to Oughterard and back and (2) using Joyce's singular cycling exercise twice.

This instance of a more or less deliberate confusion of facts (resulting either from sloppy reading or from sloppy writing) was not to remain without effects. One of these is that Daniel von Recklinghausen, who published a chronicle of Joyce's life and works in 1968, summarized the Joyces' holidays in Galway thus: "Joyce and Nora undertake a short journey to the Aran Islands (between 17 July and 7 August) and cycling trips to Clifden as well as to Oughterard cemetery, where an old flame of Nora's is buried."[10] Another victim of Ellmann's sloppiness is Brenda Maddox, who in her biography *Nora* does not mention the trip to Clifden, but writes about the shorter trip: "By bicycle Joyce cycled the fourteen miles to Oughterard and visited the graveyard of 'The Dead'."[11] Apparently Maddox mixes up Ellmann's distances: "forty" and "seventeen" converge into "fourteen"!

The next step on the way from truth to fiction is achieved by Peter Costello, who in *James Joyce: The Years of Growth 1882-1915* relates the whole affair as follows:

---

[9]   Richard Ellmann, *James Joyce*, rev. ed. (New York: Oxford University Press, 1982), p. 324 – There are some changes in the context of this passage in the second edition of Ellmann's biography (1982) from which I quote here, but these changes mainly refer to the real burial place of Michael Bodkin (in 1959, Ellmann did not yet know that such a grave existed at Rahoon cemetery) and do not affect the lines quoted, apart from the fact that the "seventeen miles" which are not in the text of the first edition (see *JJI* 335) are added. Apparently Ellmann was so confused by his own phrasing that he forgot what the "forty miles" had originally meant. The only source Ellmann gives for the information quoted is Joyce's letter to Stanislaus of 7 August.

[10]  My translation from Daniel von Recklinghausen, *James Joyce – Chronik von Leben und Werk* (Frankfurt am Main: Suhrkamp Verlag, 1968), p. 48.

[11]  Brenda Maddox, *Nora: A Biography of Nora Joyce* (London: Hamish Hamilton, 1988), p. 165.

Joyce also improved in the fresh western air; he rowed on the Corrib River some days. The pains he had complained of in Trieste were not heard of here. [...] Cycling 100 miles, through the Joyce Country to the western seaboard, Joyce interviewed the Italians involved with the Marconi transatlantic Radio Station at Clifden [...]. On Sunday, 4th August, he took himself out on his bicycle to visit the graveyard in Oughterard [...].[12]

Costello seems to have been the first one to check both the exact date of Joyce's Sunday trip and the distance from Galway to Clifden, but this still does not make him suspect that something might be wrong with the impression that Joyce cycled to Clifden, which is all the more astonishing given the fact that at the time of Costello's writing, the defects and deficiencies of Ellmann's Joyce biography had become quite well-known among Joyceans.[13] And even John McCourt, another Irishman (writing from a Triestine point of view, however), in his most recent Joyce biography falls victim again to Ellmann's suggestions by stating: "Meanwhile he [Joyce] was a bundle of energy, managing trips by bicycle to Clifden and Oughterard."[14]

Nathan Halper in an early contribution to the *James Joyce Quarterly* ended up by suspecting: "I think that Joyce never cycled to Oughterard!"[15] His argument seems to be a bit far-fetched, however, and I would like to contradict him by saying that there is no conclusive reason to doubt Joyce's having cycled to Oughterard and back on Sunday, 4 August 1912. But what did Joyce do on the very next day? I am quite sure that if he told Stannie he went to Clifden, he must have done so – but I firmly believe he did not cycle there. I believe he took the train, that other "facility of transit." After all, Joyce was quite used to travelling by train, and especially in Ireland this was a cheap way for him to get around, since he had the habit of scrounging free first-class tickets by producing pasteboard cards identifying him as a staff writer of the *Piccolo della Sera* and promising railways officials to write travel articles about the Irish west[16].

Even though there are scarcely any traces left today, in Joyce's days there was an efficient railway connection from Galway to Clifden. This line had been opened in 1895 and carried many loads of early tourists into the extreme west of Ireland until it was finally closed down in 1935. The journey went via Moycullen, Ross, Oughterard (Joyce really could have done completely without a bicycle), Maam Cross Roads, Recess and the small station at Ballynahinch (the homestead of the Martin family, one of the "fourteen tribes" of Galway). There were two trains daily on this line in 1912, leaving

---

[12]   Peter Costello, *James Joyce: The Years of Growth 1882-1915* (London: Kyle Cathie, 1992), pp. 297 f.

[13]   See Joseph Kelly, "Stanislaus Joyce, Ellsworth Mason, and Richard Ellmann: The Making of *James Joyce*," *Joyce Studies Annual* 3 (1992), pp. 98-140.

[14]   John McCourt, *The Years of Bloom: James Joyce in Trieste 1904-1920* (Dublin: The Lilliput Press, 2000), p. 184.

[15]   Nathan Halper, "The Grave of Michael Bodkin," *James Joyce Quarterly* 12.3 (Spring 1975), p. 280, note 20.

[16]   *Letters of James Joyce*, vol. II, p. 240; Ellmann, *James Joyce*, rev. ed., p. 285.

Galway at 9:00 a.m. and at 2:00 p.m., and the trip took about 80 minutes each way, with stops at all stations.[17]

Given the considerable distance from Galway to Clifden, Joyce's shaky bodily shape and the aspect of time, it seems perfectly obvious that James Joyce must have taken the train to Clifden instead of cycling. I suspected this already in an article about Joyce's adventures in Connemara[18], but only recently I discovered that I was not the first and only one to question the cycling saga. Padraic O Laoi in his slim biography *Nora Barnacle Joyce* describes the whole incident in this way:

> One day Joyce went to Clifden by train with the intention of interviewing the great Marconi and writing an article on him and his radio station for the Italian Press. He was unlucky in the trip as Marconi was out of town just then.[19]

Unfortunately O Laoi does not reveal his sources, so we may wonder if perhaps he had gathered information from relatives and acquaintances of the Barnacle family (the late Padraic O Laoi was parish priest in St. Patrick's in Galway, the parish embracing the Barnacle and Healy homes), or if he as a Galwegian simply found it obvious and beyond doubt that a trip from Galway to Clifden in 1912 would only have been undertaken by train. But be that as it may: I believe that if we carefully consider all evidence and all the questions involved here, there can not be the least doubt that O Laoi's version of the story is the only plausible one.

But what is the point of all this? Is it of any consequence at all for the reader and interpreter of Joyce's works if Joyce went to Clifden by bike or by train, if maybe he employed a donkey-driver or was transported there by a U.F.O.? Of course this question of transport does not change Joyce's texts in the least; it does not change the fact that Joyce did not get a chance to conduct an interview with Marconi ("mightif beam maircanny"[20]) and that Clifden and the extreme west of Connemara remained impenetrable for Joyce ("as softly as the loftly marconimasts from Clifden sough open tireless secrets"[21]). But what I wanted to demonstrate with this modest contribution is this:

---

[17]  I'd like to thank Patrick Larkin (who runs an internet website on the Galway – Clifden line: http://www.geocities.com/athens/atrium/3301/) for information about the timetable in 1912. I am equally indebted to Hermann Rasche (Galway), an expert in railways as well as cycling matters, for various information on the Galway – Clifden line. See also Hermann Rasche, "165 Jahre irische Eisenbahnen: Die 'Midland Great Western Railway': Galway – Clifden," *irland journal* 10.2 (March 1999), pp. 23-27.

[18]  Friedhelm Rathjen, "What Happened to Joyce in Galway and Connemara?: An Attempt to Baedekerize James Joyce," *Papers on Joyce* 6 (2000), pp. 59-65, rpt. in the present collection, pp. 27-34. For a slightly more detailed German version, see Friedhelm Rathjen, "'In the Heart of a Foulfamed Potheen District': James Joyce in Galway und Connemara," *irland journal* 9.4 (December 1998), pp. 18-29, rpt. in Friedhelm Rathjen, *Irische Reise* (Göttingen: Lamuv Verlag, 1999), pp. 107-26.

[19]  Padraic O Laoi, *Nora Barnacle Joyce: A Portrait* (Galway: Kenny's Bookshop and Art Galleries, 1982), p. 90.

[20]  James Joyce, *Finnegans Wake* (London: Faber, 1975), 408.15.

[21]  Ibid., 407.20.

there is still much in the mass of biographical data about Joyce which should not be taken for granted, and there are a lot of rumours and misconceptions about Joyce's life which deserve question marks. Richard Ellmann may have checked wagon-loads of sources when writing his biography of Joyce, but not every sentence in his book has been written really conscious of the fact that someone could draw improper con-clusions, and biographers of the next generations, even if more than willing to correct or supplement Ellmann on major affairs, always tend to copy from him uncritically in minor points. And the lesser known research done by scholars and commentators like O Laoi is always all too easily overlooked. In matters Joycean, there are no "level mac-adamised causeways," and if we think we can freewheel along, we always run the risk of suffering a puncture, perhaps even without noticing.

.

# II: Being there

# Molly Through the Garden / Reaching for the Bloom*

## A Joycean Look at John Eglinton's *Dana* Magazine

Towards the end of the "Scylla and Charybdis" episode of *Ulysses*, John Eglinton assails Stephen Dedalus for being "the only contributor to *Dana* who asks for pieces of silver"[1]. In the real-life Dublin of June 1904, Joyce was not yet a contributor to *Dana* at all; his one selection in the journal can be found in an issue of the same year in a poem entitled "Song"[2], which was to become number 7 in Joyce's *Chamber Music*. It is true, however, that Joyce, unlike all the other contributors, was paid for the poem: he received a guinea for his effort.[3]

"John Eglinton" was, of course, W.K. Magee, and he and Frederick Ryan edited *Dana*, which, fortunately, in 1970, was reprinted in a facsimile edition. Though the reproduction states on the copyright page that it is "for sale and distribution only in the United States," this author luckily found three last copies[4] on the shelves of the Hodges Figgis Bookshop, 57-58 Dawson Street in Dublin, when attending the 1992 Joyce Symposium. Thus the place where the volumes were discovered is not far from the editors' office in 1904, for the note at the bottom of the first three issues' last page runs like this: "Contributions to be addressed to The Editors, DANA, 26, Dawson Chambers, Dawson St., Dublin"[5]. The reader should note that this was the address of the Hermetic Society's Thursday evening meetings, too: "Yogibogeybos in Dawson chambers"[6].

The inventory of books that Joyce made before leaving his Trieste flat lists "*Dana* (Dublin)"[7], and it is obvious that Joyce used the journal for his work on *Ulysses*, especial-

---

* First published as the article "Molly Through the Garden / Reaching for the Bloom: A Joycean Look at Eglinton's *Dana* Magazine," by Friedhelm Rathjen, in *James Joyce Quarterly*, Volume 32, no. 1, Fall 1994, pp. 108-12.

[1] James Joyce, *Ulysses: The Corrected Text*, ed. Hans Walter Gabler (Harmondsworth: Penguin, 1986 [Student's Edition], 9.1081.

[2] See James Joyce, "Song," *Dana: An Irish Magazine of Independent Thought* 4 (August 1904), p. 124. – *Dana* was edited by W.K. Magee (John Eglinton) and Frederick Ryan and was published from May 1904 through April 1905 in Dublin by Hodges Figgis & Company, Ltd. and in London by David Nutt. This short-lived monthly journal has been reprinted as *Dana: An Irish Magazine of Independent Thought* (New York: Lemma Publishing Company, 1970).

[3] Richard Ellmann, *James Joyce*, rev. ed. (New York: Oxford University Press, 1982), p. 165.

[4] One of these copies has been given to Fritz Senn and can be inspected by scholars at the Zurich James Joyce Foundation.

[5] *Dana* 1 (May 1904), p. 32; 2 (June 1904, p. 64; 3 (July 1904), p. 96.

[6] Joyce, *Ulysses*, 9.279.

[7] Ellmann, p. 789.

ly the "Scylla and Charybdis" episode that deals with precisely the kind of literary scene whose facets are so vividly documented in *Dana*. Nearly all of the participants in Joyce's library discussion were contributors to the journal: Eglinton, of course, (who, apart from his editorship, had articles in most issues), A.E. (George Russell, who had poems as well as essays in several issues), T.W. Lyster (whose 1895 lecture on Jane Austen is printed in issues 8-11), and Oliver Gogarty (who has poems in issues 5, 7, and 10). Richard Best was no contributor, but his work for the journal *Eriu* and his translation of Arbois de Jubainville's *Cycle mythologique irlandais*[8] are mentioned in F.M. Atkinson's column "A Literary Causerie"[9].

There are many more hidden parallels, of course. In a "Literary Notice"[10], Gogarty reviews A.E.'s *New Songs* anthology that Lyster refers to in *Ulysses*: "Mr Russell, rumour has is, is gathering together a sheaf of our younger poets' verses"[11]. In this review, Gogarty praises "Mr. Colum's 'Drover', in particular," and the poem is also mentioned in "Scylla and Charybdis": "I liked Colum's *Drover*. Yes, I think he has that queer thing genius"[12]. Douglas Hyde's collection *Lovesongs of Connacht*[13] is mentioned rather critically in Ryan's article "Is the Gaelic League a Progressive Force?" ("I ask myself, is this a step forward of backward?"[14]) and approvingly in Eglinton's "The Best Irish Poem"[15]. W.B. Yeats' "Song of Wandering Aengus"[16] is referred to by Atkinson[17]), and Father Dinneen (in *Ulysses*, "Dineen"[18]) figures prominently in Ryan's "Gaelic League" article[19], as well as in Stephen Gwynn's reply "In Praise of the Gaelic League"[20].

Several contributors to *Dana* are mentioned in one way or another in "Scylla and Charybdis": coeditor Ryan ("Fred Ryan wants space for an article on economics"[21]), James Starkey (who wrote a letter under his own name[22] and poems under the pseudonym Seumas O'Sullivan[23]), George Roberts[24], Edward Dowden[25], and George Moore[26].

8    See Joyce, *Ulysses*, 9.93.
9    F.M. Atkinson, "A Literary Causerie," *Dana* 5 (September 1904), pp. 156-60, p. 157.
10   Oliver Gogarty, "Literary Notice," *Dana* 1 (May 1904), p. 32.
11   Joyce, *Ulysses*, 9.290-1.
12   Ibid., 9.301-3.
13   See Joyce, *Ulysses*, 9.514.
14   Frederick Ryan, "Is the Gaelic League a Progressive Force?" *Dana* 7 (November 1904), pp. 216-20, p. 218.
15   See John Eglinton, "The Best Irish Poem," *Dana* 10 (February 1905), pp. 296-302, p. 298.
16   See Joyce, *Ulysses*, 9.1093.
17   F.M. Atkinson, "A Literary Causerie," *Dana* 10 (February 1905), pp. 314-17, p. 316.
18   Joyce, *Ulysses*, 9.967-8.
19   See Ryan, "Is the Gaelic League a Progressive Force?" passim.
20   See Stephen Gwynn, "In Praise of the Gaelic League," *Dana* 8 (December 1904), pp. 239-44, p. 239.
21   Joyce, *Ulysses*, 9.1082-3.
22   The letter is signed "J. STARKEY, Secretary, Rural Libraries Association. 27, Dawson Chambers, Dawson Street, Dublin" – *Dana* 9 (January 1905), p. 288; this is, of course, almost the same address again as that of the *Dana* office and of A.E.'s Hermetic Society.
23   See Joyce, *Ulysses*, 9.301, 324.
24   See ibid., 9.301.
25   See ibid., 9.730.
26   See ibid., 9.274, 995.

Perhaps the appearance in Eglinton's magazine of some names and topics that are highly significant in a Joycean context is even more interesting: in the pages of *Dana*, we find mention of "the science of Plato and Aristotle"[27], of the Viceroy and "his clattering cavalcade"[28], of the *Freeman's Journal* [29], and repeatedly of Ernest Renan, Thomas Aquinas, Ignatius Loyola, and even Ibsen and William Archer. One of Eglinton's contributions is an article entitled "A Way of Understanding Nietzsche"[30] that may remind us of Buck Mulligan's "I'm the *Übermensch*"[31], just as Atkinson's review of Algernon Swinburne's collected poems – "the most interesting literary event of the moment"[32] – adds further credibility to the Swinburnian echoes in "Scylla and Charybdis" and elsewhere in *Ulysses*. In a similar way, one of O'Sullivan's poems is called "Glasnevin, October 9th 1904"[33], thus referring us to the "Hades" episode. Admirers of Nora Joyce will be pleased to find "the old fable of the barnacle goose"[34] mentioned, and all of us will be happy to know that "[i]n June, 1904, an association was formed in Dublin to promote the establishment of efficient libraries at all suitable places throughout the country"[35].

More or less direct sources for *Ulysses* are few, but these few instances should be at least noted. The June 1904 issue contains A.E.'s article "Religion and Love," which mentions "the mystery of the Logos"[36] (reappearing in the *Ulysses* phrases "magician of the beautiful, the Logos"[37] and "he thrones an Aztec logos"[38]) and the "Great Mother" and "Mighty Mother"[39] referred to in "Telemachus"[40]. Even more important is this from the "Religion and Love" article:

> Spirituality is the power of apprehending formless spiritual essences, of seeing the eternal in the transitory, and in the things which are seen the unseen things of which they are the shadow.[41]

Joyce doubtless alludes to this passage in "Scylla and Charybdis" when he writes, "Art has to reveal to us ideas, formless spiritual essences"[42], and perhaps when he includes in Stephen's interior monologue: "they creepycrawl after Blake's buttocks into eternity of

---

27    Edouard Dujardin, "The Abbé Loisy," *Dana* 1 (May 1904), pp. 18-21, p. 19.

28    Dubliniensis, "On Reasonable Nationalism," *Dana* 4 (August 1904), pp. 99-105, p. 99.

29    See Ryan, "Is the Gaelic League a Progressive Force?" p. 216.

30    See John Eglinton, "A Way of Understanding Nietzsche," *Dana* 6 (October 1904), pp. 182-88.

31    Joyce, *Ulysses*, 1.708.

32    F.M. Atkinson, "Literary Notices," *Dana* 4 (August 1904), pp. 125-28, p. 125.

33    Seumas O'Sullivan, "Glasnevin, October 9th 1904," *Dana* 7 (November 1904), p. 199.

34    F.M. Atkinson, "Literary Notices," *Dana* 3 (July 1904), pp. 93-96, p. 96.

35    F.M. Atkinson, "A Literary Causerie," *Dana* 11 (March 1905), pp. 346-48, p. 347.

36    Æ, "Religion and Love," *Dana* 2 (June 1904), pp. 45-49, p. 45.

37    Joyce, *Ulysses*, 9.62.

38    Ibid., 9.280-1.

39    Æ, "Religion and Love," pp. 45, 46.

40    See Joyce, *Ulysses*, 1.77, 80, 85, 106.

41    Æ, "Religion and Love," p. 47.

42    Joyce, *Ulysses*, 9.48-9.

which this vegetable world is but a shadow"[43]. The title of Eglinton's article in the first issue of 1905 reminds us of an essay that Joyce was to write later on: "The Islands of Saints"[44]. This piece starts with a line from Rudyard Kipling ("East is East and West is West"), and if we add Kipling's next line ("Never the twain shall meet"), it might have some consonance with Joyce's "East of the sun, west of the moon [...] Booted the twain and staved"[45].

In "Scylla and Charybdis," we also find this remark: "Our national epic has yet to be written, Dr Sigerson says"[46]. Sigerson is mentioned nowhere in *Dana*, but the problem of the unwritten national epic is everywhere in its pages – most clearly perhaps in the first sentence of the editors' "Introductory" ("the promotion of a national literature"[47]) and in R.W. Lynd's article "The Nation and the Man of Letters," which begins thus:

> THERE is one question which will scarcely be settled among us until Ireland has taken her place among the comfortable and great nations. This is the question, How far, and in what sense, ought literature to be a distinctively national affair?[48]

This quotation also includes an allusion to Robert Emmet's famous last words that are quoted at the end of Joyce's "Sirens" episode[49].

In his "Literary Causerie" column, Atkinson, on the occasion of a review of Swinburne's *A Channel Passage and Other Poems*, quotes from Genesis: "the hands are the hands of Esau, but the voice –"[50]; Stephen modifies this quotation in "Scylla and Charybdis": "I am tired of my voice, the voice of Esau"[51]. In the same issue, Eglinton has an essay entitled "Sincerity," which begins thus: "'BEWARE of that man,' said Diderot of Rousseau; 'he believes every word he says!'"[52] This may have inspired Eglinton's famous question in "Scylla and Charybdis": "Do you believe your own theory?"[53]

Some contributions to *Dana* have connections to Joyce in more mysterious ways. One of these is an article in the first issue, entitled "The Abbé Loisy"; the author of this

---

[43]  Ibid., 9.87-8.
[44]  See John Eglinton, "The Island of Saints," *Dana* 9 (January 1905), pp. 257-63. – Joyce's "Ireland, Island of Saints and Sages," of course, was delivered as a lecture in 1907 in Trieste; it is printed in *The Critical Writings of James Joyce*, ed. Ellsworth Mason and Richard Ellmann (New York: Viking Press, 1959), pp. 153-74.
[45]  Joyce, *Ulysses*, 9.413-4. – Don Gifford, with Robert J. Seidman, in *"Ulysses" Annotated: Notes for James Joyce's* Ulysses, rev. ed. (Berkeley: University of California Press, 1988), p. 220, points out that the phrase "East of the Sun, West of the Moon" is the title of a folktale collection gathered by Peter Christen Asbjörnsen.
[46]  Joyce, *Ulysses*, 9.309.
[47]  The Editors, "Introductory," *Dana* 1 (May 1904), pp. 1-4, p. 1.
[48]  R.W. Lynd, "The Nation and the Man of Letters," *Dana* 12 (April 1905), pp. 371-76, p. 371.
[49]  See Joyce, *Ulysses*, 11.1284-5, 1289-90, 1291-2, 1294.
[50]  F.M. Atkinson, "A Literary Causerie," *Dana* 7 (November 1904), pp. 221-24, p. 221.
[51]  Joyce, *Ulysses*, 9.981.
[52]  John Eglinton, "Sincerity," *Dana* 7 (November 1904), pp. 210-15, p. 210.
[53]  Joyce, *Ulysses*, 9.1065-6.

article is the inventor of the interior monologue, Edouard Dujardin, of all people![54] Another mystery concerns Moore's "Preface to a New Edition of 'Confessions of a Young Man'"[55] and the possible significance of that title in terms of Joyce's *A Portrait of the Artist as a Young Man*. Even more intriguing is my discovery of Moore's praise of Walter Pater's *Imaginary Portraits* here in the "Confessions" preface[56].

Moore's main contribution to *Dana* is his autobiographical "Moods and Memories," serialized in issues 1-6, a reflection on his Paris experiences. In one of these contributions, we find the term *"entra'ctes"*[57] that Joyce was to use (more correctly spelled) in "Scylla and Charybdis": *"Entr'acte"*[58] Even mild traces of Leopold and Molly Bloom (who do not figure in *Dana* explicitly, of course) can be found in Moore's prose; he repeatedly uses phrases like "when the chestnuts are in bloom"[59] and "this garden of rhododendrons and chestnut bloom"[60], thus involuntarily foreshadowing not only Joyce's phrase "[t]he chestnuts that shaded us were in bloom"[61] but also Molly's remembrance of the rhododendrons of Howth.[62]

The most surprising Joycean find in all the twelve *Dana* issues is a 'blooming' one too, but this time the author is not Moore but Gogarty. In *Ulysses* Joyce made use of Gogarty's more or less irreverent verse, and this poem printed in *Dana* bears witness to his ability to produce verse in both the bawdy and the sentimental manner of the day. Gogarty's poem is entitled "Molly," and the Joycean alerted by this title may perhaps get the shock of his or her life when reaching the poem's last line. The work is as follows:

MOLLY.

> Molly through the Garden
>   Laughed and played with me,
> And the gate unbarred in
>   To the rosery,

---

54 See *Dana* 1 (May 1904), pp. 18-21.
55 See George Moore, "Preface to a New Edition of 'Confessions of a Young Man'," *Dana* 7 (November 1904), pp. 200-4.
56 See ibid., pp. 201 f.
57 George Moore, "Moods and Memories: III," *Dana* 2 (June 1904), pp. 55-61, p. 57.
58 Joyce, *Ulysses*, 9.484.
59 George Moore, "Moods and Memories: I," *Dana* 1 (May 1904), pp. 5-10, p. 8.
60 George Moore, "Moods and Memories: V," *Dana* 4 (August 1904, pp. 106-10, p. 107.
61 Joyce, *Ulysses*, 14.1145.
62 Once you are alerted to Molly Bloom and rhododendrons, it seems hard not to come across cross-connections from time to time. On the occasion of a visit to Glenveagh National Park in County Donegal, Ireland, the attractions of which include three rather ethereal paintings by A.E. in Glenveagh Castle and luxuriant rhododendron gardens, I spotted one particular shrub that was labeled "RH. MOLLYANUM," thus reminding me of the rhododendronic Molly's famous posterior (see *Ulysses*, 18.53: "the usual kissing my bottom"). the fact that there is a rhododendron that sounds as though it is named after Molly's anus adds a nice irony to Joyce's identification of Molly's arse as a "cardinal point" of "Penelope" – see James Joyce, *Letters of James Joyce*, vol. I, ed. Stuart Gilbert (New York: Viking Press, 1957), p. 170. I wonder if Joyce may have known of the correct botanic name of this floral plant.

Just she said to show me
  How the roses grew,
And when she would show me,
  Ask me if I knew

Which of all was fairest,
  Crescent bud or rose,
Till I guessed the rarest
  She would not disclose.

Laughing little lady,
  All her features shone
Like a star whose body
  And whose soul are one.

So I went intending
  To please her if I could,
Pondered then, and bending
  Pointed to the bud.

But the moment after
  Saw her face illume
With a peal of laughter
  Reaching for the bloom.

                    OLIVER GOGARTY.[63]

---

[63]    Oliver Gogarty, "Molly," *Dana* 10 (February 1905), p. 308.

# Trivia ShemSamiana

## 1: Pairing Fingernails[♣]

One of the many textual details glossed by Fritz Senn in his recent German (or rather bilingual) edition of "Hades" is Bloom's "well pared" fingernails which punctuate his reaction to Boylan's appearance on the scene:

> Mr Bloom reviewed the nails of his left hand, then those of his right hand. The nails, yes. [...] My nails. I am just looking at them: well pared.[1]

Senn refers to Bloom's fingernails as being his "natural biological weapons" by means of which Bloom is able to hide his embarrassment; he remarks that "well pared" sounds exactly like 'well paired', thus expressing what Bloom intends to repress; and he quotes the line "yet it seemed as useless as the pairing of one's nails" from William Butler Yeats's *Countess Cathleen* as a possible background.[2]

One should add, however, that Bloom's well-pared nails echo another text of world literature, also by an Irish writer: in fact, by James Joyce himself. What I have in mind is Stephen's famous definition of the dramatic form in *A Portrait*[3]:

> The esthetic image in the dramatic form is life purified in and reprojected from the human imagination. The mystery of esthetic like that of material creation is accomplished. The artist, like the God of creation, remains within or behind or beyond or above his handiwork, invisible, refined out of existence, indifferent, paring his fingernails.[4]

The act of fingernail-paring here is defined as a metaphor for indifference, and indifference indeed is exactly what Bloom tries to show when examining his well-pared fingernails in Boylan's presence. In reality, he does not feel indifferent to Boylan's

---

[♣]   First published as the article "Pairing Fingernails," by Friedhelm Rathjen, in *James Joyce Quarterly*, Volume 33, no. 1, Fall 1996, pp. 115-18.

[1]   James Joyce, *Ulysses: The Corrected Text*, ed. Hans Walter Gabler (Harmondsworth: Penguin, 1986 [Student's Edition], 6.200-4.

[2]   Fritz Senn, ed., *Hades: Ein Kapitel aus dem „Ulysses": Englisch – Deutsch*, by James Joyce (Mainz: Dieterich, 1992), p. 176.

[3]   After having read this note of mine, Fritz Senn called my attention to his article "Ex ungue Leopold," *English Studies*, 48 (December 1967), pp. 537-43, where Senn already points out some facets of the relationship between the passages from *A Portrait* and *Ulysses* and (albeit embedded in a differing overall argument) draws some conclusions that are similar to some of mine. See also Senn's gloss "Well pared (*Ulysses* 92.28)" in his "Trivia Ulysseana II," *James Joyce Quarterly* 13 (Winter 1976), pp. 242 f.

[4]   James Joyce, *A Portrait of the Artist as a Young Man*, ed. Chester G. Anderson and Richard Ellmann (New York: Viking Press, 1966), p. 215.

presence at all, of course: Bloom merely enacts indifference, thus preferring the dramatic form of utterance to the lyrical and the epical ones and, in a way, playing the role of the artist who "presents his image in immediate relation to others"[5]. If Bloom's pose is not fully successful, the same must be said of Stephen's: the disturbance of mind that Bloom has to face in Boylan's presence resembles that which Stephen has to face when, in the scene immediately following his definition of the dramatic form, he is informed by Lynch: "– Your beloved is here"[6].

It is no secret to readers of *Ulysses* that at several points of the novel the silent musings of Bloom and Stephen coincidentally correspond to each other. What makes our pair of fingernail-paring scenes different from those instances of carefully woven coincidence, however, is that Stephen's pa[i]ring scene is to be found in *A Portrait*: in this case, the network spun by Joyce in order to connect his protagonists does not limit itself to the pages of *Ulysses*. This might lead to the conclusion that the duplicity of both scenes is an accidental one – a conclusion that is definitely wrong, as can be shown by examining the contexts of both scenes.

In both cases, the character forcing the protagonist to pull himself together and play the role of the fingernail parer is located near the entrance of a public building. Blazes Boylan in *Ulysses* is seen saluting the passing cab from "the door of the Red Bank"[7], and Emma Clery, Stephen's beloved, stands "near the entrance door"[8] of the National Library, "on the steps of the colonnade"[9]. In both cases, not only jealousy but also a certain element of emptiness is involved. When Stephen catches sight of Emma, "[h]is mind, emptied of theory and courage, lapse[s] back into a listless peace"[10]; Bloom, following his musings on the nails, sends "his vacant glance over [his fellow-passengers'] faces"[11]. This glance may even recall Stephen's "turning his eyes towards her from time to time"[12].

The most compelling intertextual coincidence, however, precedes the fingernail-paring. Stephen, before defining the forms of art, once more recurs to Lessing's *Laokoon* and the art of sculpture: "– Lessing, said Stephen, should not have taken a group of statues to write of. The art, being inferior, does not present the forms I spoke of distinguished clearly one from another"[13]. Statues, on the other hand, figure prominently in the "Hades" chapter of *Ulysses*. Immediately preceding Blazes Boylan's appearance, Bloom's mind reflects on "Sir Philip Crampton's memorial fountain bust. Who was he?"[14] This is exactly the same bust that Stephen reflects on when reaching out for his

---

5    Ibid., p. 214.
6    Ibid., p. 215.
7    Joyce, *Ulysses*, 6.198.
8    Joyce, *A Portrait of the Artist as a Young Man*, p. 215.
9    Ibid., p. 216.
10   Ibid., p. 216.
11   Joyce, *Ulysses*, 6.209-10.
12   Joyce, *A Portrait of the Artist as a Young Man*, p. 215.
13   Ibid., p. 214.
14   Joyce, Ulysses, 6.191.

definition of the dramatic artist as the indifferent God of creation, paring his fingernails: *"Is the bust of Sir Philip Crampton lyrical, epical or dramatic?* "[15]

There is no doubt that when Joyce put together the Crampton bust and the fingernail-paring motif in "Hades" he intended to compose a special kind of *déjà lu*. Interestingly enough, the "Hades" episode of *Ulysses* itself is to a certain degree written in the modes of the dramatic art defined in *A Portrait*: the episode (more than the preceding ones) consists mainly of the characters' dialogue and Bloom's interior monologue, and the artist as narrator who has refined himself out of existence in a way is a dead artist, a narrator having gone to Hades. The artist himself is beginning to be as lifeless and as indifferent to his surroundings as a cold statue – statues nevertheless don't have to pare their fingernails.

## 2: Why Lambay?[*]

In the "Oxen of the Sun" episode of *Ulysses*, Buck Mulligan proposes to set up a national fertilizing farm, and for this purpose "he had resolved to purchase in fee simple for ever the freehold of Lambay island from its holder, lord Talbot de Malahide"[1]. Mulligan's paste-board cards have already been printed: *"Mr Malachi Mulligan. Fertiliser and Incubator. Lambay Island*"[2]. We may wonder, however, why Lambay has been chosen for this enterprise.

I believe that the answer is two-fold. First of all, Mulligan is mistaken: in 1904, Lambay Island was no longer owned by Lord Talbot de Malahide. In 1888, the island had been sold to Count James Considine[3], who resold it some years later. And in what year exactly? In the *Ulysses* year, as Kenneth McNally tells us in his *The Islands of Ireland*: "In 1904 Lambay again changed hands when Mr Cecil Baring (later Lord Revelstoke) became the new owner after seeing the island advertised for sale in *The Field*."[4] The advertisement must have been noticed by Buck Mulligan (and by the author of *Ulysses*), too; the weekly newspaper where it appeared is by no means unfamiliar to the world of *Ulysses*: "Bought the *Irish Field* now"[5], Bloom once muses.

So, the fact that Lambay Island was for sale in 1904 is one part of the answer to our question. The other one is that in those days Lambay must have really been a place

---

[15]     Ibid, p. 214.

[*]     First published as the article "Why Lambay?" by Friedhelm Rathjen, in *Joyce Studies Annual* Volume 1995, pp. 168 f. Copyright © 1995 by the University of Texas Press. All rights reserved.

[1]     James Joyce, *Ulysses: The Corrected Text*, ed. Hans Walter Gabler (Harmondsworth: Penguin, 1986 [Student's Edition], 14.681-3.

[2]     Ibid., 14.660.

[3]     This is the year given by Kenneth McNally in his *The Islands of Ireland* (London: Batsford, 1978), p. 143. Don Gifford with Robert J. Seidman in their *"Ulysses" Annotated: Notes for James Joyce's "Ulysses"* (Berkeley: University of California Press), p. 426, give 1878 as year of purchase.

[4]     McNally, p. 143.

[5]     Joyce, *Ulysses*, 8.339.

of fertility already. For centuries, rabbits had been trapped on the island in considerable numbers for sale, but according to Kenneth McNally "even the extent of this trade was insufficient to control the rate of increase and it was necessary to kill some 24,000 over a two-year period from 1904-6."[6] Again the *Ulysses* year comes into play.

Buck Mulligan, then, would not have been the first fertilizer on Lambay Island, had he, instead of Lord Revelstoke, purchased the isle in 1904: first came the rabbits. Rabbits are weapons of fertility, so to speak, as is noted in *Finnegans Wake*, too: "It's too screaming to rizo, rabbit it all! [...] O but you must, you must really!"[7] Less than two pages later in the *Wake*, we reach our island again: "Werra where in ourthe did you ever pick a Lambay chop as big as a battering ram? Ay, you're right."[8]

## 3: Ascot or Epsom?♣

The King of the Newsboys appears on the very first page of the "Aeolus" episode of *Ulysses*: "Davy Stephens, minute in a large capecoat, a small felt hat crowning his ringlets, passed out with a roll of papers under his cape, a king's courier"[1]. In *Finnegans Wake*, "Dav Stephens"[2] reappears, and Adaline Glasheen in her *Third Census* tells us what this Dublin character has been famous for in his lifetime: "Every year he dressed up like a gentleman and went to the Derby."[3]

Maurice Gorham in the caption to a photograph of Stephens, however, tells the story slightly different:

> For many years he sold his papers at Kingstown (Dun Laoghaire) where the mailboats come in; he was on chatting terms with crowned heads and other distinguished visitors; and every year he took the boat himself and crossed to Ascot, where he found many friends.[4]

If Gorham is right and Glasheen is wrong, it follows that there is a minute crux in the realism of *Ulysses*. The Ascot Races take place in June every year, and the Ascot Gold Cup of 1904 was run on Bloomsday, June 16, as every reader of *Ulysses* will know. This

---

[6]  McNally, p. 145.

[7]  James Joyce, *Finnegans Wake* (London: Faber, 1975), 206.15-6.; see also 4.15-6.: "Phall if you but will, rise you must."

[8]  Ibid., 208.2-4.

♣  First published as the article "Ascot or Epsom?" by Friedhelm Rathjen, in *Joyce Studies Annual* Volume 1995, pp. 169 f. Copyright © 1995 by the University of Texas Press. All rights reserved.

[1]  James Joyce, *Ulysses: The Corrected Text*, ed. Hans Walter Gabler (Harmondsworth: Penguin, 1986 [Student's Edition], 7.28-30; see also 15.1122.

[2]  James Joyce, *Finnegans Wake* (London: Faber, 1975), 300.n2.

[3]  Adaline Glasheen, *Third Census of "Finnegans Wake": An Index of the Characters and Their Roles* (Berkeley: University of California Press, 1977), pp. 271 f.

[4]  *Ireland from old Photographs*, intro. and commentaries by Maurice Gorham (London: Batsford, 1971), n.p., illustration no. 206.

means that if Davy Stephens went to the races in 1904 indeed, he was decidedly unable to pass out of the offices of the *Freeman's Journal* on Bloomsday.

Two different conclusions seem possible: either Glasheen is right and the race that Davy Stephens went to annually was the English Derby at Epsom indeed (which was run on June 2 in 1904), or we have to allow for an oversight on Joyce's (or perhaps Bloom's?) part. After having long tried in vain to obtain final evidence in the Ascot vs. Epsom case, at long last I came across what seems to be the decisive source, namely the autobiography of Davy Stephens (written not by himself but by a ghostwriter), where it is stated rather unmistakably: "This year, on account of the war, I had to go racing at Newmarket instead of on Epsom Downs, and it was nothing to the grand old Derby days of yore"[5] – what a pity! I must admit that I for my part would rather have preferred evidence in favour of Ascot: this would have meant another subtle link between Leopold Bloom, Throwaway, and all the dark horses of Bloomsday.

## 4: Daedalean Crash on Bloomsday ♣

Statistically speaking, exactly 0.27 percent of all events in world history must have happened on 16 June, and this surely means that it would be nonsense to connect each and every historical Bloomsday event with Joyce's *Ulysses*. In some cases, however, a connection is suggested by the nature of the event in question, and one of these may be the death of Pilâtre de Rozier on 16 June, 1785, reported by Arno Schmidt (of all people) in his novella *Dark Mirrors*: "I raised a hand in honour of Pilâtre de Rozier, crashed on 16. 6. 1785, the first in that long series, unprejudicial to Icarus"[1]. Pilâtre de Rozier was the first person who transformed the myth of Icarus into history: as a *montgolfière* pilot, he died in what seems to have been the very first fatal air crash when his balloon caught fire. Obviously, this fits in with the Daedalus-Icarus motif introduced by Joyce in the name of his autobiographical hero: Stephen, son of Dedalus, suffers his crash on Bloomsday, too.

## 5: In Pieces ♣

Marcel Proust is a focus of much of early Beckett's thinking, and therefore even Beckett's short and occasional "Proust in Pieces" (a review of Albert Feuillerat's *Comment Proust a composé son roman* written in 1934) should be handled and examined with

---

[5]     *The Life and Tiomes of Davy Stephens. The Renowned Kingstown Newsman*, online at <http://www.chaptersofdublin.com/books/General/dstephens.htm>, chapter VI: "Davy goes racing and visits London."

♣     First published as the article "Daedalean Crash on Bloomsday," by Friedhelm Rathjen, in *James Joyce Quarterly*, Volume 33, no. 1, Fall 1996, pp. 115.

[1]     Arno Schmidt, *Dark Mirrors*, *Nobodaddy's Children*, trans. John E. Woods (Normal, IL: Dalkey Archive Press, 1995), pp. 177-236, p. 191.

♣     Previously unpublished.

care. Towards the end of the review, Beckett defends the non-straightforwardness of Proust's *Recherche*:

> His material, pulverized by time, obliterated by habit, mutilated in the clockwork of memory, he communicates as he can, in dribs and drabs.[1]

Interestingly enough, most of the terms used here to describe Proust's method can be found in Beckett's short story "Yellow" from *More Pricks than Kicks*, too. Belacqua, striving to keep ideas away from the "posterns of the mind," has developed a plan:

> His plan [...] was not to refuse admission to the idea, but to keep it at bay until his mind was ready to receive it. Then let it in and pulverise it. Obliterate the bastard [...], tear it into pieces like a priest.[2]

And then, two pages further down, "then he would admit the idea and blow it to pieces."[3] Who goes to pieces – Belacqua? An idea forcing itself into Belacqua's mind? Or rather Proust, forcing itself into Beckett's mind as a priest? At the least we may say that Proust is present here – and his "dribs and drabs" are present, too. For Belacqua, the sun is a "dribble of time"[4]; the sun, on the other hand, is also "that creature of habit,"[5] thus representing the very obliterative mechanism which Proust was striving to avoid. By the way, the colour of the sun is yellow and thus present in the story's title, too.

It seems that in "Yellow" Beckett has already begun to turn the Proustian system upside down. Proust wants to forget (i.e., to pulverize, to obliterate, and to mutilate) in order to find and experience and enjoy anew, whereas Beckett's fictional voices pulverize and obliterate and mutilate ideas in order not to forget but rather to bleach these by constantly keeping everything at bay under the sun and burning life and immediacy out of the ideas. Beckett's sun is always shining on the nothing new, and the nothing new is what Beckett prefers to the constant renewal of Proustian experience.

## 6: Sam Remembering Ringelnatz ♣

Since its publication in *Disjecta* in 1983, Samuel Beckett's famous German letter of July 9, 1937 to Axel Kaun has been widely discussed by Beckett scholars, but the letter's very motive, Kaun's suggestion that Beckett might translate poems by Joachim Ringelnatz (1883-1934), is seldom mentioned and never examined – and quite rightly so, as Beckett

---

[1]   Samuel Beckett, "Proust in Pieces," *Disjecta: Miscellaneous Writings and a Dramatic Fragment*, ed. Ruby Cohn (London: John Calder, 1983), pp. 63-65, p. 65.

[2]   Samuel Beckett, "Yellow," *More Pricks than Kicks* (London: Pan / Picador, 1974), pp. 143-57, p. 148.

[3]   Ibid., p. 150.

[4]   Ibid., p. 152.

[5]   Ibid., p. 151.

♣   Previously unpublished.

in the letter itself dismisses Ringelnatz as a rhyme coolie and refuses to act as his translator. This, however, is not in every respect the end of Beckett's interest in Ringelnatz.

In June 1985, nearly half a century after having written his letter to Axel Kaun, Beckett stayed in Stuttgart for ten days to direct the TV version of *What Where*. At the end of the farewell dinner on the last night, Beckett was asked by cameraman Jim Lewis if he had any idea for their next joint project. Instead of an answer, Beckett recited a German poem:

> In Hamburg lebten zwei Ameisen,
> Die wollten nach Australien reisen.
> Bei Altona auf der Chaussee
> Da taten ihnen die Beine weh,
> Und da verzichteten sie weise
> Dann auf den letzten Teil der Reise.[1]

(Interlinear trans.: "In Hamburg there lived two ants / who wanted to travel to Australia. / Near Altona on the avenue / their legs were hurting, / So wisely they relinquished / the final bit of the journey.")

This nonsense poem, entitled "Die Ameisen" ("The Ants"), is by Joachim Ringelnatz, of all people, and the fact that Beckett remembered the exact wording fifty years after having read (and perhaps tried to translate) the poem indicates that dismissal was not Beckett's exclusive reaction to Ringelnatz's verse. Maybe that in this instance Beckett's memory was backed up by his being familiar with Hamburg and Altona from his travelling impressions in the winter of 1936. Beckett in particular must have known that Altona (incorporated into Hamburg in 1937) was connected to the adjoining metropolis through a railway line, just like Foxrock was to Dublin. In a way, Mercier and Camier who want to leave Dublin but break their journey in Foxrock thus suffer the same fate as the couple of Ringelnatz's ants.

---

[1]    Walter D. Asmus, "All Gimmicks Gone?" *Theater heute* 27.iv (April 1986), pp. 28-30, p. 30. This is one of the most famous poems of Ringelnatz and was originally published in his early collection *Die Schnupftabaksdose: Stumpfsinn in Versen und Bildern* (The Snuff-box: Stupidity in Verse and Pictures) in 1912.

# Horses versus Cattle in *Ulysses**

In his contribution to *Papers on Joyce* 3, Rafael I. García León has attempted a survey of the role played by horses and equine images in *Ulysses*.[1] His survey could have been much more fruitful and less casual, however, if he had not chosen to isolate equine references from references to other animals. For a full understanding of the role played by horses in *Ulysses* it seems essential to also consider the role played by cattle, as I would like to show briefly in this article.

As early as the "Nestor" episode (art: "History"; symbol: "Horse," according to Joyce[2]), equine allusions are beginning to be complimented by bovine ones. Pictures of dead horses ("Framed around the walls images of vanished horses stood in homage"[3]) illustrate the history which is represented by Deasy and which, for Stephen, "is a nightmare from which I am trying to awake"[4], thus turning the nightmare into a "night-*mare*,"[5] i.e., a dark horse – but Deasy, albeit quite unintentionally, at the same time provides Stephen with the very means to awake from both nightmares and horses. From Deasy, Stephen receives a tool of bovine strength – Deasy's letter on foot and mouth disease: "Allimportant question. In every sense of the word take the bull by the horns. Thanking you for the hospitality of your columns"[6]. Bulls and hospitality are indeed mighty weapons to overcome horses as well as racism, if Stephen manages to be that "bullockbefriending bard"[7] that he feels he will become in Buck Mulligan's eyes.

In the next episode, "Aeolus," the dualism of horses / history versus cattle / hospitality is explored further. Horses remain to be signposts to the bad dream of Ireland's past: "The whitemaned seahorses, champing, brightwindbridled, the steeds of Mananaan"[8]. However, Stephen remembers to have been awakened from this nightmare by a better kind of dream: "After he woke me last night same dream or was it? Wait.

---

[*]     First published as the article "Horses Versus Cattle in *Ulysses*," by Friedhelm Rathjen, in *Joyce Studies Annual* Volume 2001, pp. 172-75. Copyright © 2001 by the University of Texas Press. All rights reserved.

[1]     Rafael I. García León, "Reading *Ulysses* at a Gallop," *Papers on Joyce* 3 (1997), pp. 3-8.

[2]     For a synoptical comparison of the "Linati Schema" and the "Gorman-Gilbert Plan," see Richard Ellmann, *"Ulysses" on the Liffey* (London: Faber and Faber, 1972), charts following p. 188.

[3]     James Joyce, *Ulysses: The Corrected Text*, ed. Hans Walter Gabler (Harmondsworth: Penguin, 1986 [Student's Edition], 2.300.

[4]     Ibid., 2.377.

[5]     Vincent Cheng, "White Horse, Dark Horse: Joyce's Allhorse of Another Color," *Joyce Studies Annual* (1991), p. 106.

[6]     Joyce, *Ulysses*, 2.335-7.

[7]     Ibid., 2.431.

[8]     Ibid., 3.56-7.

Open hallway. [...] In. Come. Red carpet spread. You will see who"[9]. Obviously this is a dream of hospitality – and this is a dream of the man from the east whom Stephen will meet soon, i.e., Leopold Bloom.

It is quite misleading to see horses as "one of the many features that make Bloom and Stephen similar"[10] – what really contributes to the union of Bloom and Stephen is rather the fact that both reject equine images in favour of bovine ones. To be sure, Bloom in the "Lotus Eaters" episode encounters a horse – but he does not like the image:

> Mr. Bloom went round the corner and passed the drooping nags of hazard. No use thinking of it any more. Nosebag time. [...] Poor jugginses! Damn all they know or care about anything with their long noses stuck in nosebags. Too full for words. Still they get their feed all right and their doss. Gelded too: a stump of black guttapercha wagging limp between their haunches.[11]

This passage indicates that for Bloom, horses are connected with nonfertility, with sterility. Bloom himself, however, is clearly dissociated from the horse image, and for this reason Bantam Lyons, in order to get a racing tip from Bloom, has to misunderstand his "I was just going to throw it away"[12]: what Bantam Lyons gets from Bloom seems to be a tip but is not; Bloom seems to get associated with horse imagery but in reality is not.

What Bloom is inobtrusively associated with is rather the cattle imagery of *Ulysses*. When in "Scylla and Charybdis" Buck Mulligan – himself "equine"[13] – mistakes Bloom for a homosexual, Stephen silently associates Bloom with the "Manner of Oxenford"[14] and thus indirectly makes him a friend of himself, "the bullockbefriending bard"[15]. In the "Sirens" episode, Blazes Boylan is trying to usurp Bloom's bovine role, but he remains unsuccessful and is linked to equine images instead:

> By Bachelor's walk jogjaunty Blazes Boylan, bachelor, in sun in heat, mare's glossy rump atrot, with flick of whip, on bounding tyres: sprawled, warmseated, Boylan impatience, ardentbold. Horn. Have you the? Horn. Have you the? Haw haw horn.[16]

Boylan's horn here is a false one, for he, the son of a horse dealer, is associated with horses throughout the chapter[17], and we have to remember that horses are linked to

---

[9]   Ibid., 3.365-9.
[10]  García León, 5.
[11]  Joyce, *Ulysses*, 5.210-8.
[12]  Ibid., 5.534.
[13]  Ibid., 1.15.
[14]  Ibid., 9.1212.
[15]  Ibid., 2.431.
[16]  Ibid., 11.524-7.
[17]  See David J. Piwinski, "The Image of the Bleeding Horse in James Joyce's *Ulysses*," *Papers on Language and Literature* 26.2 (1990), pp. 285 f.; García León, 5 f.

sterility by the passage above quoted from the "Lotus Eaters" episode. The image of the mare that repeatedly joins the description of Boylan on his way to Molly is always an image of sluggishness, prostration and exhaustion:

> Blazes Boylan's smart tan shoes creaked on the bar-floor, said before. [...] Slower the mare went up the hill by Rotunda, Rutland square. Too slow for Boylan, blazes Boylan, impatience Boylan, joggled the mare.[18]

Bloom, on the other hand, is still the man of (at least potential) fertility: "No son. Rudy. Too late now. Or if not? If not? If still?"[19] Lenehan and Joe are definitely wrong when in "Cyclops" they say of Bloom, "He's a bloody dark horse himself "[20]. Bloom is not, he is neither dark nor a horse; he belongs to the realm of bovine images and the brightness of sun and son; he belongs to the title imagery of the "Oxen of the Sun" episode. In this episode of fertility –"Send us bright one, light one, Horhorn, quickening and womb-fruit"[21] – Bloom is the one to defend fertility against the sterility of his drinking companions who, led by equine Buck Mulligan, vote for "Copulation without population"[22].

Exactly this – copulation without population – is what the horsepower man Boylan is exercising with Molly, but hospitable Bloom is the true owner of the horn – the horn of the bull and the horn of fertility. At the end of the day, Molly is obviously satisfied that she has had some fun with Boylan, but what she does not like is exactly horseness: "one thing I didnt like his slapping me behind going away so familiarly in the hall though I laughed Im not a horse or an ass am I I suppose he was thinking of his fathers"[23]. Although Molly appreciates Boylan's strength, in the end she has to realize that he is remarkably short of the juices of fertility:

> No I never in all my life felt anyone had one the size of that to make you feel full up [...] whats the idea making us like that with a big hole in the middle of us or like a Stallion driving it up into you [...] still he hasn't such a tremendous amount of spunk in him [...].[24]

Bovine Bloom still is the fruitful, blooming man. Horses are hoarse, but cattle can boil over like a kettle with the water of life. It's Bloom that boils, not "Boylan impatience"[25].

---

[18]  Joyce, *Ulysses*, 11.761-6.
[19]  Ibid., 11.1067.
[20]  Ibid., 12.1558.
[21]  Ibid., 14.2.
[22]  Ibid., 14.1422.
[23]  Ibid., 18.122–24.
[24]  Ibid., 18.149–54.
[25]  Ibid., 11.526.

# Thorne Smith in the *Wake**
## Arno Schmidt's Neglected Recommendation

In the post-war reception of James Joyce in Germany, the role played by the novelist Arno Schmidt (1914-79) can hardly be overestimated. Starting with his harsh critique of Georg Goyert's translation of *Ulysses* in 1957 (which eventually led to Hans Woll-schläger's new translation), Schmidt wrote a number of essays on Joyce which still today have not lost their impact on German readers' conception of Joyce's works, especially *Finnegans Wake*. In contrast to this, Schmidt's readings of the *Wake* have left virtually no traces in Joyce scholarship, and the reasons are quite obvious: being a strongly original writer himself, Schmidt imposed his own eccentric conceptions of the literary work of art on Joyce rather than looking for Joyce's conceptions, and, moreover, Schmidt tried to overcome his 'anxiety of influence' by wilfully disparaging Joyce's character, the professional Joyce exegets, and in part also Joyce's works, especially certain aspects of *Finnegans Wake*.[1] According to Schmidt, the scene of *Finnegans Wake* is laid in Trieste rather than Dublin, and the whole book deals with nothing else but the rivalry of James and Stanislaus Joyce over Nora Barnacle. Although Schmidt's discoveries seem to have been taken seriously by most of his readers in Germany, it is only too natural that the international community of Joyce scholars ignored Schmidt.

Some of Schmidt's incidental discoveries, however, deserve more attention than they have received so far, and one of these is Schmidt's identification of Thorne Smith as a background for at least one passage in the *Wake*. Smith, a popular American novelist of the 1920s and 1930s, is virtually unknown to *Wake* commentators from Glasheen and Atherton to McHugh, and this gave Schmidt a most welcome opportunity to brag with his own knowledge and at the same time ridicule the professional Joyce scholars on the grounds that they did not even notice the most obvious allusions.[2]

Thorne Smith had been a favourite author of Schmidt's since at least the late 1940s. Several of Smith's novels are to be found in Schmidt's personal library, and allusions to the *Topper* novels in particular can be found in the whole of Schmidt's

---

\*    First published as the article "Thorne Smith in the Wake: Arno Schmidt's Neglected Recommendation," by Friedhelm Rathjen, in *Papers on Joyce* No. 2, 1996, pp. 93-98.

[1]    See my article "Arno Schmidt's Utilization of James Joyce: Some Basic Conditions," *James Joyce Quarterly* 30.1 (1992), pp. 85-90; rpt. in the present collection, pp. 173-78.

[2]    Examples of Arno Schmidt's and also Vladimir Nabokov's tendency to ridicule profess-sional Joyce scholarship in order to install their own conception of Joyce and his work can be found in my article "Die Gunst des Verlesens: Zur Frage des Umgangs von Nabokov und Schmidt mit Joyce," Gregor Strick (ed.), *Zettelkasten 14: Jahrbuch der Gesellschaft der Arno-Schmidt-Leser 1995* (Frankfurt am Main: Bangert & Metzler, 1995), pp. 147-72; rpt. in Friedhelm Rathjen, *Dritte Wege: Kontexte für Arno Schmidt und James Joyce* (Scheeßel: Edition ReJoyce, 2006), pp. 109-26.

oeuvre from *Brand's Haide* (1950) through to *Julia* (1979). Schmidt must have been highly attracted by Smith's extremely comical mixture of turbulent plots and burlesque situations, undermined by an underground tendency towards misanthropy and escapism.

Thorne Smith, born in Annapolis in 1892, made a career in the advertising business and started writing in World War I, when, as an editor of the Naval Reserve Magazine *Broadside*, he authored a series of funny stories collected after the war in *Biltmore Oswald* (1918) and *Out O'Luck* (1919). Subsequently he lived in Greenwich Village, published a collection of verse (*Haunts and By-Paths*, 1919), and returned into the advertising business. Thorne Smith did not come into his own, however, until he wrote his best-remembered novel *Topper: A Ribald Adventure* (1926; with a sequel, *Topper Takes a Trip*, 1932), which was an immediate commercial success and eventually led to its screen adaptation by Norman Z. McLeod, starring Cary Grant, Roland Young and Constance Bennett. (The film versions of the *Topper* novels, however, are rather disappointing to most fans of the books.[3]) The plot of the novel centres around an aging, henpecked bank clerk, Cosmo Topper, who buys a second-hand sportscar and subsequently has to deal with the ghosts of the former owners, George and Marion Kerby, who have been killed in a road accident but live on in the fourth dimension and are able to materialize for limited periods. Throughout the novel, seemingly driverless cars are racing along the highway, liquids are being poured into nothing in mid-air, and suitcases are floating masterless through hotel halls. Most of Thorne Smith's novels are variations of the basic idea that the characters' nature and appearance are grotesquely disunited: in *Turnabout* (1931), husband and wife change bodies but not personalities; the protagonists of *The Stray Lamb* (1929) and *Skin and Bones* (1933) are transformed into animals and a skeleton respectively; Greek stone statues in a museum are turned into human beings (*The Nightlife of the Gods*, 1931), and a commuter ferry-boat by mistake discharges a group of well-respected citizens in a nudists' camp (*The Bishop's Jaegers*, 1932). The remainder of Smith's novels are: *Dream's End* (1927), *Did She Fall?* (1930), a children's book *Lazy Bear Lane* (1931), *Rain in the Doorway* (1933), and *The Glorious Pool* (1934).[4] Thorne Smith died in 1934 in Sarasota, Florida, from apoplexy of the heart; an unfinished novel, *The Passionate Witch*, was completed by Norman Matson and published in 1941.

Although allusions to the *Topper* novels can be found in almost all of Arno Schmidt's books, it is only in his Joyce essays that Schmidt gives any details regarding the significance of Smith's works; it seems that when Schmidt discovered traces of Thorne Smith in *Finnegans Wake*, he took this as a most welcome confirmation of his own esteem for the American novelist. In a short essay written in 1964, Arno Schmidt argues that anyone who is irritated by the *Wake* simply suffers from lack of reading:

---

[3]     I am indebted to Rudi Schweikert for this and more information.

[4]     A bibliographical listing is given by Peter Arendt, "'Ach, ich hör auf: Sie *kennen* das Alles nicht': Einige Anmerkungen zu Thorne Smith," *Schauerfeld: Mitteilungen der Gesellschaft der Arno-Schmidt-Leser* 8.2 (1995), pp. 5-12. In 1980, six of Smith's novels have been reprinted by Ballantine Books, New York, but all are out of print again.

"wird doch z.B. die S. 434 f. sogleich durchsichtig, wenn man THORNE SMITH kennt."[5] Schmidt's discovery that pages 434 and 435 of *Finnegans Wake* should be read in the light of Smith's books is unfolded in detail in his radio essay "Das Buch Jedermann," written on the occasion of the twentyfifth anniversary of Joyce's death.[6] I would like just to report Schmidt's suggestions, using not only the radio essay but also the facsimile edition of Schmidt's personal copy of the *Wake*[7]; we will, however, have to reject most of these suggestions afterwards:

Thorne Smith in person is present in the "would-do performer, *oleas* Mr Smuth"[8], and a few lines down we can spot an "autocart"[9] which Schmidt in a marginal note in his *Wake* copy identifies as Topper's important sportscar (formerly owned by the Kerbys). Topper in person appears in "the icepolled globetopper is haunted"[10]: in Smith's book, the pedantic Topper is haunted (albeit affectionately) by the ghost-like vagabond Marion Kerby. Several details of Joyce's text seem to refer to *The Night Life of the Gods*. In "the *Smirching of Venus?*"[11] a goddess is explicitly named, and the following phrase, "asking with whispered offers in a very low bearded voice"[12], is wrongly identified by Schmidt as being a quotation from Smith's *Night Life*.[13] A few lines down Joyce seems to merge the *Night Life* and *The Bishop's Jaegers* into one: "the frecklessness of the giddies nouveautays"[14] is translated by Schmidt into the 'recklessness of the goddess's nudities', thus connecting the godliness of the *Night Life* with the topic of nudism that is to be found in Smith's later book, and the same combination occurs again in "the undraped divine"[15]. Schmidt in his radio essay also suggests that the "back beautiful"[16] is owned by Josephine Duval, heroine of *The Bishop's Jaegers*. The nouns of this book's title, moreover, are mentioned in "Bussup Bulkeley"[17] and "always jaeger for

5     Arno Schmidt, "‹Meine Bibliothek›," *Bargfelder Ausgabe*, vol. III/4 (Zurich: Haffmans, 1995), pp. 361-68, p. 364. English translation: "Page 434 f., for example, becomes immediately transparent, as soon as you know THORNE SMITH."

6     Arno Schmidt, "Das Buch Jedermann: James Joyce zum 25. Todestage," *Bargfelder Ausgabe*, vol. II/3 (Zurich: Haffmans, 1991), pp. 231-56, pp. 245-47.

7     *Arno Schmidts Arbeitsexemplar von Finnegans Wake by James Joyce* (Zurich: Haffmans, 1984), pp. 434 f.

8     James Joyce, *Finnegans Wake* (London: Faber, 1975), 434.35-6.

9     Ibid., 434.31.

10     Ibid., 434.12-3.

11     Ibid., 435.2-3.

12     Ibid., 435.3-4.

13     In the margin of his copy of the *Wake*, Schmidt locates this quotation on p. 157 of his copy of *The Night Life of the Gods* (Harmondsworth: Penguin, 1960). Unfortunately I have not been able to obtain a copy of this edition yet. Anyhow, we will see below that for reasons of chronology, this phrase simply can not be a quotation from Thorne Smith.

14     Joyce, *Finnegans Wake*, 435.11-2.

15     Ibid., 435.14-5.

16     Ibid., 435.14.

17     Ibid., 435.11.

a thrust"[18] respectively, and the English translation of German *Jäger* is "hunter"[19]. And one more reference to *The Bishop's Jaegers*: the 'artist's model' hidden in "won't you be an artist's moral and pose in your nudies"[20] according to Schmidt is van Dyke, a character in Smith's novel.

Unfortunately Arno Schmidt did not have any detailed knowledge of the genetics of *Finnegans Wake*. The passage in which all these possible references occur is part of chapter III.2 of *Finnegans Wake*, a chapter that was put aside by Joyce as early as April, 1926, when all of Thorne Smith's books except *Topper* had not even been written, and the chapter was printed in *transition* no. 13 in the summer of 1928, three years before *The Night Life of the Gods* and four years before *The Bishop's Jaegers*. If Schmidt is right indeed in identifying Thorne Smith as a vital source in the *Wake* passage in question, Joyce must have written or at least heavily revised this passage at a comparably late stage and fit the revisions into a text that originally had been considered finished already.

Let us take a close look at the genetics of the passage in question. The following is the final book version of *Finnegans Wake* 443.27-435.16; I introduce square brackets in order to identify all words and phrases that are still missing in the 1928 *transition*[21] printing:

> [...] Jonas in the Dolphin's Barncar [with your meetual fan, Donveyed Covetfilles, comepulsing paynattention spasms between the averthisment for Ulikah's wine and a pair of pulldoors of the old cupiosity shape]. There you'll fix your eyes darkled on the autocart of the bringfast cable but here till youre martimorphysed please sit still face to face. For if the shorth of your skorth falls down to his knees pray how wrong will he look till he rises? Not before Gravesend is commuted. But now reappears Autist Algy, [the pulcherman and would-do performer, **oleas Mr Smuth**,] stated [by the vice crusaders] to be well known [**to all the dallytaunties**] in and near the ciudad of Buellas Arias, taking you to the playguehouse to see the *Smirching of Venus* and asking [with whispered offers] in a very low bearded voice, with a nice little [**tiny**] manner and in a very nice little [**tony**] way, won't you be an artist's moral and pose in your nudies as a local esthetic before voluble old masters, introducing you[, left to right the party comprises,] to hogarths [like] and[22] Bottisilly and Titteretto and Vergognese and Coraggio [with their extrahand Mazzaccio, **plus the usual bilker's dozen of dowdy-cameramen**]. And the volses of lewd Buylan[,] for innocence! And the

---

18 Ibid., 435.14.

19 Ibid.

20 Ibid., 435.5.

21 James Joyce, "Continuation of a Work in Progress," *transition* 13 (July, 1928), pp. 5-32, p. 9. See *The James Joyce Archive*, ed. Michael Groden et alii (New York: Garland, 1978), vol. 61, p. 29.

22 *transition* 13 reads: "hogarths and Bottisilly." In the process of textual revision, Joyce changes this into "hogarths like and Bottisilly" (*The James Joyce Archive*, vol. 61, p. 356), but the final wording is "hogarths like Bottisilly" (Joyce, *Finnegans Wake*, 435.7).

phyllisophies of Bussup Bulkeley. [**O, the frecklessness of the giddies nouveautays! There's many's the icepolled globetopper is haunted by the hottest spot under his equator like Ramrod, the meaty hunter, always jaeger for a thrust.** The back beautiful, the undraped divine! And Suzy's Moedl's with their Blue Danyboyes!] All blah!

This synoptical version clearly shows that Schmidt was partly but not wholly right. Contrary to all expectations, both the "*Smirching of Venus*" and "Bussup Bulkeley" have been in the text already before Joyce could ever have heard of Thorne Smith, and mysteriously the same is true of the "very low bearded voice" which Schmidt identifies as quotation from the *Night Life*. On the other hand it seems that Joyce realized that the presence of both Venus and a bishop allowed the insertion of Smith-related material into this passage. The insertions that I have put in square brackets in the above quotation date from at least three different stages of revisions between 1933 and 1937: revisions on marked pages of *transition* 13[23]; revisions on another (apparently third) set of *transition* 13 pages[24]; revisions on two sets of galleys for *Finnegans Wake*[25]. For convenience sake, I have used bold-face type in order to identify all insertions that date from Joyce's revisions on the first set of *transition* 13 pages; these first revisions include all the most vital references to Thorne Smith, namely "Mr Smuth" himself and the cluster of references at the end of the passage. Both these insertions can be traced further to sheets no. 13 and 10 respectively of a batch of extradraft notes compiled by Joyce in 1933-34[26]. These sheets belong to a special part of the batch of notes which consists mainly of units transferred directly from notebooks VI.C.2 and VI.C.3, and these notebooks again have to be dated approximately 1933-34[27]. It should be noted, however, that in these notebooks, there is no trace of the original notes for the units in question, which makes it appear quite probable that both phrases originate from the very time of Joyce's compiling the extradraft notes.

From all this we may well conclude that Arno Schmidt was basically right in identifying Smithian overtones in "Mr Smuth," "the icepolled globetopper" and "hunter" / "jaeger": when Joyce took notes for these phrases, Smith's books had already been published, and maybe Smith himself was dead already. All of Schmidt's suggestions that deal with *Wake* material not printed in bold-face type in the above quotation, on the other hand, including Schmidt's detection of what he believed to be a direct quotation from Smith, have to be rejected on chronological grounds. Thorne Smith seems to have been discovered late by Joyce, but not too late. Suffice it to say that if the same can be said of Smith's being discovered by the Joyceans, this is entirely owing to Arno Schmidt.

---

[23]    *The James Joyce Archive*, vol. 61, pp. 29 and 213.
[24]    Ibid., vol. 61, pp. 356 f. and 566.
[25]    Ibid., vol. 62, pp. 41-43 and 287-89.
[26]    Ibid., vol. 61, pp. 130 and 126.
[27]    See ibid., vol. 61, pp. x-xi.

# Chancelation & Transincidence[*]
## How to Deal With Coincidentals in Translating *Finnegans Wake*

Dylan Thomas once remarked that the magic in a poem is always accidental – Thomas himself, however, in his poetical works again and again found ways to increase the probability of these accidents to happen, and the same is a vital part of the task of the *Finnegans Wake* translator. Coincidence is not always something that just happens or does not happen; coincidence rather is something that can be arranged (or even forced) to happen.

Joyce himself obviously found lots of ways to arrange chance and coincidence in the process of composing *Finnegans Wake*, but he was luckier than the translator in that he as an original author could take advantage of preexististing cases of coincidence, whereas the translator – obliged to somehow imitate Joyce's original cases of coincidence in the respective target language, where the word material usually does not lend itself to exactly the same coincidental overlappings of sounds and spellings – has to continually find means to increase the probability of coincidences to happen. The most important means to do so is the increasement of plurability: the translator has to increase the totality of chances, i.e., the number of elements from which to select those that show the best possible approximation to the cases of coincidence that occur in Joyce's text.

An example of such an increasement of chances is the way I handled Joyce's neologism "cropse"[1], a blending of 'crop' and 'corpse'. The German translation of 'crop' is *Feldfrucht*, the German translation of 'corpse' is *Leiche* – if we had to restrict ourselves to this material, however, there would be no chance at all for the original sound coincidence to happen again in the target language. We have to multiply our chances by preparing lists of alternative German renderings of 'crop' and 'corpse': in addition to *Feldfrucht* possible equivalents for the former could be *Ernte* (harvest), specifications like *Kartoffeln* (potatoes), *Getreide*, *Korn* (grains) or plural forms of these like *Früchte* or *Körner*, the latter could be rendered not only as *Leiche* but also as *Leichnam, Kadaver, sterbliche Überreste* or (speaking of bodies in general, either dead or alive) [p. 26:] *Leib* or *Körper*. In order to make the coincidence we are looking for more easily recognizable, let's arrange these alternatives of translational raw material in column form:

---

[*] First published as the article "Chancelation and Transincidence: How to Deal with Coincidentals in Translating *Finnegans Wake*," by Friedhelm Rathjen, in *Papers on Joyce* No. 4, 1998, pp. 25-28.
[1] James Joyce, *Finnegans Wake* (London: Faber, 1975), 55.08.

| English: | crop | + | corpse |
|----------|------|---|--------|
| German: | Feldfrucht | | Leiche |
| | Ernte | | Leichnam |
| | Kartoffel(n) | | Kadaver |
| | Getreide | | sterbliche Überreste |
| | Frucht, Früchte | | Leib |
| | Korn, **Körner** | | **Körper** |

At this point the coincidence of word material we are looking for is finally achieved: *Körner* and *Körper* can easily be melted into "Körnper."[2]

The increasement of the plurality of possibilities, i.e., of the variety of raw materials, is achieved by processes of transforming, transposing, transferring etc. the first and most obvious guesses into a catalogue of alternative elements from which to choose. Almost every act designated by a 'trans'-prefixed verb can help in this process. Translation of third languages, for example, proved helpful when I had to deal with "Mahazar ag Dod"[3], a Joycean blending of 'Mother of God' and the Armenian words for 'mortal' and 'dirty': by using the Italian instead of the Armenian language, I found the solution "Mortal Gottas"[4] which blends the German *Mutter Gottes* with the Italian words for 'mortal' and 'the gout' (which, of course, is not dirty but shares with dirt connotations of decay).

The cases of coincidence mentioned thus far are all cases of voluntary coincidence. When translating passages from the *Wake*, however, I inevitably also fall victim to involuntary coincidences. Ulrich Blumenbach in his M.A. thesis finds high praise for my rendering of "retempter"[5] as "Redammptor"[6] on the grounds that this includes an allusion to the Dammtor railway station in Hamburg which, as Blumenbach has found out, was opened in 1866 on 16 June, of all dates[7] – a nice coincidence that I definitely did not dream of when working on my translation.

Translations of passages from *Finnegans Wake* can easily be used for a kind of test case: to what extent can elements of Joyce's original text that the translator did not

---

[2] Friedhelm Rathjen, unpublished translation of Joyce, *Finnegans Wake*, p. 55, used for Anthony Burgess, *Joyce für Jedermann: Eine Einführung in das Werk von James Joyce für den einfachen Leser*, trans. Friedhelm Rathjen (Frankfurt am Main: Frankfurter Verlagsanstalt, 1994).

[3] Joyce, *Finnegans Wake*, 389.32.

[4] Friedhelm Rathjen, trans., „Mamalujo," James Joyce, *Finnegans Wake Deutsch: Gesammelte Annäherungen*, ed. Klaus Reichert and Fritz Senn (Frankfurt am Main: Suhrkamp, 1989), pp. 220-37, p. 226.

[5] Joyce, *Finnegans Wake*, 154.6.

[6] Friedhelm Rathjen, trans., „Der Mauchs und Der Traufen," Joyce, *Finnegans Wake Deutsch*, pp. 124-31, p. 126.

[7] See Ulrich Blumenbach, *Üb-ersetzungen aus dem Anglo-wakischen ins Germano-wakische: Untersuchungen zum Problem der Übersetzbarkeit von James Joyces „Finnegans Wake"* (M.A. thesis, Free University of Berlin, 1990), p. 49.

notice nevertheless be traced in his target language version? Not everything, of course, survives the translation process, but I have already discovered in my German versions patterns and structures of Joyce's text I am sure I did not notice until after my translation was finished. For one example, let's have a look at the very first page of the *Wake*:

> riverrun, past Even and Adam's, from swerve of shore to bend of bay, brings us by a commodius vicus of recirculation **back** to Howth Castle and Environs.
>
> Sir Tristram, violer d'amores, fr'over the short sea, had **pass**encore rearrived from North **Arm**orica on this side the scraggy isthmus of Europe Minor to wielderfight his **penis**olate war: nor had topsawyer's rocks by the stream Oconee exaggerated themselse to Laurens County's gorgios while they went doublin their mumper all the time: nor avoice from afire bellowsed mishe mishe to tauftauf thuartpeatrick: not yet, though venissoon after, had a kidscad **butt**ended a bland old isaac: not yet, though all's fair in vanessy, were sosie sesthers wroth with twone nat**hand**joe. Rot a peck of pa's malt had Jhem or Shen brewed by arclight and rory end to the reggin**brow** was to be seen ringsome on the aqua**face**.[8]

I did not realize until recently that at least eight words designating parts of the body (printed in bold-face type for convenience sake in the quotation above) are more or less hidden in these lines. When translating this passage more than ten years ago, I definitely did not notice this – but still, seven German words designating parts of the body found their way into my translation:

> Flußgefließe, schleunigst Ev' und Adam passiert, vom Strandgestreun zum Buchtgebeug, führt uns im com**mund**iösen Wickelwirken des Rezirkulierens zurück zur Burg von Howth con Entourage.
>
> Sir Tristram, Widerholer d'amoore, von jenseits der Kurzsee, war passimkorps aus Nord**arm**orika rückgelangt an diese Seite den rauhen Isthmus von Kleineuropa um seinen **penis**olieren Krieg zu fehderführen: noch hatten Topfsawyers Felsen am Oconeelauf einanders aufgeworfen zu Laurensbezirks-**geäug**iern während sie die ganze Zeit ihre Unzoll verdopplinten: noch neStimmede aus deFeuerne michsiemaschsie blaßgebalgt um Dubistpaetrick taufzutaufen: noch nicht, obwohl hirschnell danach, hatte ein Knirpskniff einen dünkelnobelalten Isaak butterseicht bedickerendet: noch nicht, obwohl man's ja mag vannerstdie Eiteln kleiden, zürnten sosie Schwesthern zweinem Nathaundjoe. Nücht einen Viertelscheffel von Pas Malz hatte Jhem oder Shen bis zum Boginnlicht ge**brau**t und rötaurig Ende zum Gegen**brauen** war allerherund zu sehen auf der Aqua**fratz**.[9]

---

[8]   Joyce, *Finnegans Wake*, 3.1-14; bold-face type added.
[9]   Friedhelm Rathjen, trans., „Der Anfang," Joyce, *Finnegans Wake Deutsch*, p. 44; bold-face type added.

Some items (like the 'face' in "aquaface," the 'brow' in "regginbrow" and the 'penis' in "penisolate"), of course, translate themselves when the translator handles the surface value of the source language text with care, but in my German rendering I find at least two words for parts of the body (a mouth in "comm**und**iösen" and a manneristic word for eyes in "Laurensbezirks**geäug**iern") the appearance of which is completely unplanned: these are instances of sheer coincidence.

Maybe only a texture like *Finnegans Wake* allows this to happen to such an extent, the reason being that not only the translator has to increase the plurality of possibilities for coincidences to happen but that Joyce himself [p. 28:] during the composition of *Finnegans Wake* has already increased the totality of (possible) meanings, the probability that things 'fit' or can be made to 'fit' and up to a certain degree translate themselves without even being noticed by the translator. All the more unanswerable remains the question as to where we can draw the line between author's intentions, voluntary coincidences that the author arranged or at least approved of and involuntary coincidences that happen unnoticed.

# Translating Names, Titles and Quotations[*]
## Ten Practitioners' Rules, Derived from and Applied to
## German Renderings of *Ulysses* and *Finnegans Wake*

for Gerhard Friesen,
mennonite poet

## 1: Names

If you had to translate "Fritz Senn" into English, what would you come up with? My old Muret-Sanders dictionary (printed before World War I) explains that "Fritz" is an abbreviated form of "Friedrich" (or of Friedrich Wilhelm or even Friedhelm, as I would like to add) and gives "Fred" as the English equivalent. Wildhagen-Héraucourt's *German English Dictionary* of 1965 translates "Fritz" as both "Fred" and "Freddy" and also tells us that "der alte Fritz" in English is either "Old Fred" or "Frederick the Great." And how about Fritz Senn's last name? Wildhagen and Héraucourt translate "Senn" as (or rather transpose it into) "Alpine herdsman"; in Muret-Sanders, I find the variant "Alpine cowherd." Or should we prefer to translate the name "Senn" into English by using one of the misspellings that Senn has fallen victim to over the years? There's a variety of these: "Sin, Sen, Zen, Zimm, Senft, etc."[1]

Luckily nowadays there is not the slightest necessity to translate proper names, and so Fritz Senn is always Fritz Senn, at least in Western languages. (In, say, Japanese or Russian, however, even Fritz Senn would look quite different.) The stability of names while crossing borders is a relatively new achievement; less than a century ago, things looked quite different: you could be born as, say, Giorgio or Lucia and still be called George or Lucy elsewhere. If your last name was Joyce, you could even be joking about your name's German version being "Freud." And if you wrote a novel entitled *Ulysses* (which itself is a translated name and in some cases even has suffered re-translation[2]),

---

[*]   First published as the article "Translating Names, Titles and Quotations: Ten Practitioners' Rules, Derived from and Applied to German Renderings of *Ulysses* and *Finnegans Wake*," by Friedhelm Rathjen, in *A Collideorscape of Joyce: Festschrift for Fritz Senn*, edited by Ruth Frehner and Ursula Zeller (Dublin: Lilliput Press, 1998), pp. 407-26.

[1]   "Interview with Fritz Senn, May 1994," *Inductive Scrutinies: Focus on Joyce*, ed. Christine O'Neill (Dublin: Lilliput Press, 1995), pp. xii-xix, p. xviii.

[2]   Thomas Warburton's Swedish translation of *Ulysses* (first published in 1946), for example, and Aloys Skoumal's Czech translation (published in 1976) bear the title *Odysseus*. Some German critics (Arno Schmidt being the most notorious one) have opted for replacing the German title *Ulysses* by "Odysseus" on the grounds that whereas Ulysses is the most common form of the Greek hero's name in English tradition, Odysseus is much more common in German. There is, however, an (albeit minor) tradition in Germany, too, of

with one of the characters named Stephen Dedalus, you had a good chance that your German translator (Georg Goyert, in this case) would rename this character "Stephan Dädalus."

The most obvious reason for rejecting Goyert's "Stephan Dädalus" is that *Ulysses* is located in a real and (basically, at least) realistically treated city, namely Dublin, where nobody has ever heard of a native citizen called either "Stephan" or "Dädalus." Unfortunately the same can be said of the name "Dedalus" in Joyce's original. Claire A. Culleton, who in her *Names and Naming in Joyce* claims that "verisimilitude was one of Joyce's governing principles" and that "Joyce was careful to people his texts with names that maintained the nominal integrity of his works, names that believably fit the milieu of Dublin during the particular era in which his book was set"[3], has been taken to task by Michael Patrick Gillespie for this statement on the grounds of what Gillespie calls "the Dedalus / Daedalus anomaly"[4]. Joyce's decision to use his own immature pseudonym "Stephen Daedalus" for one of his major characters is undoubtedly one of the few mishaps in the formation of his artistic devices – but at least he has made things a little bit better by changing "Daedalus" into "Dedalus" in the process of rewriting *Stephen Hero* into *A Portrait of the Artist as a Young Man*. Georg Goyert was the one to make things worse again. It seems, however, that Goyert's decision to Germanize the name followed directly from the fact that it was non-Irish and non-realistic already: he left the other major characters' names unchanged, even the name of Leopold Bloom, which would lend itself perfectly to a Germanization in the form of "Blum." (Arno Schmidt, the German writer and would-be Joycean, who voted for "Odysseus" as the correct German title of the novel, habitually spells the novel's hero "Leopold Blum.")

So – my first and major rule for the handling of names in translation is this:

• Never change or modify a name unless there is a good reason for changing it.[5]

Unfortunately there is a variety of good reasons that may interfere with the translator's wish for conservation. Some of these reasons have to do with effects, but most have to do with a name's background, and in most cases conforming the background is the overriding principle. Unless the background consists in a realistic setting (which always

---

using the Latin form, mostly with the spelling "Ulyses"; there are two poems entitled "Ulysses," for example, by Samuel Christian Pape, a mediocre romantic poet favoured by Arno Schmidt, of all people.

3   Claire A. Culleton, *Names and Naming in Joyce* (Madison: University of Wisconsin Press, 1994), p. 14.

4   Michael Patrick Gillespie, "What's in a Name?," *James Joyce Literary Supplement* 10.1 (Spring 1996), p. 3.

5   This is my version of a rule that Fritz Senn has put down in "Seven Against *Ulysses*," *James Joyce Quarterly* 4.3 (Spring 1967), pp. 165-93, p. 181: "Surnames, as a rule, are not tampered with, but the rule is often broken." I intend my rule to be valid for first names, too. – Remarks on translating names are also included in Senn's "*Ulysses* in der Übersetzung," *Nichts gegen Joyce: Joyce Versus Nothing: Aufsätze 1959-1983*, ed. Franz Cavigelli (Zurich: Haffmans, 1983), pp. 207-43, esp. pp. 236-38.

tends to support our first rule), it is easier for a translator to forget that rule and ask himself how a name's effects in one language might be best reproduced in another. There are some cases where the translator – depending on his personal tastes – may find it best to change a name in order to achieve the effects of the original version in the target language. For example, one may not like Christian Enzensberger's translating "Humpty Dumpty" into "Goggelmoggel" and the "Jabberwocky" into a "Zipferlake" in his German version of Lewis Carroll's *Through the Looking-Glass* (and I definitely don't like it), but this depends largely on taste, and we cannot reject Enzensberger's decisions solely on the grounds of the overriding background principle – because there *is* no such background here. Enzensberger's rendering of "Thelma bboggs" as "Selma Kkloo" and of "Hyam's" as "Wertheim" in his translation of Samuel Beckett's *More Pricks than Kicks* stories[6], however, is an obvious violation of the overriding background rule: Beckett's stories are set against a more or less realistic Dublin background.

There are, however, other backgrounds that sometimes interfere with that of the setting. One of these is that of inconsistent but nonetheless binding naming traditions. Let's have a look at a name catalogue from "Cyclops" in order to illustrate this point:

> Father John Murphy, Owen Roe, Patrick Sarsfield, Red Hugh O'Donnell, Red Jim MacDermott, Soggarth Eoghan O'Growney, Michael Dwyer, Francy Higgins, Henry Joy M'Cracken, Goliath, Horace Wheatley, Thomas Conneff, Peg Woffington, the Village Blacksmith, Captain Moonlight, Captain Boycott, Dante Alighieri, Christopher Columbus, S. Fursa, S. Brendan, Marshal MacMahon, Charlemagne, Theobald Wolfe Tone, the Mother of the Maccabees, the Last of the Mohicans, [...], Muhammad, the Bride of Lammermoor, Peter the Hermit, Peter the Packer, [...], Angus the Culdee, Dolly Mount, Sidney Parade, [...], Adam and Eve, Arthur Wellesley, Boss Croker, Herodotus, Jack the Giantkiller, Gautama Buddha, Lady Godiva, The Lily of Killarney [...].[7]

This list comprises of real and realistic Irish names, historical names from various backgrounds, biblical names, and what in German are called *sprechende Namen* ('speaking names'), such as "Captain Moonlight," as well as non-names. In English, *sprechende Namen* (by their technical term: *aptronyms*) comes close to symbolic names. Non-names are labels functioning as names, such as "the Village Blacksmith," "the Last of the Mohicans" or "The Lily of Killarney"; these are translated by both Georg Goyert and Hans Wollschläger in their German versions of *Ulysses*. The realistic (or sometimes – as with "Dolly Mount, Sidney Parade" – mock-realistic) names remain unchanged (apart from a typo in Goyert's text) in accordance with our first rule; even components like

---

[6]    See Friedhelm Rathjen, "Dubliner Zentralklosett: Zu Christian Enzensbergers Übersetzung von Samuel Becketts Prosasammlung *More Pricks than Kicks*," *die horen* 168 (1992), pp. 133-39, rpt. in Friedhelm Rathjen, *weder noch: Aufsätze zu Samuel Beckett* (Scheeßel: Edition ReJoyce, 2005), pp. 125-33.

[7]    James Joyce, *Ulysses: The Corrected Text*, ed. Hans Walter Gabler (Harmondsworth: Penguin, 1986 [Student's Edition]), 12.178-97.

"Red," "Joy," "Moonlight" are treated strictly as names and therefore not translated. Items like "Peter the Packer" and "Angus the Culdee" are separated into proper name (which remains unaltered) and supplementary identification (which, strictly speaking, is not subject to our first rule and therefore translated by both Goyert and Wollschläger). What remains is this:

> Goliath, [...], Dante Alighieri, Christoph Columbus, [...], Karl der Grosse, [...], Mohammed, [...], Adam und Eva, [...], Herodotus, [...] Gautama Buddha [...].[8]
> Goliath, [...], Dante Alighieri, Christoph Columbus, [...], Karl der Große, [...], Mohammed, [...], Adam und Eva, [...], Herodot, [...] Gaudama Buddha [...].[9]

These are all names from history and / or scripture. Names from backgrounds like these often take different forms in different languages, and this leads us to our second rule, which in such cases overrides the first one:

- If you have to deal with a historical, biblical, mythical or literary name which has different forms in different languages, always be sure to use the one that is customary in the target language, unless there is a good reason for sticking to the form in the source language.

As you may have noticed, Georg Goyert in the above example did not stick to the rule in one case: he left the Latin form "Herodotus" (customary in English) unchanged, although the old Greek historian is always called "Herodot" in German.

Sticking to this second rule sometimes causes some trouble, e.g., when an author uses a biblical or historical character as a foil to / for the characters of a realistically set novel, but the worst possible solution always is to charge ordinary characters with uncommon name forms in your translation where they are ordinarily named in the original. British kings may usually be called Georg, Heinrich, Jakob in German, but most German readers will prefer reading of "Henry VIII" to having a character in an English novel bear the name "Heinrich." (Luckily in this field at least, things are beginning to change: nobody in Germany calls the present Prince of Wales "Prinz Karl.")

Although consistency of your translation would be a nice thing to have, it is sometimes more elegant to deviate from your own rules in order to achieve more conformity with the original (all the more so in the case of *Ulysses* and *Finnegans Wake*, both of which are novels that deliberately sacrifice homogeneity and purity an the altar of eclecticism and even bastardization). A good example is William Shakespeare's saying, quoted by Stephen in "Scylla and Charybdis": *"William the conqueror came before Richard III"*[10]. Georg Goyert in his translation sticks to our second rule and therefore misses the point: *"Wilhelm der Eroberer kam vor Richard III"*[11]. Of course "Wilhelm der Eroberer" is

---

8     Georg Goyert, trans., *Ulysses*, by James Joyce, 2 vols. (Munich: dtv, 1966), p. 334.

9     Hans Wollschläger, trans., *Ulysses*, by James Joyce (Frankfurt am Main: Suhrkamp, 1979), p. 411.

10    Joyce, *Ulysses*, 9.637.

11    Goyert, trans., *Ulysses*, p. 229.

the correct translation of "William the conqueror," but nevertheless this version does not fit into the context, as Shakespeare is *not* called "Wilhelm Shakespeare" in German. Hans Wollschläger therefore breaks our rule, translates "William the conqueror" into a bastard version unheard of before, but thus manages to make the sentence work and at the same time make the identity of the conqueror in question absolutely clear for the German reader: "*William der Eroberer kam vor Richard III*"[12].

As has been stated before, our second rule applies to names from literary works as well: Shakespeare's characters, for example, sometimes bear different names in different languages. The most famous case – in the German language, at least – is Bottom, the weaver from the *Midsummer Night's Dream*, who in the standard German translation is called "Zettel." Literally translated, this name means "slip of paper" (which is quite something other than a bottom); luckily neither Bottom nor Zettel appears in *Ulysses*, and we may leave the problem of dealing with the intricacies of this case to anyone who may want to try to translate Arno Schmidt's novel *Zettel's Traum* into English.

A problem that the translator of *Ulysses* does have to deal with is the fact that in German, "Sinbad the Sailor" is "Sindbad der Seefahrer." Where Joyce has „Sinbad the Sailor and Tinbad the Tailor and Jinbad the Jailer and Whinbad the Whaler"[13], Goyert tells us of "Sindbad dem Seefahrer und Tindbad dem Teefahrer und Jindbad dem Jefahrer und Windbad dem Wehfahrer"[14] and Wollschläger of "Sindbad dem Seefahrer und Tindbad dem Teefahrer und Findbad dem Feefahrer und Rindbad dem Rehfahrer"[15]. Of course a "Whaler" is neither "Wehfahrer" nor "Rehfahrer," but both translators stick to the formal operations going on in the text (Goyert a little bit more clumsily than Wollschläger) and ignore quite rightly the question of whether the tailor's tailorship may be of importance elsewhere in this or any other Joycean text. I myself was less lucky, because I had to translate Anthony Burgess's book *Here Comes Everybody*. In one of his *Wake* chapters, Burgess uses the formula "FROM SINBAD THE SAILOR TO TINBAD THE TAILOR"[16] in introducing his reader to the sailor / tailor theme of *Finnegans Wake* II.3. My solution is a rephrasing of the formula ("VON SINDBAD DEM SEEMANN ZU NINDBAD DEM NÄHMANN"[17]) plus an explanatory endnote – notes are always possible in secondary literature (which in itself is merely

---

12    Wollschläger, trans., *Ulysses*, pp. 282 f.
13    Joyce, *Ulysses*, 17.2322-3.
14    Goyert, trans., *Ulysses*, p. 760.
15    Wollschläger, trans., *Ulysses*, p. 938.
16    Anthony Burgess, *Here Comes Everybody: An Introduction to James Joyce for the Ordinary Reader* (London: Faber, 1965), p. 231.
17    Anthony Burgess, *Joyce für Jedermann: Eine Einführung in das Werk von James Joyce für den einfachen Leser*, trans. Friedhelm Rathjen (Frankfurt am Main: Frankfurter Verlagsanstalt, 1994), p. 294. – The title of this translation is yet another instance of giving up in the face of translation problems. "Here Comes Everybody," one of the names given to HCE in the *Wake*, could be rendered as "Hier Chauffiert Einjeder," but this doesn't seem fit to stand as a book's title.

explanatory) but should be avoided in primary texts which – even in translation – should work without being explained.

With the permutations of "Sinbad the Sailor," we have already entered a sphere where a name stops being just a name, i.e., something arbitrary meant only to designating someone, and instead becomes capable of also describing that someone. *Sprechende Namen* play an important role in the onomastic structure of *Ulysses* (and, even more so, of *Finnegans Wake*), and this again requires us to restrict the validity of our rules and to establish new ones. I have stated elsewhere

> that (1) in naming major characters Joyce gave priority to realistic and illusionistic names, while in naming minor characters (and especially in name catalogues) he increasingly tended towards using symbolic and even undisguisingly speaking names, and that (2) the less a chapter or passage is ruled by neutral representational realism the more Joyce's naming habits show a tendency toward oversubscribing characterization and even parodistical distortion.[18]

In short: less realism means more *sprechende Namen* and vice versa. We may from this deduce our third rule for dealing with Joyce's names in translation:

- If a name is a 'speaking name' or is clearly symbolic, don't hesitate to translate the surface value into your target language – but if the name in question shows any traces of background (similarities to realistic names and / or names with a tradition), be sure to create this background in your solution, too.

The names "Doctor Diet and Doctor Quiet"[19] are 'speaking names' through and through, so Georg Goyert is justified in forgetting all background and rendering this phrase as "Doktor Diät und Doktor Ruhe"[20] – were it not for the missing sound pattern which in 'speaking names' is of considerable importance. Hans Wollschläger has a better solution: "Doktor Pfleg und Doktor Heg"[21]. In the case of "sir Frederick the Falconer"[22], things are less clear: although the article "the" identifies this name as a *sprechender Name*, "Falconer" could be a real family name instead of a profession or activity. At first glance, Goyert's "Sir Frederik der Falkner"[23] therefore sounds less convincing than Wollschläger's "Sir Frederick der Falconer"[24]. The real person behind Joyce's naming, however, is Sir Frederick Richard Falkiner (1831-1908), who appears

---

[18]   Friedhelm Rathjen, "Blame the Names," *James Joyce Literary Supplement* 5.1 (Spring 1991), p. 9. This is a review of Andreas Palme, *Die Personennamen im Ulysses: Eine Studie zur literarischen Onomastik bei James Joyce* (Erlangen: Palm & Enke, 1990); although the conclusion I quote here is mine and not Palme's, his book has been of considerable help in tracing the mechanics at work.

[19]   Joyce, *Ulysses*, 14.1402.

[20]   Goyert, trans., *Ulysses*, p. 483.

[21]   Wollschläger, trans., *Ulysses*, p. 595.

[22]   Joyce, *Ulysses*, 12.1121.

[23]   Goyert, trans., *Ulysses*, p. 363.

[24]   Wollschläger, trans., *Ulysses*, p. 448.

elsewhere in *Ulysses* under his correctly spelled name[25] (unchanged in Goyert's as well as Wollschläger's translation). In this case, the German "Falkner" is much more adequate than the English "Falconer" that Wollschläger preserves.

A problem with 'speaking names' is that sometimes the quality of being a name is beginning to disappear. This is the case once in "Oxen of the Sun," where Joyce's catalogue "Mr Cavil and Mr Sometimes Godly, Mr Ape Swillale, Mr False Franklin, Mr Dainty Dixon, Young Boasthard and Mr Cautious Calmer"[26] is weakened by Goyert: "der Sophist und der Manchmal-Fromm, der gierige Saufaus und der falsche Freisasse, der treffliche Dixon, der Prahler und der vorsichtige Beruhiger"[27]. These are no longer names at all, because Goyert decides to completely skip the "Mr" (which he usually translates as "Herr"). Wollschläger (who usually leaves the "Mr" in its appropriate place) is much stronger in this case: "Der Herr Krittle Frisch und der Herr Manchmal Gottsförchtig, der Herr Nacheffer Sauffaus, der Herr Freisaß Falsch, der Herr Geck Dixon, Jung Prahlhans und der Herr Fürsichtige Besennftiger"[28].

Not each and every name that is (or looks like) a 'speaking' one must be changed. In most cases, Goyert and Wollschläger agree with each other when deciding which names *not* to alter. These include the following[29]:

> Leopold Bloom, Buck Mulligan, Kinch, Strongbow, M'Intosh, Fresh Nelly, Henry Tudor, Pisser Burke, Vera Verity, Nasodoro, Silversmile, Silberselber, Flipperty Jippert, Penrose, Mary Shortall, Jimmy Pidgeon, Shotover, Gummy Granny, Skin-the-Goat, Mr Goodbody, Ramsbottom

Surprises are few here. Since nobody knows yet what "Kinch" is really meant to mean, both translators were certainly wise in leaving this name untouched. Luckily "Pisser" in German means exactly what it means in English, so there is not the least reason to fumble around with "Pisser Burke." "Strongbow" and "Skin-the-Goat" are historically correct names which should not be changed unless there is a really strong reason; "Penrose" and "Ramsbottom" and "Mr Goodbody" sound like 'speaking names' but are fixed in the background of realism and must not be translated. What could have been translated, however, is "Jimmy Pidgeon," and the same could be said of "Silversmile,"

---

[25]   See Joyce, *Ulysses*, 8.1151.
[26]   Ibid., 14.468-70.
[27]   Goyert, trans., *Ulysses*, p. 452.
[28]   Wollschläger, trans., *Ulysses*, p. 555.
[29]   For practical reasons, I give no citation for the lists that follow. These and more names can be most easily located in the text by using either Wolfhard Steppe's *A Handlist to James Joyce's "Ulysses": A Complete Alphabetical Index to the Critical Reading Text* (New York: Garland, 1986) (for the Gabler edition) or Shari and Bernard Benstock's *Who's He When He's at Home: A James Joyce Directory* (Urbana: University of Illinois Press, 1980) (for the 1961 Random House edition). For converting these editions to the German translations, Dieter Rudolph's *The Pages of Ulysses: A synoptical comparison of the pagination of different editions and translations of James Joyce "ULYSSES"* (Frankfurt am Main: privately printed, 1985) is most useful.

were it not for the fact that this name appears in the list of Bloom's multilingual silver children, a list that in the English original includes a German "Silberselber," for example, so that a German translation can just as well include an English name.

The following is a list of names that suffer some kind of change in both Goyert's and Wollschläger's translation[30]:

> Jove (GG: Zeus, HW: Jupiter), Thomas Aquinas (GG: Thomas von Aquino, HW: Thomas von Aquin), Turko the Terrible (GG and HW: Turko der Schreckliche), Plain Jane (GG: Ernstes Mädchen, HW: Fade Liese), Ballocky Mulligan (GG: Klöterich Mulligan, HW: Wallachi Mulligan), Toby Tostoff (GG: Toby Abgänger, HW: Toby Kaltbauer), Chickabiddy (GG: Herzblättchen, HW: Schnuckiputzi), Throwaway (GG: Weggeworfen, HW: Flugblatt), Edward Guelph-Wettin (GG: Eduard Welf-Wettin, HW: Edward Welf-Wettin), Dame Fashion (GG: Dame Mode, HW: Göttin Mode), Father Cantekissem (GG: Vater Cantekissene, HW: Pater Kathischißmus), Tommy Tittlemouse (GG: Schäker, HW: Nippeljipper), Cunty Kate (GG and HW: Fotzen-Kate)

As can be clearly seen here, changes in names are restricted to either names with a historical or literary background that calls for change or 'speaking names' in the full sense of the word. Goyert's "Ernstes Mädchen" is an interesting case, for this is not only a misunderstanding of what "Plain Jane" means but also a de-naming of the original version: "Ernstes Mädchen" is no name a all. The same can be said of some of the (few) cases where Goyert changes a name and Wollschläger does not:

> Stephen Dedalus (GG: Stephan Dädalus), (Prince) Albert Edward (GG: Albert Eduard), Deadwood Dicks (GG: Bande Räubergesindel), Victoria (GG: Viktoria), Hoppy Holohan (GG: Hümpeleinundertig Holohan), Blephen (GG: Blephan), Penelope Rich (GG: Penelope Reich)

"Bande Räubergesindel" is a de-naming of the "Deadwood Dicks"; "Hümpeleinundertig Holohan" is a very clumsy (and unintelligible) rendering of "Hoppy Holohan"; "Penelope Reich" is more than problematic because "Penelope Rich" is not a 'speaking name' but rather a historically correct name that should not be fumbled around with, as long as Joyce himself does not do so.

Overall, however, Goyert changes less than Wollschläger. The following is a sample list of names that are translated by Wollschläger but not by Goyert:

> Sceptre (HW: Szepter), Rightaway (HW: Flugpfeil), Jacky Tar (HW: Jan Maat), sir Fopling Popinjay (HW: Sir Dummbatsch Geckerich), sir Milksop Quidnunc (HW: Sir Geilhans Nasweis), Ananias Praisegod Barebones (HW: Ananias Preisegott Knochendürr; typo in GG: Praisegold), Slipperslapper (HW: Schlappschluffen), Handy Andy (HW: Witzbold), Dubedat (HW: Disedat)

---

[30]   GG = Georg Goyert; HW = Hans Wollschläger.

An interesting point is Wollschläger's rendering of "Sceptre" (a horse running in the Gold Cup race) as "Szepter," a translation that seems absolutely unnecessary, for although "Sceptre" is a 'speaking name', it does not really act as one but rather sticks to the realism of horse-naming. Moreover, even a German reader unfamiliar with the English language will recognize what "Sceptre" means. A third objection against "Szepter" is that this translation establishes an inconsistency, as the name of another horse, "Shotover," is not translated by Wollschläger, as can be seen from our first list. The case is different, however, with the rendering of yet another horse name, "Rightaway," as "Flugpfeil": this is made necessary by the fact that Wollschläger (in order to make Bantam Lyons's momentous misunderstanding work in the German text) has to render "Throwaway" as "Flugblatt." Goyert, on the other hand, makes "Throwaway" read "Weggeworfen" but leaves "Rightaway" as it is, thus showing once more that he has no ear for sound structures.

In *Finnegans Wake* the problems in dealing with names are more severe even than in *Ulysses*: where Joyce always speaks in different tongues at the same time, all names increasingly sound like 'speaking names'. Not all are, however, and in principle, we have to apply the same rules that are valid for translating names from *Ulysses*. As just one example I'd like to introduce what arguably is the most problematic name translation that can be found in my own renderings of *Wake* material. In "Mamalujo" we find these sentences: "Mind mand gunfree by Gladeys Rayburn! Runtable's Reincoroporated. The new world presses"[31]. "Gladeys Rayburn" is not quite a realistic name, but it sounds nearly like one; this means that rendering "Gladeys" as, say, "Freudäuglein" would be a violation of all rules. Joyce takes the real first name 'Gladys' and adds just one letter. In my version, I have done the same, but since this seemed impossible with 'Gladys', I have taken the liberty of replacing it with another name. I admit that this is always and by definition a problematic solution, but my reinsurance is that according to Glasheen's *Census*, "Gladeys Rayburn" is a name that is not connected with any other item inside or outside the *Wake*. Moreover, I made sure that the name I chose – Augusta – is easily recognizable for the German reader but – and this is important! – nevertheless fits into an English-language background. Adding a single letter, my solution is "Auglusta"; lust seems to have something to do with glad eyes. The last name, "Rayburn," is even trickier. In noticing the "new world" as a focus of the passage in question, I read "Reincorporated" as a reference to 'reincarnated', "gunfree" as a bilingual 'gone früh' and "Rayburn" as 'reborn'. My aim in translating the name therefore was to make it recall the German 'Wiedergeburt' and at the same time sound at least a little bit like something that is conceivable as an English family name. My solution is "Widdergabbart"; the whole passage in my version reads as follows: "Minne Manne Gehtfrüh von Auglusta Widdergabbart! Tabelrenntes Reinkarpitalgesellschaft. Druck der neuen Welt."[32]

31  Joyce, *Finnegans Wake*, 287.35-6.
32  Friedhelm Rathjen, trans., "Mamalujo," James Joyce, *Finnegans Wake Deutsch: Gesammelte Annäheruungen*, ed. Klaus Reichert and Fritz Senn (Frankfurt am Main: Suhrkamp, 1989), pp. 220-37, p. 224.

## 2: Titles

Translating *Finnegans Wake* 287.35-36 includes dealing not only with a name but also with a film title: "Mind mand gunfree" according to McHugh's *Annotations* refers to the film *My Man Godfrey*.[33] Not knowing if (and with what title) this film may have been translated into German, I modelled my "Minne Manne Gehtfrüh" upon the English title. Strictly speaking, this is a violation of my first rule of title-translating, for this rule runs like follows:

- If the text that you have to translate includes titles, always use the target language title of the work in question, unless there is a good reason for sticking to the original version.

Contrary to names, titles are usually translated. The ordinary reader in Germany knows Margaret Mitchell's best-selling novel as *Vom Winde verweht* rather than *Gone with the Wind*; every English speaking reader prefers speaking of Halldór Laxness's *Atom Station* to speaking of his *Atómstöðin*; Fyodor Dostoyevsky's most famous novel is known to the English public as *Crime and Punishment* and to the German public as *Schuld und Sühne*, and scarcely anyone would recognize this novel if referred to as *Prestupleniye i nakazaniye*. Since, however, a new German translation of Dostoyevsky's novel has appeared recently, bearing the new title *Verbrechen und Strafe*, it is quite possible that before long this will be the standard title in Germany. There are a lot of cases where a work of literature is translated more than once into the same language, and this can make things quite complicated. There are still some people in Germany, definitely no Joyce experts, who sometimes refer to Joyce's *Jugendbildnis* or a volume of verse by the same author entitled *Am Strand von Fontana*. We have to add a second rule to our first one:

- If there are different titles for the work in question in the target language, use the title of the standard translation, unless there is a good reason for choosing another.

Such a good reason may under certain circumstances be presented by the fact that the standard (or, even worse, the only) translation bears an inadequate title. As a general rule, however, even bad titles, if they are known to the readership, are preferable to good titles that are your own invention. Sometimes – but not automatically – these can be instances where it is wisest to stick to the original title.

Let us see whether or not Goyert and Wollschläger submit to our rules. Perhaps the most famous instance of title-quoting in *Ulysses* is the catalogue of Bloom's books. The following is just a small portion of that list in the original and both German versions:

---

[33]  See Roland McHugh, *Annotations to "Finnegans Wake"* (London: Routledge & Kegan Paul, 1980), p. 387.

*Philosophy of the Talmud* (sewn pamphlet).

Lockhart's *Life of Napoleon* (cover wanting, marginal annotations, minimising victories, aggrandising defeats by the protagonist).

*Soll und Haben* by Gustav Freytag (black boards, Gothic characters, cigarette coupon bookmark at p. 24). [...]

*In the Track of the Sun* (yellow cloth, titlepage missing, recurrent title intestation).[34]

*Philosophy of the Talmud* (broschiertes Pamphlet).

Lockart's *Life of Napoleon* (ohne Einbanddecke, Randbemerkungen, Siege des Helden werden verkleinert, Niederlagen übertrieben).

*Soll und Haben* von Gustav Freytag (schwarze Pappe, Fraktur-Buchstaben, Bildchen aus Zigarettenschachtel als Lesezeichen bei Seite 24). [...]

*In the Track of the Sun* (gelbe Leinwand, Titelseite fehlt, laufende Titelangabe auf jeder Seite).[35]

*Philosophy of the Talmud* (geheftete Broschur).

Lockharts *Life of Napoleon* (Deckel nicht mehr vorhanden, Randbemerkungen, Siege der Hauptfigur verkleinernd, Niederlagen vergrößernd).

*Soll und Haben* von Gustav Freytag (schwarzer Pappband, Frakturschrift, Zigarettenbildchen als Lesezeichen auf S. 24). [...]

*In the Track of the Sun* (gelbes Leinen, Titelseite nicht mehr vorhanden, wiederkehrende Titelintestierung).[36]

Surprisingly enough, neither Goyert nor Wollschläger translates the titles. (Goyert even leaves the apostrophe in the misspelled "Lockart's" in its place, although this is clearly not part of the title.) One conceivable reason is that in this case, the titles refer not to works in immaterialized form but rather to books in their physical presence – this alone, however, is not reason enough for violating our rules, for this would also apply to "the Capel street library copy of *The Woman in White*"[37], a novel that would most probably never have been on the shelves of a Dublin library in German translation. Both translators, however, as we will see further on, translate Collins's title into German. The reason for the fact that the titles of Bloom's books have not been translated can best be tracked via the Gustav Freytag title in the list: *Soll und Haben* is German in both Goyert's and Wollschläger's versions, simply because it is German in Joyce's original already. The inclusion of "*Soll und Haben* by Gustav Freytag" in the list indicates that Joyce wanted to cite all titles in the language that the books Bloom owns are written in; had Bloom owned, say, only French-language books, Joyce would have given us a list of French titles which, of course, should have remained French in any German translation. The rule that applies here is this one:

---

[34] Joyce, *Ulysses*, 17.1380-96.
[35] Goyert, trans., *Ulysses*, p. 727.
[36] Wollschläger, trans., *Ulysses*, p. 89.
[37] Joyce, *Ulysses*, 10.368.

- Titles that in the original appear in a third language must always remain unchanged in your translation.

"*Soll und Haben* by Gustav Freytag" is meant to show that Bloom has read this book in the German language (albeit up to page 24 only); the reader of a German *Ulysses* translation would necessarily miss this point, unless the translators either leave all English titles in English or find any kind of compensation – an additional remark in the book's description, e.g., saying 'in German'. Both translators have understandably opted against such a compensatory solution and thus preferred not to translate the English titles here – which, however, causes some minor problems elsewhere in the novel, as we will see later.

If this really is the reason for the non-translated titles, English titles should be properly translated elsewhere in Goyert's and Wollschläger's versions. Let's check this my means of "the evolutionary theories of Charles Darwin, expounded in *The Descent of Man* and *The Origin of Species*"[38]. Wollschläger translates: "die Evolutionstheorien von Charles Darwin [...], wie sie in der *Abstammung des Menschen* und der *Entstehung der Arten* dargelegt waren"[39], using the well-known German titles of Darwin's writings; Goyert, however, does not follow our rules: "die Evolutionstheorien Charles Darwins, wie er sie in *The Descent of Man* und *The Origin of Species* darstellt"[40]. Goyert's own rule runs absolutely counter to ours: throughout *Ulysses*, he leaves innumerable titles of both unknown and well-known books unaltered, thus rendering the text of *Ulysses* more difficult for the German reader without gaining anything in return. And he also renders his own task as translator more difficult, for his decision not to translate titles leads to several pitfalls into which Goyert every now and again stumbles.

Among the titles that Goyert refuses to translate are those of Shakespeare's plays, well-known to German readers and theatre-goers under the titles of the Schlegel-Tieck translation. All titles consisting of just two names with an "and" in between, however, in Goyert's text are graced by a German "und," which leads to absurd bilingual lists such as "*King Lear, Othello, Hamlet, Troilus und Cressida*"[41]. Moreover, Goyert does translate formulations that make use of but are no longer titles. In Stephen's "When Rutlandbaconsouthamptonshakespeare or another poet of the same name in the comedy of errors wrote *Hamlet*"[42], Goyert renders "comedy of errors" as "Komödie der Irrungen"[43]. When Stephen in a similar way uses the title of a book (practically unheard of by German readers) by Robert Greene ("He had a good groatsworth of wit"[44]),

---

[38] Ibid., 17.1644-5.
[39] Wollschläger, trans., *Ulysses*, p. 910.
[40] Goyert, trans., *Ulysses*, p. 736.
[41] Ibid., p. 222.
[42] Joyce, *Ulysses*, 9.865-7.
[43] Goyert, trans., *Ulysses*, p. 237.
[44] Joyce, *Ulysses*, 9.245.

Goyert does *not* translate this phrase: "Er besass einen *good groatsworth of wit*"[45]. Wollschläger, who as a rule translates all titles, has no problems here: "Er besaß einen guten Groschenwert Witz"[46].

Dealing with titles of works that have never been translated into the target language is slightly more difficult than dealing with well-known and well-translated titles. One could argue with good reason that in such cases all titles should remain untranslated, but I personally opt for a rule that is more complicated:

- If there is no existing version of a title in your target language, well-known titles may sometimes best remain untranslated, but titles of works that only a few experts have heard of should always be translated into the target language. In all cases make sure that readers who know the original title have no difficulties in recognizing the work in question in your newly translated title.

If, for example, in an English text that you have to translate *Finnegans Wake* is mentioned, don't feel obliged to imitate Arno Schmidt and twaddle of "Finnegans Totenwacht" but rather stick to *Finnegans Wake*; if *"Ruby: the Pride of the Ring"*[47] is mentioned, however, you'll be best off with *"Ruby: der Stolz der Arena"*[48] or *"Ruby: Der Stolz der Arena"*[49]. The fact that in this case Goyert unexpectedly translates the title unfortunately does not mean that he respects our third rule in title translation – there are other cases where he again refuses to translate unknown titles. "Mr Justice Madden in his *Diary of Master William Silence*"[50] in his version is rendered as "Richter Madden in seinem *Diary of Master William Silence*"[51], and even Hans Wollschläger here refuses to translate the title[52], maybe because of the obvious problems of translating the name "William Silence."

The result is that in Goyert's translation, there is a total confusion of inadequate rules, leading inevitably to a general inconsistency. When Joyce mentions *Paradise Lost* and *The Sorrows of Satan*[53], Goyert, contrary to his rules, uses the standard translation ("das *Verlorene Paradies*") and an adequate rendering of a seemingly untranslated title ("*Die Sorgen Satans*"[54]) respectively; Wollschläger does exactly the same[55], but according to his rules. When in the vicinity of "the *Merry Wives*" (which in Goyert's translation are reduced to "den *Merry wives*") the long forgotten pamphlets *"Hooks and Eyes for Believers'*

---

45     Goyert, trans., *Ulysses*, p. 217.
46     Wollschläger, trans.,*Ulysses*, p. 268.
47     Joyce, *Ulysses*, 4.346.
48     Wollschläger, trans.,*Ulysses*, p. 90.
49     Goyert, trans., *Ulysses*, p. 75.
50     Joyce, *Ulysses*, 9.582-3.
51     Goyert, trans., *Ulysses*, p. 227.
52     See Wollschläger, trans., *Ulysses*, p. 281.
53     Joyce, *Ulysses*, 9.19-20.
54     Goyert, trans., *Ulysses*, p. 210.
55     See Wollschläger, trans., *Ulysses*, p. 259.

*Breeches* and *The Most Spiritual Snuffbox to Make the Most Devout Souls Sneeze*"[56] are mentioned, Goyert (possibly mistaking these titles for Joycean forgery) translates: "*Haken und Ösen für die Hosen der Gläubigen* und *Die sehr geistliche Schupftabakdose, nach deren Gebrauch die sehr frommen Seelen niesen*"[57]. (Wollschläger translates the titles using historical language that suits the purpose: "*Haken und Ösen für eines rechten Gläubigen Beinkleid* und *Die sehr geistliche Schnupftabakdose, davon die frommen Seelen ein herzhaft Niesen sollen haben*"[58].) The "Capel street library copy of *The Woman in White*"[59] mentioned before is not only translated by Goyert, but also translated with disregard to the then standard German title: Wilkie Collins's novel was translated by C. Büchele in 1862 under the title *Die weiße Frau*, but Goyert uses "*Frau in Weiss*"[60] as his German title. Ironically enough, Goyert's severest critic, Arno Schmidt, when publishing his translation of the Collins novel, used the title *Die Frau in Weiß* indeed, thus making Goyert's solution correct at last (not in accordance with Goyert's own rule, but in accordance with our rules at least). Another problem caused by Goyert's non-translational approach is that he always translates titles that are not marked as such – "Japhet in search of a father"[61] is rendered as "Japhet auf der Suche nach einem Vater"[62] – and sometimes even fails to notice titles as such – "Twenty years asleep in Sleepy Hollow"[63] is reduced to an insignificant "Schlief zwanzig Jahre im Schlaftal"[64].

Inconsistencies of this kind can also be found in Wollschläger's translation, however. As has been noted before, the title *In the Track of the Sun* from Bloom's bookshelf remains untranslated in both Goyert's and Wollschläger's translation. In "Calypso," there is a reference to this book: "in the track of the sun. Sunburst on the titlepage"[65]. Both translators Germanize this passage and thus inevitably obscure the reference for the German reader: "über die Sonnenbahn. Mit Sonnenaufgang auf dem Titelblatt"[66]; "Auf den Spuren der Sonne. Der Sunburst auf dem Titelblatt: Aufgang des Glanzes"[67]. The only possible solution to this problem would have been to translate the titles of Bloom's library, too.

The titles discussed so far all belong to the field of literature. With titles from other fields, things are sometimes slightly different. Titles of journals, newspapers and to a certain degree radio programmes are usually not translated, as in most cases these titles add to the atmosphere of a text's setting rather than working as a foil for possible

---

[56] Joyce, *Ulysses*, 9.806-9.
[57] Goyert, trans., *Ulysses*, p. 235.
[58] Wollschläger, trans.,*Ulysses*, p. 289.
[59] Joyce, *Ulysses*, 10.368.
[60] Goyert, trans., *Ulysses*, p. 259.
[61] Joyce, *Ulysses*, 1.561.
[62] Goyert, trans., *Ulysses*, p. 24.
[63] Joyce, *Ulysses*, 13.1114-5.
[64] Goyert, trans., *Ulysses*, p. 425.
[65] Joyce, *Ulysses*, 4.99-100.
[66] Goyert, trans., *Ulysses*, p. 68.
[67] Wollschläger, trans.,*Ulysses*, p. 81.

allusion-hunting and background-acknowledgment. Titles from classical music are sometimes translated and sometimes not, depending largely on questions of tradition and convention that the translator should stick to as far as possible. Titles of pop songs that may occur in post-Joycean literature should obviously never be translated, as these songs are always known internationally by their original (mostly English) titles. This, however, does not apply to the abundance of popular music titles in the works of Joyce. Let's have a look at a few examples of how Goyert and Wollschläger deal with such titles.

"And *The Last Rose of Summer* was a lovely song"[68]: Thomas Moore's well-known song is included by Friedrich von Flotow in his light opera *Martha*, and therefore it is no wonder that both Goyert ("Und *Letzte Sommerrose* wäre auch ein herrliches Lied"[69]) and Wollschläger ("Und *Die letzte Sommerrose* war auch ein wunderschönes Lied"[70]) use the same German version of the song's title. The same can be said of the "*Lily of Killarney*"[71] which in both translations is rendered as "*Lilie von Killarney*"[72]. This seems to run counter to Goyert's general rule of not translating titles, but apparently he restricts the validity of his rule to literary titles – song titles are always translated in Goyert's version. Thus "*The Night before Larry was Stretched*"[73] is rendered as "*Die Nacht bevor man Larry henkte*"[74] by Goyert, whereas Wollschläger's version runs: "*Die Nacht, bevor Larry gehenkt ward*"[75]. Rather inelegant is Goyert's rendering of Joyce's "as he trudged to Romeville whistling *The Girl I left behind me*"[76], where Goyert fails to mark the title as a title: "als er zu Fuss nach Romeville wanderte und pfiff: Das Mädchen, das ich schnöd verliess"[77]. Hans Wollschläger's version manages better to indicate that what Stephen is referring to is a tune's title rather than just a line from a song: "als er nach Romeville stapfte und dabei pfiff: *Das Mädchen, das zurück ich ließ*"[78].

There is one case where Wollschläger, in contrast to Goyert, chooses not to translate a song title. "*The Croppy Boy*. Our native Doric"[79] in Goyert's version reads "*Der junge Rebell*. Unsere dorische Ausdrucksweise"[80], whereas Wollschläger translates: "*The Croppy Boy*. Unser heimatliches Dorisch"[81]. There are no less than three good reasons for voting in favour of Wollschläger's solution: firstly, it is possible to view 'the Croppy

---

68    Joyce, *Ulysses*, 11.1178.
69    Goyert, trans., *Ulysses*, p. 632.
70    Wollschläger, trans.,*Ulysses*, p. 398 f.
71    Joyce, *Ulysses*, 13.1213.
72    Goyert, trans., *Ulysses*, p. 429; trans. Wollschläger, p. 532.
73    Joyce, *Ulysses*, 12.542-3.
74    Goyert, trans., *Ulysses*, p. 344.
75    Wollschläger, trans.,*Ulysses*, p. 425.
76    Joyce, *Ulysses*, 9.246-7.
77    Goyert, trans., *Ulysses*, p. 217.
78    Wollschläger, trans.,*Ulysses*, p. 268.
79    Joyce, *Ulysses*, 11.991.
80    Goyert, trans., *Ulysses*, p. 318.
81    Wollschläger, trans.,*Ulysses*, pp. 391 f.

Boy' as a proper name and act according to our first name translation rule; secondly, "Our native Doric" requires a title that not only is but also sounds Irish (albeit Anglo-Irish); thirdly, the song is a relatively well-known one and may well have been encountered by non-native English speakers who, however, would never recognize it via the title *"Der junge Rebell."*

In *Finnegans Wake*, translating titles (like everything else) is even more complicated than in *Ulysses*. The main problem is that there is scarcely any title in the *Wake* that has not undergone some kind of distortion, and this makes it seem all the more important to stick to our rules in order to enable the reader to recognize as much as possible. For example, *"Gorotsky Gollovar's Troubles"*[82], clearly identified as a title by the use of italics, must be translated not at face-value ('Gorotsky Gollovars Ärger' or something like that) but rather in a way that recalls *Gulliver's Travels*, which in German is called *Gullivers Reisen*. My solution here is *"Gorotsky Gollovars Scherereisen"*[83], blending 'Reisen' with 'Scherereien'. Luckily *Gulliver's Travels* is well-known in Germany, and always under the same title. A much trickier case is *"pippap passage"*[84], referring to Browning's *Pippa Passes*, a play that is relatively unknown to German readers. The only German translation of Browning's play was published in 1903 under the title *Pippa geht vorüber*, but this title is even less familiar to German readers than the original one, so I decided to model my German version on the original Browning title: *"Pippappassage"*[85]. Still trickier is *"Spice and Westend Woman"*[86], Joyce's transformation of Wyndham Lewis's *Time and Western Man*. The problems for the translator into German are at least threefold: firstly, the German word for 'spice' ('Gewürze') does not resonate with the German word for 'space' ('Raum'); secondly, the correct German equivalent for 'Western man' would be something like 'der Mann des Abendlandes' or 'der abendländische Mensch' which makes it virtually impossible to introduce a "Westend"; and thirdly, there is no German translation of *Time and Western Man* on which to rely. Exactly this, the absence of any German translation, however, gave me the licence to play around freely with the material I had to face. I'm afraid that my solution – *"Rahm und die Frau des Westends?"*[87] – will not be recognizable for most German readers, but I hope that at least those few readers who might perhaps recognize the original Wyndham Lewis title may gain some fun out of my version.

Before moving on to the problems of quotations, let's have a brief look at a special kind of title list that is included in the *Wake* – the list of the unofficial episode titles of *Ulysses*, somewhat garbled in the *Wake* machine:

---

[82]     Joyce, *Finnegans Wake*, 294.18-9.
[83]     Friedhelm Rathjen, "Die verdreckteste Sacke die jemals hörbetrüben ward," unpublished translation of *Finnegans Wake*, pp. 282-304.
[84]     Joyce, *Finnegans Wake*, 301.7.
[85]     Rathjen, "Die verdreckteste Sacke die jemals hörbetrüben ward."
[86]     Joyce, *Finnegans Wake*, 292.6.
[87]     Rathjen, "Die verdreckteste Sacke die jemals hörbetrüben ward."

Ukalepe. Loathers' leave. Had Days. Nemo in Patria. The Luncher Out. Skilly and Carubdish. A Wondering Wreck. From the Mermaids' Tavern. Bullyfamous. Naughtsycalves. Mother of Misery. Walpurgas Nackt.[88]

In Dieter Stündel's trial-translation, this list is rendered as follows:

UKarlIpso. Lotessers Blatt. Hart D's. Niemand im VaterLand. Die läßtRieh gonnen. 's Kühla und Kar üb dies. Schwimännde Fellsehn. Von der Sehjuck-frauens Tabärne. Pulli Fee muß. Nau sieh kacka. Mucksen des SohnenGockels. Walkirkis Nackt.[89]

The main problem of Stündel's translation here (as elsewhere) is that Stündel always translates only one level of Joyce's wording and twists this with his own additions and not with Joyce's other levels. In most cases the level he chooses is simply the episode title (which, by the way, in most cases is also a proper name); in at least one case the episode title is not even reproduced correctly: "Schwimännde Fellsehn" is modelled over 'schwimmende Felsen', whereas the correct German equivalent is "Irrfelsen." In Joyce's "Mother of Misery," moreover, the "Oxen of the Sun" episode is hinted at mainly via the Mater ("Mother") Misericordiae ("Misery") Hospital (although, ironically, the scene of the episode is not laid here but in its twin hospital, the National Maternity). Stündel duplicates the syntactical structure half-heartedly and, it seems, uncomprehendingly and needs material not employed by Joyce here (the sun-god of "Sohnen-Gockels" referring to Helios) in order to make the reference work. I hope that in my own version of the episode list, I have managed to stick more convincingly to Joyce's title's structure, references, and overtones:

Ukalepe. Lotter läßt es. Hatt' es. Nemo in Patria. Eßt Ransgehend. Skönner und Kehrübtisch. Ein Wirrender Fetzen. Aus der Nixentaverne. Bullyfamos. Naun-sinnkälba. Mutter der Misere. Walpurg als Nackt.[90]

## 3: Quotations

Titles appearing in a work you have to translate are in themselves always quotations already; in principle, titles have to be handled just like quotations and quotations just like titles by the translator, and so our first rule for translating quotations sounds very much like the first rule for translating titles:

- Quotations in the source text you are translating must always appear in a target language version in your translation, unless there is an exceptionally good reason for sticking to the original; if satisfactory target language versions of the quotations exist, use them.

---

[88]  Joyce, *Finnegans Wake*, 229.13-6.

[89]  Dieter H. Stündel, *Finnegans Wehg: Kainnäh ÜbelSätzZung des Wehrkeß fun Schämes Scheuß* (Darmstadt: Häusser, 1993), p. 229.

[90]  Burgess, *Joyce für Jedermann*, p. 282.

The most frequent of all exceptionally good reasons for sticking to the original version is that a quotation in the source text is in a language different from the text's source language. Our second rule for translating quotations, therefore, equals another rule that we have heard already:

- Quotations that appear in a third language in the original must always remain unchanged in your translation.

The third and final rule concerns the usage of existing target-language versions of quotations; this time, however, I'd like to propose a rule that is quite different from the one we have established for translating titles:

- In case there are different versions of the quotation in question in the target language, in the case of well-known quotations try to use the version that is best remembered (in most cases this will be the standard translation); if, however, the quotations are more or less unknown, use the one that suits your purposes best or feel free to forge a translation of your own.

The difference between titles and quotations is that titles resemble proper names, in that they are aimed primarily at identification, whereas quotations are primarily aimed at explanation. Even though some-times the crucial point for using quotations may be to boast a wide range of different texts an author has got at his or her disposal, this seldom depends on using particular versions of the quoted texts. (I'm speaking of quotations in literature here, definitely not of quotations in secondary sources.)

In the "Scylla and Charybdis" episode of *Ulysses*, for instance, one of Padraic Colum's poems is discussed: "Yeats admired his line: *As in wild earth a Grecian vase*"[91]. Surprisingly both Georg Goyert and Hans Wollschläger leave the quotation in English[92], although there is hardly an exceptionally good reason for their doing so. Maybe both translators didn't want to contradict Yeats's admiration of Colum's style by giving us a clumsy translation of the quoted line, but even then it would have been the translator's task to produce a German version of the line that replicates the style of the original – say, 'Wie in wilder Erd' ein Griechenväslein' or something like that. It may even be possible that a German version of Colum's poem has been printed in some collection of Irish verse, but according to our rules 1 and 3, it is unnecessary to use such a practically unknown version.[93]

In another case, however, Goyert obscures things exactly by *not* sticking to the original version of a quotation. In "Scylla and Charybdis," Best talks about Oscar

---

[91]    Joyce, *Ulysses*, 9.304-5.

[92]    See Goyert, trans., *Ulysses*, p. 219; trans. Wollschläger, p. 270.

[93]    Sometimes there are even cases where it would be highly problematic for a German translator of *Ulysses* to use the original German version of a text quoted by Joyce in a very free English translation. For an example, see Fritz Senn, "Beyond the Lexicographer's Reach: Literary Overdetermination," *Inductive Scrutinies*, pp. 216-25, pp. 221 f. (re Joyce, *Ulysses*, 11.665: a quote from the English version of Flotow's *Martha*).

Wilde's "*Portrait of Mr W.H.* where he proves that the sonnets were written by a Willie Hughes, a man all hues"[94]. The Hughes / hues homophone, a quotation from Wilde, is literally untranslatable into German, but Goyert nevertheless decides to translate the quotation (although he does not translate the easily translatable title): "Das *Portrait of Mr. W.H.*, in dem er beweist, dass die Sonette von einem Willie Hughes geschrieben wurden, einem Mann, der auch Jude sein kann"[95]. This awkward rendering is completely unintelligible, and therefore Wollschläger is right in preferring the makeshift solution of not translating Wilde's homophones at all: "Das *Porträt von Mr. W.H.*, worin er nachweist, daß die Sonette von einem Willie Hughes geschrieben wurden, einem *man all hues*"[96]. Admittedly this version is unintelligible, too, for a reader completely unfamiliar with the English language, but at least some of the readers may make out what the point is here.

Goyert's refusal to stick to Joyce's (or rather Wilde's) English wording is all the more surprising, since in several other places Goyert tends to unnecessarily leave English quotations in his text. For example, Shakespeare's line "*That beetles o'er his base into the sea*"[97] is reprinted untranslated in Goyert's version[98], whereas Wollschläger uses Schlegel-Tieck's standard German Shakespeare translation: "An den Felsen, *der in die See nickt über seinen Fuß*"[99]. And again, Goyert tends to be inconsistent; the *Cymbeline* quotation at the end of "Scylla and Charybdis" – "*Laud we the gods / And let our crooked smokes climb to their nostrils / From our bless'd altars*"[100] – in Goyert's translation is replaced by this rather clumsy rendering: "*Loben wir die Götter, / Und von gesegneten Altären steig' krauser Opferrauch / Hinauf in ihre Nasen*"[101]. Maybe Goyert simply did not know where the quotation came from; Wollschläger definitely does know and uses the Schlegel-Tieck translation again[102]. In an essay written after having completed his translation, Wollschläger has disclosed what standard translations he chose for two vital sources of quotations in *Ulysses*:

> Daß die Bibel- und die Shakespeare-Allusionen in der Übersetzung eine adäquat eindeutige Gestalt haben können, ist möglich nur aufgrund der Tatsache, daß beide Quellen einmal durch Übersetzungen ins Deutsche gekommen sind, die im Lauf der Zeit die unveränderliche Prägnanz von Originalen angenommen haben: durch Luther und die Schlegel-Tieck-Ausgabe.[103]

---

[94]    Joyce, *Ulysses*, 9.523-4.

[95]    Goyert, trans., *Ulysses*, p. 226.

[96]    Wollschläger, trans.,*Ulysses*, p. 278.

[97]    Joyce, *Ulysses*, 1.567-8.

[98]    See Goyert, trans., *Ulysses*, p. 24.

[99]    Wollschläger, trans.,*Ulysses*, p. 28.

[100]    Joyce, *Ulysses*, 9.1223-5.

[101]    Goyert, trans., *Ulysses*, p. 247.

[102]    See Wollschläger, trans., *Ulysses*, p. 304.

[103]    Hans Wollschläger, "Am Ende eines 'Welt-Alltags'," *ensemble* 7 (October 1976), pp. 156-68, pp. 167 f.

This sounds quite convincing; we may wonder, however, if a decidedly Protestant version of the Bible really is ideal as a means of reproducing the decidedly Catholic background of Joyce's biblical quotations and allusions.

In case of the innumerable quotations from English and Irish songs, nursery rhymes and similar material, the problem for the translator is quite different: in almost every instance, there are no given German versions, and if the translator neither wants to replace the original songs and rhymes with existing German language songs and rhymes (which is always problematic, for this tends to shift the realistic setting from a place in Ireland to a place in Germany) nor simply wants to replicate the English wording (which always looks like unconditional surrender), he or she has to translate everything on his or her own. There are very few cases, however, where it is possible to fall back upon adequate target language materials. In "Oxen of the Sun," for example, the following rhyme is quoted: *"Pope Peter's but a pissabed. / A man's a man for a' that"*[104]. Wollschläger simply translates these lines — *"Papst Peter, der leidet an Bettpisserei, / Denn Mann bleibt Mann, ahoi!"*[105] – without paying any attention to the fact that this is a variation on Robert Burns's poem "For A' That and A' That" which is well known as a folk song. Its melody, in fact, is used in Germany as a musical setting for Ferdinand Freiligrath's poem "Trotz alledem und alledem"; Georg Goyert seems to have recognized this, for he makes use of the phrase "trotz alledem" in his rendering of the rhyme from *Ulysses*: *"Papst Peter pisst ja nur ins Bett. / Ein Mann ist ein Mann trotz alledem"*[106]. Here, Goyert is on the right track – if only he had had an ear for sound and rhythm, he might have been able to find the ideal solution.

In *Finnegans Wake*, most quotations have already undergone a process of both distortion and dispersion, and this tends to make them all the harder to translate and harder still for the reader of any translation to recognize. The following is a passage from *Finnegans Wake* I.1:

> Shize? I should shee! Macool, Macool, orra whyi deed ye diie? of a trying thirstay mournin? Sobs they sighdid at Fillagain's chrissormiss wake, all the hoolivans of the nation, prostrated in their consternation and their duodisimally profusive plethora of ulculation. There was plumbs and grumes and cheriffs and citherers and raiders and cinemen too. And the all gianed in with the shoutmost shoviality. [...] He's stiff but he's steady is Priam Olim![107]

There are at least six popular songs that in one way or other are quoted in this passage: "Pretty Molly Brannigan" ("Arrah, why did ye die?"), "Finnegan's Wake," "Hooligan's Christmas Cake" ("There were plums and prunes and cherries / Raisins and currants and cinnamon too"), "Johnny I Hardly Knew You" ("With drums and guns, and guns and drums"), "Phil the Fluter's Ball" ("And they all joined in with the utmost joviality"),

---

[104]  Joyce, *Ulysses*, 14.649-50.
[105]  Wollschläger, trans., *Ulysses*, p. 563.
[106]  Goyert, trans., *Ulysses*, p. 458.
[107]  Joyce, *Finnegans Wake*, 6.13-23.

and "Brian O'Linn." The translator, however, cannot simply translate the lines of these songs, for he must always simultaneously try to consider and translate all the other material with which the song quotations are blended. Taken this for granted, Harald Beck's version is a considerable success, in that at least some of the songs are somewhat recognizable:

> Schize? Kannst fei wohl schaugen! Macool, Macool, hach was mußtest du sterben? an so nem verkorkten durstag mortgen? Schluckzer säufztens bei Füllagains christmasscwake, die hooligauner all im land, gebeugt in bestürzung und verzwölfelt schwappendem jammerschwall. Da gab's zwetschkerl, plaumann und kirschner, zitt'rauner und weinträuber, auch zimmterer dazu. Und alle fielens ein mit grölßter faustgelassenheit. [...] Steif aber standfest ist Priam Olim![108]

As you will notice, some of the song quotations here can only be saved by using the original English word material – a method that always seems justifiable when dealing with the multilingual *Wake*, as long as you don't take this procedure too far. Dieter Stündel, on the other hand, reduces the multi-linguality of the *Wake* to a text that consists almost only of German-language material. This, however, is not the only reason why song quotations in his version are quite hard to recognize:

> Schaiße? Ich soldte es sargen! Markkuhl, Markkuhl, order wirrum biest du krähpiert? an so einem druckenen Dunnerstag Murgen? Schluckzer seifzen sieh bei Filligrans blödsinnlicher TortenWache, all die Hallewamse der Naktion, und sie prostttratierten in irrer Bestürzung und ihre Zwölfzallichkeit proddelziehrte ein ÜbellMass an Plärrerei. Da gab es FlauMänn und Mannderln und Cherryfs und Bossköppe und Rüber und sogar Zimteasten. Und sie alle schlimmten in das schöckste Ginderascha ein. [...] Er war steiff, doch er war standhaft wie einst immay![109]

In my own translation of this passage, I have tried to use literal translations of the song quotations into German and have also attempted to add to the musicality of the text by observing the given rhythmic structures. At the same time, however, I have been careful not to sacrifice the non-musical elements of Joyce's texture in favour of the songs:

> Säuftserg? Sollt ich siehen! Macool, Macool, ochjäh waruum tatst du'n sterbuun? von 'nem stöhnen Durstertagsorgen? Schlucktzerr säuftsen sie echtsinnd bei Füllneurins Weinwachtswürg, alle Hoolifans der Nation, dahingestrecknist in ihrer Verstürzung und ihrem verdutzend übelschwänklichen Trüberfluß der Heuligkeit. Da gab's Pflaumeln und Gezwetsche und Kirscherrn und Chorinthner und Rohsündner und Zimperlinge dazu. Und die allemachten mit mit fäusterster Heiserkeit. [...] Er ist steif und ist doch stetig das ist Priam Olim![110]

---

[108]    Harald Beck, trans., "Der Anfang," Joyce, *Finnegans Wake Deutsch*, pp. 27-35, p. 30.
[109]    Stündel, *Finnegans Wehg*, p. 6.
[110]    Friedhelm Rathjen, unpublished translation of Joyce, *Finnegans Wake*, 6.13-28, written at Fritz Senn's request for the Zurich James Joyce Foundation's Hyperwake project in 1991.

In a way, the whole text of *Finnegans Wake* consists of quotations – the *Wake* continually quotes from printed an unprinted sources of the most various nature, always including itself. One may even argue that the most vital quotations to be found in the *Wake* are the quotations from itself, and if the translator makes sure always to translate these self-quotations in a way that they are recognizable as such, his or her translated version will be the perfect reproduction of the *Wake*'s structure of repetition and variation.

Fritz Senn, in his recent article on repetition in Joyce, has identified seven instances where the text of *Finnegans Wake* quotes the first sentence of *A Portrait of the Artist as a Young Man*[111]:

1. "One's upon a thyme and two's behind their lettuce leap"
2. "There was once upon a wall and a hooghoog wall a was"
3. "Eins within a space and a wearywide space it was"
4. "O, fibbing once upon a spray what a queer and queasy spree it was"
5. "Once upon a drunk and a fairly good drunk it was"
6. "Once upon the grass and a hopping high grass it was"
7. "One's apurr a puss a story about brid and breakfedes"

Before examining German renderings of these phrases, we should have a look at the quoted sentence itself and its translations into German:

James Joyce:      "Once upon a time and a very good time it was"[112]
Georg Goyert:     "Vor vielen, vielen Jahren – war das eine herrliche Zeit – "[113]
Klaus Reichert:   "Es war einmal vor langer Zeit und das war eine sehr gute Zeit"[114]

The German translation generally agreed upon as being the standard one is Reichert's, so we should compare all German versions of the *Wake* phrases to this one.

The only German translator to have dealt with all the *Wake* phrases in question is Dieter Stündel. His versions read thus[115]:

1. "Äß war ein Mahl und zwei ist hinterm Lassens blattFeen"
2. "Da war einstwalls und ein riessicker Wall e war"
3. "Es wirr einmalz vor lunger Breit und das waar eine sähgutte Breit"

[111]   Joyce, *Finnegans Wake*, 20.23-4, 69.6-7, 152.18, 319.14-5, 453.20, 516.1-2, 597.16-7 respectively. – See Fritz Senn, "'The Same Renew': *Finnegans Wake* as a Chamber of Echoes," Andreas Fischer (ed.), *Repetition* (Tübingen: Narr, 1994), pp. 191-206, p. 194.

[112]   James Joyce, *A Portrait of the Artist as a Young Man*, ed. Chester G. Anderson and Richard Ellmann (New York: Viking Press, 1966), p. 7.

[113]   James Joyce, *Jugendbildnis*, trans. Georg Goyert (Zurich: Rhein-Verlag, n. d.), p. 8.

[114]   James Joyce, *Ein Porträt des Künstlers als junger Mann*, trans. Klaus Reichert (Frankfurt am Main: Suhrkamp, 1972), p. 7.

[115]   Stündel, *Finnegans Wehg*, pp. 20, 69, 152, 319, 453, 516, 597 respectively (same pagination as Joyce's original text).

4. "Oh, und fiedelte es war einmalz, was für ein queerer und quählerischer Spars es war"
5. "Es wahr einwahl vor lunger Zeugt und das wahr eine sörgutte Zeugt"
6. "Es war einmal ein Gras und ein hüpf hoch Gras war es"
7. "Es war einmal eine Geschichte über Bett und Frühstück"

The words "Once upon a time" employed by Joyce in all of the phrases in question correspond to Reichert's "Es war einmal vor langer Zeit," which means that this is the exact wording that should be present in the renderings of all the *Wake* phrases. The "vor langer Zeit" part, however, is missing in Stündel's versions of phrases 1, 2, 4, 6 and 7, which means that in these cases his renderings quote the well-known fairy-tale opening 'Es war einmal' but not necessarily Joyce's *Portrait*. In phrases 2, 4 and 6, this imperfection is made good for by some kind of rendering of the "and a very good time it was" of Joyce's *Portrait* formula, so that Stündel's versions of phrases 1 and 7 only lack any convincing connection to the first sentence of *A Portrait*. The same can be said of Joyce's own phrasings, however: the original phrases 1 and 7 are not necessarily connected with *A Portrait* and can well be understood as referring to the fairy-tale formula and nothing else. (In addition we may note that Ulrich Blumenbach and Reinhard Markner, too, in their rendering of phrase 7 – "Eins warr einmusch eine Geschichte vom Hotel Ungarni und Paricombattieren und Kuschkuß"[116] – quote only the formula "Es war einmal" and not Reichert's continuation "vor langer Zeit.")

If we check Reichert's translation against Joyce's original version, we find that whereas Joyce concludes his phrase with the "it was" (and repeats this syntactical decision in the *Wake* phrases 2, 3, 4, 5 and 6), Reichert puts his "das war" in front of "eine herrliche Zeit." Stündel, however, follows Reichert's standard German rendering in phrases 3 and 5 only; strictly speaking, his versions of phrases 2, 4 and 6 are violations of the rule to follow the standard target language translation of the quoted passage.

Phrase 3 has been rendered by four other German translators, too:

Ingeborg Horn: "Einst wast inmal ein raum und ein schwerweiter raum ist das"[117]

Robert Weninger: "Einst war einall und alts ein raomfassend all"[118]

Friedhelm Rathjen: "Eins war womal in weitem Raum und das gar ein leerweiter Raum"[119]

Klaus J. Schönmetzler: "Einst war imall im weiten-breiten Raum"[120]

---

[116]    Ulrich Blumenbach and Reinhard Markner, unpublished translation of *Finnegans Wake* IV.

[117]    Ingeborg Horn, trans., "Schem, Schaun: Quisquiquock," Joyce, *Finnegans Wake Deutsch*, pp. 73-115, p. 99.

[118]    Robert Weninger, trans., "The Mookse and the Gripes," Joyce, *Finnegans Wake Deutsch*, pp. 116-23, p. 116.

[119]    Friedhelm Rathjen, trans., "Der Mauchs und Der Traufen," Joyce, *Finnegans Wake Deutsch*, pp. 124-31, p. 124.

[120]    Klaus J. Schönmetzler, trans., "*... ein sitzam Saeculi Phönis": Sechs deutsche Annäherungen an Finnegans Wake von James Joyce* (Bad Aibling: privately printed, 1987), p. [5].

If we check the criteria addressed before, we find that Horn, Weninger and Schön-metzler deviate from Reichert's wording in that their versions all lack an equivalent of "vor langer Zeit," and that Horn deviates from Reichert's wording in that her version puts the "ist das" (being the equivalent of Reichert's "das war") in the wrong place, whereas in Weninger's and Schönmetzler's versions this part of the phrase is totally absent. Only Stündel's version and my own sufficiently quote the structure of the *Portrait* phrase underlying the *Wake* phrase – and as for the translation of Joyce's semantic twistings ("time" becomes "space," "upon" becomes "within"), I may be forgiven if I frankly boast of being closer to the original version than Stündel.

### 4: And more...

Something is always lost in translation, the well-known saying goes, and the translator of Joyce in particular is always struggling hard to keep the loss as small as possible. Maybe he or she can find some relief in a key remark by Salman Rushdie: "It is normally supposed that something gets lost in translation; I cling, obstinately, to the notion that something can also be gained."[121] This, however, does not mean that the translator is entitled to put into his translation anything he wants, and this leads me to my last rule:

- If you want to put something into your translation that is absent from the original and that is not meant to be an apt compensation for something that is inevitably lost in the process of translation, always be sure that you act like a skilled smuggler: although a reader who is really keen to find what you are smuggling should have a chance to do so, a reader looking for nothing should equally have the chance to find nothing.

As an example of the translator-smuggler in action, I'd like to reveal a case where I have smuggled not a quotation and not a title but perhaps a name into a translation of mine. The text in question – Christopher Buckley's novel *Thank You for Smoking* – has nothing to do with Joyce, but maybe the name has. At one point in the novel there is a passage that in the original runs thus:

> "NHK – Japanese TV – did an interview with him. He was very good on second-hand smoke. He's really got that down cold. He'll get face time in Tokyo. I'm certain."
> "That won't do us a whole lot of good in Peoria."
> "Well..." So Erhardt was next. Twenty years of devoted service to science and *auf Wiedersehen*, you're history, Fritz.[122]

---

121 Salman Rushdie, "Imaginary Homelands" (written in 1982), *Imaginary Homelands: Essays and Criticism 1981-1991* (London: Granta / Penguin, 1992), pp. 9-21, p. 17. This remark is repeated nearly verbatim in Rushdie's novel *Shame* (London: Pan / Picador, 1984), p. 29.

122 Christopher Buckley, *Thank you for Smoking* (New York: Random House, 1994), p. 15. – Maybe Buckley's novel does have something to do with Joyce, after all; see p. 73: "For a second there it looked like she was going to say yes, yes I will, yes."

My rendering of this passage is a faithful translation – at least for every reader who does not look for smuggled goods:

„NHK – das japanische Fernsehen – hat ein Interview mit ihm gemacht. Er war ziemlich gut in Sachen Passivrauchen. Da hat er ihnen wirklich den Wind aus den Segeln genommen. Der wird in Tokio Gesichtszeit kriegen. Da bin ich sicher."
„Das wird uns in Peoria nicht viel Gutes einbringen."
„Na ja..." Also war Erhardt der nächste. Zwanzig Jahre hingebungsvoller Dienst an der Forschung, und dann *auf Widdersenn*, jetzt bist du Geschichte, Fritz.[123]

Latin Quarter hats off to Him, the Fürst of Fritzerland!

---

[123] Christopher Buckley, *Danke, daß Sie hier rauchen*, trans. Friedhelm Rathjen (Zurich: Haffmans, 1996), pp. 23 f. – For my rendering of the possible quotation from Molly's soliloquy, see p. 99: "Eine Sekunde lang sah es so aus, als würde sie ja sagen, ja, ich will, ja."

# Sprakin sea Djoytsch?*
## *Finnegans Wake* into German

Arno Schmidt, the German novelist, read *Finnegans Wake* in early 1960 and needed a whole decade to overcome the anxiety of influence resulting from that experience. One of Schmidt's dialogical radio essays on Joyce, "Der Triton mit dem Sonnenschirm," written in 1961, focuses on the translatability of *Finnegans Wake* and incorporates fragments from Schmidt's own *Wake* translation begun in 1960 and abandoned soon after. At the end of the "Triton" essay, Schmidt's speaker B. declares:

> Ich will es ganz vorsichtig formulieren; aber ich möchte doch dabei bleiben: *das englische Original ist für den deutschen Leser völlig undiskutabel!* – Der kann nur hoffen, daß eine vermittelnde, leidlich klare, menschlich=umschreibende und reichlich kommentierende Verdeutschung, ihm, früher oder später, einen Begriff davon gibt, was mit FW beabsichtigt war.[1]

> [I want to formulate it quite carefully; but I'd like to stick to it: *for the German reader, the English original is completely out of question!* – He can only hope that sooner or later a mediatory, fairly clear, humanly rewriting and amply annotating Germanization will give him an idea of what was intended with FW.][2]

And speaker C. retorts:

> Ist es arg ketzerisch, wenn mir unwillkürlich die Bemerkung entkommt, daß jegliche *Um*=schreibung, in eine andere Sprache, besser sein wird, als das Original=selbst?[3]

> [Is it severely heretical, if I cannot help the remark escaping my lips, that each and every *re*=writing into another language will be better than the original=itself?]

"Sehr gut," replies speaker B.

Very well, then, every *Wake* translation better than the original – I freely admit that mine is not; it is unmistakably worse than the original, and we may well conclude that my *Wake* translations are not *Wake* translations in Arno Schmidt's sense of the word. What I intend when translating bits of *Finnegans Wake* is not to mediate or to

---

\* First published as the article "Sprakin sea Djoytsch? *Finnegans Wake* into German," by Friedhelm Rathjen, in *James Joyce Quarterly*, Volume 36, no. 4, Summer 1999, pp. 905-16.

1 Arno Schmidt, „Der Triton mit dem Sonnenschirm (Überlegungen zu einer Lesbarmachung von FINNEGANS WAKE von James Joyce)," *Bargfelder Ausgabe*, vol. II/3 (Zürich: Haffmans, 1991), pp. 31-70, p. 69.

2 My translation; all subsequent translations from Schmidt's radio essay are mine.

3 Schmidt, p. 69.

clarify or to rewrite humanly or to annotate the original, but rather to produce a basically German text that is as unclear and inexplicated (and, if possible, as inexplicable) as Joyce's text. In order to achieve this aim, I decidedly do not apply any theory concerning the question of what *Finnegans Wake* may be about – or, in Arno Schmidt's term: I do not have any reading-model.

For Schmidt, establishing a reading-model was essential to dealing with the Wake: „bevor Sie an die Lektüre von FW gehen, tun Sie gut, das ein= oder andere Lesemodell zu wählen [before you set to reading FW, you better choose one reading-model or the other]"[4]. When Klaus Reichert in his review of Schmidt's Joyce essays heartily dismissed Schmidt's odd interpretations as hardly justifiable, Schmidt's „These vom Lesemodell, das, um übersetzen zu können, zuerst zu erstellen sei [thesis of the reading-model which has to prepared at first in order to attempt a translation]"[5] was the only one that Reichert found reasonable. I for my part would like to contradict both Reichert and Schmidt: if you want to translate you strictly have to avoid any reading-model, any interpretation of what's going on in *Finnegans Wake*. You have to understand nothing. You have to look at Joyce's text with as little understanding as possible and translate Joyce's sentences into sentences that you don't understand either.

What I am talking about is not the "tricky problem" referred to by members of the Frankfurt *Wake* translation group – "how to translate those words that one simply does not understand."[6] Of course I'd like to 'understand' every single word – or, to be more precise, to 'understand' what is present in a given word and a given sentence; but as translator I should not understand *why* it is present there. Basically, this is the difference between shape and meaning, between knowledge and understanding: the ideal translator of *Finnegans Wake* knows everything about the text but understands nothing; the ideal translator memorizes the whole of the text, recognizes in any given word or sentence from the *Wake* every echo of other words or sentences inside or outside the *Wake*, recognizes all syntactical, semantic or linguistic structures and tries to transfer as many as possible of these into the translation that he is working on without asking himself why Joyce might have chosen these structures instead of others. And I freely admit that I myself am surely not the ideal translator: I understand nothing indeed, but I also know little – scarcely more than McHugh & Company are able to tell me.

The ideal translator – knowing everything, understanding nothing – tries to reproduce everything he or she knows in his translated version; that person doesn't succeed, of course, but keeps on trying, and the only hierarchy that the translator will know is the hierarchy between translatable and intranslatable bits of knowledge on the

---

4     Ibid., p. 54.
5     Klaus Reichert, "Der Doktor Allwissend," *Frankfurter Allgemeine Zeitung*, 17 March 1970); rpt. in Hans-Michael Bock (ed.), *Über Arno Schmidt. Rezensionen vom „Leviathan" bis zur „Julia"* (Zurich: Haffmans, 1984), pp. 178-80, p. 180.
6     Elisabeth Ruge, Reinhard Schäfer and Dirk Vanderbeke, "Digressions of the Book for Allemannen," Geert Lernout (ed.), *European Joyce Studies 2:* Finnegans Wake: *Fifty Years* (Amsterdam: Rodopi, 1990), pp. 37-45, p. 45.

text. On the other hand, the Schmidtian translator – the one who believes that he or she understands something because of having a reading-model – must inevitably establish a different kind of hierarchy: the one between information that is understood and information that is not understood; between information that supports a reading-model and information that doesn't; between what is felt to be important in Joyce's text and what is felt to be unimportant (or even disturbing). It is obvious that this translator will translate the hierarchy that he or she has established in the text but not the nonhierarchical text that every reader has a legal claim to when opening *Finnegans Wake* – or a translation of *Finnegans Wake* – for the first time.

The *Wake* translation that I have in mind is not the kind of reading-aid, of course, that Arno Schmidt wants the translator to supply the reader with – or, rather, it should only be a reading-aid for someone who is unable to read English well enough (like myself: I started translating bits of the *Wake* in order to supply myself with a text that I was able to read as fluently as a native speaker of the English language is able to read the original) but not a reading-aid for someone who wants to know something about *Finnegans Wake* without reading *Finnegans Wake* itself. For Arno Schmidt, Finnegans Wake looked like a "Zerrgestalt," a 'shape of distortion,' that was in need of rectification: of what Schmidt called an "Entzerrung ins Deutsche."[7] What I have in mind when attempting to translate bits of *Finnegans Wake* is completely different; it is what I have elsewhere called "eine 'Transzerrung'"[8]: a 'transdistortion,' in effect, I want to transfer the Joycean distortion into a version that has German bits of language where the original version has English ones but which is quite as distorted as the original.

As long as we don't know what *Finnegans Wake* is all about (if it is about anything at all and not merely something itself), we can never be sure what might get lost if we change anything in the text. Therefore the translator should change as little as possible: don't translate freely if there's a way to translate more pedantically; don't feel obliged to use good German style in your translation where bad German style is nearer to the original sentence structure (this, by the way, is why I believe that being a good translator and being a good *Wake* translator are two things completely different, if not opposite to each other); try to replicate every Joycean pun, double-talk, allusion, sound-effect or whatever occurs in the text, and try to replicate it in exactly the same place where it occurs in the original (maybe the place is of importance – you don't know, of course, because you don't understand).

Thus, my way of translating *Finnegans Wake* is, first, to separate the layers of information found in the original; second, to translate all bits of information into

---

[7]  Schmidt, p. 70.

[8]  Friedhelm Rathjen, „Nöö, Euer Maddetät! Überlegungen zu Status und Theorie der Schmidtschen *Finnegans-Wake*-Übersetzungen und ein Gegenentwurf," Rudi Schweikert (ed.), *Zettelkasten 10: Aufsätze und Arbeiten zum Werk Arno Schmidts: Jahrbuch der Gesellschaft der Arno-Schmidt-Leser 1991* (Frankfurt am Main: Bangert & Metzler, 1991), pp. 197-229, p. 220; rpt. in Friedhelm Rathjen, *Bargfeld Transfer: Studien zu Arno Schmidt als Übersetzer und Transformator* (Scheeßel: Edition ReJoyce, 2010), pp. 123-43.

German; and third, to amalgamate again as much of these translated bits of information as possible. This procedure may sound simple (which it is in theory only) and inevitable, but you should note that some people prefer methods that are completely different. Some people prefer to select just the most obvious layer of the text and cut off everything else; this seems to be Philippe Lavergne's method. Some people prefer to select the least obvious layer of the text and present this layer in highly stylized fashion; this is Arno Schmidt's method. Some people select the most obvious layer of the text, translate this layer alone and pour out completely new and inappropriate coprophile puns over this layer; this is Dieter Stündel's method. Some people separate all layers of information, translate these, and put these bits of information one behind the other instead of amalgamating everything; this is a method used by more or less everyone to various degrees (sometimes even by myself), but this, too, is one of the many ways to destroy *Finnegans Wake*, while pretending to translate it: the special feature of the *Wake* is not that a lot of different things are said in this book but that these things are always said at the same time.

Enough of all this theoretical swaggering: let's take a look at the practice itself. In order to demonstrate the inevitably different results of different approaches to translating *Finnegans Wake*, I'd like to quote all hitherto published German versions of a single paragraph from the Wake: the concluding paragraph of the Mookse and Gripes fable from chapter I.6. In Joyce's original version, this paragraph reads as follows (I have portions to facilitate comparison to the German versions):

> Then Nuvoletta reflected for the last time in her little long life and she made up all her myriads of drifting minds in one. She cancelled all her engauzements. She climbed over the bannistars; she gave a childy cloudy cry: *Nuée! Nuée!* A <u>lightdress</u> fluttered. She was gone. And into the river that had been a stream (for a thousand of tears had <u>gone eon her and come on her</u> and <u>she was stout and struck on dancing</u> and <u>her muddied name</u> was Missisliffi) there fell a tear, a <u>singult</u> tear, the loveliest of all tears (I mean for <u>those crylove fables fans</u> who are '<u>keen</u>' on the prettypretty commonface <u>sort of thing you meet by hopeharrods</u>) for it was a <u>leaptear</u>. But the river tripped on her by and by, lapping as though her heart was brook: *Why, why, why! Weh, O weh! I'se so silly to be flowing but I no canna stay!* [9]

In the years 1978-83 Robert Weninger attempted a German version of the fable that was subsequently published as an appendix to his book *The Mookse and The Gripes*.[10] Weninger's version of the paragraph in question reads as follows:

> Dann reflektierte Nuvolisa zum letzten male in ihren kleinen langen leben und sie beschloß all ihre myriaden treibender gedanken in einem. Sie sagte ab ihre verabschleierjungen. Sie überstieg die ballustars; sie entließ einen kindlich wollkichten

9    James Joyce, *Finnegans Wake* (London: Faber, 1975), 159.6-18.
10   Robert Weninger, *The Mookse and The Gripes: Ein Kommentar zu Joyces „Finnegans Wake"* (Munich: edition text + kritik, 1984), pp. 210-18.

schrei: *Nuée! Nuée!* Ein <u>lichtkleid</u> flatterte. Sie war fort. Und zum strome hin welcher eine bächlichkeit gewesen (denn tausend tränen waren <u>ihr eongeströmt und ihr rheingeflossen</u> und <u>sie war erstarkt und versessen aufs tanzen</u> und <u>ihr trüber name</u> lautete Missiliffi) tröpfelte eine träne, ein <u>alleinic</u> trahen, die lieblichste aller tränelein (ich meine für <u>jene liebesdorn fabeln anhänger</u> die <u>sich ‚bekleistern'</u> für die ganzschön schöne allstägliche <u>sorte dinger die man vor hoffhortens trifft</u>) denn es war ein <u>schalttrahr</u>. Aber die stromung reisste an ihr anbei und vorbei, bespülend als sei ihres herzens glut gerinnsalt: *Why, why, why! Weh, O weh! Bin zwar so töricht zu strömen, nur find nie ich bleibe!*[11]

In 1987, there was a private publication of Klaus J. Schönmetzler's trial translation from the *Wake*, including a version of the fable ending as follows:

Da bespiegelte Nuvoletta sich zum letzten Mal in ihrem kleinen langen Leben und sammelte die Myriaden ihrer driftenden Gedanken all in eins. Sie löste all ihre Verflichtungen. Sie überkletterte die Ballusterne; und sie schrieb mit wolkenwehem Kinderklang: *Nuée! Nuée!* Ein <u>Lichthemd</u> flatterte. Sie war dahin. Und in die Strömung die ein Strom war (denn ein Jahrtausend Tränen <u>ging eon sie hin und kommt noch über sie</u> und sie <u>war stark und wild aufs Tanzen</u> und <u>ihr Muddername</u> war Missiliffi) fiel eine Träne, eine <u>seufzige</u> Träne, die lieblichste aller Tränen (ich meine das für all <u>die Crylove-Fabelfreunde</u>, die auf all die nettenkleinen Gemeinfrätzlein „<u>scharf</u>" sind, und auf alldie <u>Sachen, wie man sie in Karstadt an der Quelle kriegt</u>), denn es war <u>eine hüpfende Schaltjahrsträne</u>. Doch die Strömung tripfelte nach und nach über sie, auch wenn ihr Herz gebrooken war: *Why, why, why! Weh, O weh! Ach, i sollde nimmer fließen, und bleib doch nicht, wo ich steh!*[12]

A German translation of the whole of *Finnegans Wake* I.6 has been undertaken by Ingeborg Horn in 1986-88. Her version of our paragraph reads as follows:

Dann reflektierte Nuvoletta zum letzten mal in ihrem kleinen langen leben und sie beschloß alle ihre myriaden driftender geistesverfassungen in einer einzigen. Sie kündigte all ihre engazemente. Sie kletterte übers sternengeländer; sie gab einen kindigen wolkigen schrei von sich: *Nuée! Nuée!* Ein <u>lichthemd</u> flatterte. Sie war dahin. Und in den fluß der ein bächlein gewesen war (denn ein tausend von tränen waren <u>ihr eon gegangen und an gekommen</u> und <u>sie war dickflüssig und stockte beim tanzen</u> und <u>ihr beschmutzter name</u> war Missiliffi) da fiel eine träne, eine <u>singultne</u> träne, die lieblichste von allen tränen (Ich meine für <u>jene liebesleidfabelnfans</u> <u>mit ihrer ‚leidenschaft'</u> für die hübschhübsche gemeinfratzenhafte <u>sorte von thing die du bei hoffharroden antriffst</u>) denn es war <u>jahr eine sprungträne</u>. Doch

11   Robert Weninger, trans., "The Mookse and the Gripes," in James Joyce, *Finnegans Wake Deutsch: Gesammelte Annäherungen*, eds. Klaus Reichert and Fritz Senn (Frankfurt am Main: Suhrkamp, 1989), pp. 116-23, p. 123; underlinings added.

12   Klaus J. Schönmetzler, trans., "... *ein sitzam Saeculi Phönis*": *Sechs deutsche Annäherungen an Finnegans Wake von James Joyce* (Bad Aibling: privately printed, 1978), p. [11 f.]; underlinings added.

die fluß trippte über ihr um und um, schlucksend als sei ihr das herz zerbachen: *Why, why, why! Weh, O weh! I'se so silly to be flowing but I no canna stay!*[13]

In Dieter H. Stündel's German version of *Finnegans Wake* (composed from 1974 to 1991 and published in 1993), the paragraph in question reads:

> Dann übelleckte Wöllkehlschön zum leckzten Mal in ihrem kurzen, langen Leben und sie vereinickte all ihre Myriaden triebender Gedanken zu einem einzigen. Sie sargte alle ihre Verabredunkeln ab. Sie klettete über das Gländster; sie gab einen kindisch wölkischen Schrei von sich: *Nuckht Nuckht!* Ein <u>LichtKleid</u> flattate. Sie war fort. Und in den Fluß, der ein Bach gewesen war (vor eintausönnt Zjähren waren <u>Äonsie geströmt und inn sie geflossen</u>, und <u>sie war gekräftigt und begierig aufs Tanzen</u> und <u>ihr Mättschen-Name</u> war MissisLiffi), fiel eine Träne, eine <u>einzärne</u> Träne, die lieblichste allah Tränen (ich meine <u>jene kreischlieb Fabel Freunde</u>, die auf die hübschhübsche abgegoschene <u>Sorte vom Dink</u> ,scharff' sind, <u>die man vor Saufhäusern antrifft</u>) denn es war ein <u>SchälltNarr</u>. Aber der Fluß drüppte sich an ihr vorbei und bei und bespielte sie so, als sei ihr Herz zerbächen: *Warum, warum, warum! Weh, Oh weh! Isse so sümmlich su strömen, aba ich kannich blaiben!*[14]

When I undertook my own translation of the fable in 1984, I relied heavily on Weninger's detailed commentary but wilfully neglected his translation. My version of the fable reads thus:

> Dann reflektierte Nuvoletta zum letzten Mal in ihrem kleinlangen Leben und sie sammelte all ihre Myriaden schweifender Sinne in einem. Sie annullierte all ihre Verflechtungen. Sie klettere über die Bannerstellarden; ihr entfuhr ein kindiger wolkiger Schrei: *Nuée! Nuée!* Ein <u>Sachtgewind</u> flatterte. Sie war fort. Und in die Fließende die ein Wässerchen gewesen (denn tausend Zähren waren <u>äon sie eingegangen und über sie gekommen</u> und <u>sie war zäh und aufs Tanzen verfallen</u> und <u>ihr erdiglicher Name</u> war Missisliffi) fiel eine Zähre, eine <u>einzeufzge</u> Zähre, die lieblichste aller Zähren (ich meine für <u>jene Krygen-und-Lieven-Fabel-Fanatiker</u> die ,zum klaquen scharf' auf die hübschhübsch geschönlichen <u>Dinge</u> sind <u>die man aufs Harrodewool wo threffen kann</u>) denn es war ein <u>Schaltzährchen</u>. Doch die Fließende trippelte auf ihrem Herbald und Fortbei weg, leckend als sei ihr Herz bruchig: *Nein, nein, nein! Sprich, O sprich! Isses mir auch blöd zu fließen bleiben canna ich nicht!*[15]

I don't want to attempt a full analysis of all these versions here: such an undertaking could easily fill a whole book (and still be incomplete). Instead, I will provide the

---

13    Ingeborg Horn, trans., "Schem, Schaun: Quisquiquock," in Joyce, *Finnegans Wake: Deutsch*, pp. 73-115, p. 106; underlinings added.

14    Dieter H. Stündel, trans., *Finnegans Wehg: Kainnäh ÜbelSätzZung des Wehrkeß fun Schämes Scheuß* (Darmstadt: Häusser, 1993), p. 159; underlinings added.

15    Friedhelm Rathjen, trans., "The Mookse and the Gripes," in Joyce, *Finnegans Wake: Deutsch*, pp. 124-31, p. 131; underlinings added.

reader with a brief synopsis of the most important of my considerations when striving for the best possible German equivalents of the words and phrases that I have underlined in the above quotations. In each case, I list Joyce's original wording, the components, and overtones of these phrases plus German translations of these components, a few additional overtones not present in Joyce's phrases that I decided to include as a compensation for Joycean particles that were unpreservable in my version, and finally the wording that is to be found in my translation, complemented with my fellow translators' versions in order to facilitate comparative analysis by the reader. The translator's analysis of Joyce's phrases results in a catalogue of particles, not all of which are synthesizable again in the German version, and I have marked the particles that made it into my final version so that the reader can easily distinguish between what has been preserved and what got lost. If the reader checks the versions of the other translators, too, in most cases he or she will find that either their analyses of what is present in Joyce's phrases or the techniques they preferred when synthesizing their findings again must have been different from mine. For the most part, this results in a reduction of overtones, caused at least in part by the translators' explicitly or implicitly applying a reading model, which leads them to establish a hierarchy of different meanings and to come to easy decisions as to what is 'important' and what may be left out. I must admit, however, that my colleagues' versions may contain covert overtones that I am too narrow-minded to recognize because obviously I do not know these versions as thoroughly as I know my own. This is why I don't want to attempt to reconstruct the decisions of fellow translators; instead, the following synopsis merely summarizes my own translation decisions in handling nine tricky details of Joyce's paragraph:

| 1. *FW* 159.9: | "lightdress" |
|---|---|
| → 'nightdress' = German *Nachthemd*, *Nachtkleid*, <u>*Nachtgewand*</u> | |
| → 'light' = German a) *Licht* (meteorology), b) *leicht*, <u>*sachte*</u> | |
| addition: <u>*Wind*</u> (meteorology) | |
| Rathjen: | "Sachtgewind" |
| Weninger: | "lichtkleid" |
| Schönmetzler: | "Lichthemd" |
| Horn: | "lichthemd" |
| Stündel: | "LichtKleid" |

| 2. *FW* 159.11: | "gone eon her and come on her" |
|---|---|
| → "eon" = German <u>*Äone*</u> | |
| → "gone" / "come" = German <u>*gegangen*</u> / <u>*gekommen*</u> | |
| Rathjen: | "äon sie eingegangen und über sie gekommen" |
| Weninger: | "ihr eongeströmt und ihr rheingeflossen" |
| Schönmetzler: | "ging eon sie hin und kommt noch über sie" |
| Horn: | "ihr eon gegangen und an gekommen" |
| Stündel: | "Äonsie geströmt und inn sie geflossen" |

| 3. *FW* 159.11-12: | "she was stout and struck on dancing" |
|---|---|
| → alliteration: "<u>st</u>out" / "<u>st</u>ruck" | |
| → "struck" also "fallen down" = German *ge<u>fallen</u>* | |
| Rathjen: | "sie war <u>z</u>äh und aufs Tan<u>z</u>en verfallen" |
| Weninger: | "sie war erstarkt und versessen aufs tanzen" |
| Schönmetzler: | "sie war stark und wild aufs Tanzen" |
| Horn: | "sie war dickflüssig und stockte beim tanzen" |
| Stündel: | "sie war gekräftigt und begierig aufs Tanzen" |

| 4. *FW* 159.12: | "her muddied name" |
|---|---|
| → 'muddy' = German *schmutzig, trüb, <u>erdig</u>* | |
| → 'married name' = German *Ehename, <u>ehelicher Name</u>* | |
| Rathjen: | "ihr erdiglicher Name" |
| Weninger: | "ihr trüber name" |
| Schönmetzler: | "ihr Muddername" |
| Horn: | "ihr beschmutzter name" |
| Stündel: | "ihr MättschenName" |

| 5. *FW* 159.13: | "singult" |
|---|---|
| → 'single' = German *alleinig, einzeln, <u>einzig</u>* | |
| → Lat. *singultus* = German *<u>seufzen</u>* | |
| Rathjen: | "einzeufzge" |
| Weninger: | "alleinic" |
| Schönmetzler: | "seufzige" |
| Horn: | "singultne" |
| Stündel: | "einzärne" |

| 6. *FW* 159.14: | "those crylove fables fans" |
|---|---|
| → 'to cry' = German *weinen*; 'love' = German *Liebe, <u>lieben</u>* | |
| → Ivan <u>Kry</u>lov's fables | |
| addition: German *sich <u>kriegen</u>* = 'to marry' (standard end of books) | |
| Rathjen: | "jene Krygen-und-Lieven-Fabel-Fanatiker" |
| Weninger: | "jene liebesdorn fabeln anhänger" |
| Schönmetzler: | "die Crylove-Fabelfreunde" |
| Horn: | "jene liebesleidfabelnfans" |
| Stündel: | "jene kreischlieb Fabel Freunde" |

| 7. *FW* 159.14: | "'keen'" |
|---|---|
| → 'keen on' = German *erpicht auf, <u>scharf auf</u>* | |
| → 'keen' (Irish mourning habit) = German *Toten<u>klage</u>* | |
| addition: *<u>klaquieren</u>* | |

| Rathjen: | "'zum klaquen scharf'" |
| --- | --- |
| Weninger: | "sich 'bekleistern'" |
| Schönmetzler: | "'scharf'" |
| Horn: | "mit ihrer 'Leidenschaft'" |
| Stündel: | "'scharff'" |

**8. *FW* 159.15:** "sort of thing you meet by hopeharrods"
→ 'at haphazard' = German *per Zufall, <u>aufs Geratewohl</u>*
→ 'to hope' = German *hoffen*
→ 'Hope Bros' and '<u>Harrods</u>' = London department stores
→ 'to meet somewhere' = German *(irgend)<u>wo</u> (an)<u>treffen</u>*
addition: '<u>Woolworth</u>' = English department store, known in Germany

| Rathjen: | "Dinge [...] die man aufs Harrodewool wo threffen kann" |
| --- | --- |
| Weninger: | "sorte dinger die man vor hoffhortens trifft" |
| Schönmetzler: | "Sachen, wie man sie in Karstadt an der Quelle kriegt" |
| Horn: | "sorte von thing die du bei hoffharroden antriffst" |
| Stündel: | "Sorte vom Dink [...], die man vor Saufhäusern antrifft" |

**9. *FW* 159.16:** "a leaptear"
→ 'leap' = German *hüpfen, Sprung*
→ 'leapyear' = German *Schaltjahr*, diminutive *<u>Schaltjährchen</u>*
→ 'tear' = German *Träne*; obs. / poet. *Zähre*, diminutive *<u>Zährchen</u>*

| Rathjen: | "ein Schaltzährchen" |
| --- | --- |
| Weninger: | "ein schalttrahr" |
| Schönmetzler: | "eine hüpfende Schaltjahrsträne" |
| Horn: | "jahr eine sprungträne" |
| Stündel: | "ein SchälltNarr" |

In ist listing of only isolated particles of the text, this synopsis naturally disregards the problems of intratextual cross connections. Therefore, as a final example, let us take a look at the italicized phrase at the end of our paragraph: „*Why, why, why! Weh, O weh! I'se so silly to be flowing but I no canna stay!*" Joyce here refers back to a phrase that is to be found a few pages earlier in the text: „*My, my, my! Me and me! Little down stream don't I love thee!*"[16] Every translator should keep the structure that these phrases reveal when arranged in stanza form:

*My, my, my! Me and me!*
*Little down stream don't I love thee!*
*Why, why, why! Weh, O weh!*
*I'se so silly to be flowing but I no canna stay!*

---

[16]   Joyce, *Finnegans Wake*, 153.7-8.

The perfect translation of this stanza is done by Ingeborg Horn; she simply repeats the English words in her German text, thus preferring a non-translation to a clumsy one – like the one submitted by Robert Weninger:

> *Mein, mein, mein! Mich und mich!*
> *Winzig brauner straum lieb ich nicht dich!*
> *Why, why, why! Weh, O weh!*
> *Bin zwar so töricht zu strömen, nur find nie ich bleibe![17]*

Schönmetzlers attempt is even clumsier and surely the least poetic:

> *Mei, mei, mei! Mein und mein!*
> *Kleiner brauner Traum, ich lieb dich!*
> *Why, why, why! Weh, O weh!*
> *Ach, i sollde nimmer fließen, und bleib doch nicht, wo ich steh![18]*

Dieter H. Stündel even dares to present his reader with a version which has lost all rhyme and reason without gaining anything in return:

> *Moi, moi, moi! Mir und mir!*
> *Leines fraunes Bäcklein, lieb ich dich nicht!*
> *Warum, warum, warum! Weh, Oh weh!*
> *Isse so sümmlich su strömen, aba ich kannich blaiben![19]*

In my own version, I tried to preserve not only rhythm, meter, and rhyme scheme but also the allusion to the song "Little brown jug don't I love thee" (which in German would have to be *Kleine braune Kanne, lieb' ich dich nicht*) sowie and the *canna* (Latin for 'reed') in the last line. The result reads as follows:

> *Mein, mein, mein! Mich und mich!*
> *Kleins kaums Träumch lieb ich dich nicht!*
> *Nein, nein, nein! Sprich, O sprich!*
> *Isses mir auch blöd zu fließen bleiben canna ich nicht![20]*

I hope that this is proof enough that, although translating *Finnegans Wake* admittedly tends to be a fairly frustrating job, some *Wake* translators really hide all the light of their profession under a bushel: every translation surely has to be worse than the original (let Arno Schmidt say what he may), but no translation has to be worse than no translation at all.

---

[17] Weninger, trans., pp. 116 and 123; stanza arrangement added.
[18] Schönmetzler, trans., pp. [5] and [12]; stanza arrangement added.
[19] Stündel, trans., pp. 153 and 159; stanza arrangement added.
[20] Rathjen, trans., pp. 125 and 131; stanza arrangement added.

# In Principle, Beckett is Joyce
# (and Schmidt is Schmidt)✵
## The Magic Triangle
## and Giordano Bruno's *Coincidentia Oppositorum*

## I: In Principle, Beckett is Joyce

Many scholars have compared the works of Samuel Beckett with those of James Joyce, but the first one to do so seems to have been Beckett himself. His comparison nevertheless did not focus on similarities but on differences (if not opposites). In his famous German letter of 1937 Beckett informs the addressee Axel Kaun of his artistic dream to "eliminate language"[1] and of his artistic aim to achieve what he calls a "literature of the unword"[2]. This apotheosis of the unword, of wordlessness is opposed to what Beckett sees in Joyce:

> With such a program, in my intention, the latest work of Joyce has nothing whatever to do. There it seems rather to be a matter of an apotheosis of the word. Unless perhaps Ascension to Heaven and Descent to Hell are somehow one and the same. How nice it would be to be able to believe that that indeed was the case.[3]

✵    This full version first published as the article "In Principle, Beckett is Joyce (and Schmidt is Schmidt): The Magic Triangle and Giordano Bruno's *Coincidentia Oppositorum*," by Friedhelm Rathjen, in *Dritte Wege: Kontexte für Arno Schmidt und James Joyce* (Scheeßel: Edition ReJoyce, 2006), pp. 137-51. Parts previously published as the articles "Maximal Joyce is a State of Beckett: Joyce, Beckett, and Bruno's *Coincidentia Oppositorum*" in *In Principle, Beckett is Joyce*, edited by Friedhelm Rathjen (Edinburgh: Split Pea Press, 1994), pp. 99-112, "The Magic Triangle: James Joyce, Samuel Beckett, Arno Schmidt," in *Samuel Beckett: Endlessness in the Year 2000 / Samuel Beckett: Fin sans fin en l'an 2000*, edited by Angela Moorjani and Carola Veit (= *Samuel Beckett Today / Aujourd'hui* 11, Amsterdam / New York: Rodopi, 2002), pp. 92-99, and "Magiczny trójkąt: James Joyce, Samuel Beckett, Arno Schmidt," translated by Katarzyna Spiechlanin, in *od Joyce'a do liberatury*, edited by Katarzyna Bazarnik (Kraków: Universitas, 2003), pp. 45-61.

1    Samuel Beckett, "German Letter of 1937," trans. Martin Esslin, *Disjecta: Miscellaneous Writings and a Dramatic Fragment*, ed. Ruby Cohn (London: John Calder, 1983), pp. 170-73, p. 172.

2    Ibid., p. 173.

3    Ibid., p. 172; I have altered Esslin's mistranslation of "Absicht" as "opinion" and of "schön" as "beautiful" to "intention" and "nice" respectively. In spite of these mistakes, Esslin's translation on the whole is fairly accurate – in contrast to the translation and discussion of portions of the letter offered by Ed Jewinski, "James Joyce and Samuel

How nice it would be indeed – and I am tempted to contradict Beckett: in a way heaven and hell *are* one and the same, or, at least, reverse sides of one and the same medal.

One and the same: this is a phrase that occurs elsewhere in Beckett's work, and in that case the conception that lies behind the phrase is not rejected. In "Dante ... Bruno . Vico .. Joyce" Beckett sums up Bruno: "There is no difference, says Bruno, between the smallest possible chord and the smallest possible arc, no difference between the infinite circle and the straight line. The maxima and minima of particular contraries are one and indifferent." And Beckett continues:

> Minimal heat equals minimal cold. Consequently transmutations are circular. The principle (minimum) of one contrary takes its movement from the principle (maximum) of one another. Therefore not only do the minima coincide with the minima, the maxima with the maxima, but the minima with the maxima in the succession of transmutations. Maximal speed is a state of rest. The maximum of corruption and the minimum of generation are identical: in principle, corruption is generation.[4]

The principle in question here is Bruno's identity of opposites principle, of course, and at least metaphorically this principle fits the Joyce / Beckett relationship. Isn't it tempting to adapt Beckett's wording for our purpose? 'Minimal Joyce equals minimal Beckett. Consequently transmutations are circular. The principle (minimum) of Beckett takes its movement from the principle (maximum) of Joyce. Maximal Joyce is a state of Beckett. The maximum of Beckett and the minimum of Joyce are identical: in principle, Beckett is Joyce.'

I believe that we don't have to limit such an identification to the metaphorical level. Beckett's work looks extremely different from Joyce's work, but this very dissimilarity itself is the result of Beckett's being connected with Joyce. The Joycean influence does not manifest itself in direct Joycean traces that can be found in Beckett's work but rather in the absence of any superficial traces: Joyce was Beckett's starting point not in the sense of Joyce's showing Beckett where to go but in the sense of Beckett's realizing what to avoid: he had to avoid the Joycean "apotheosis of the word" in order to create something of his own. Beckett's work therefore is reciprocally connected with Joyce's: the greater the impact of Joyce, the more it is left blank in Beckett's work, and this is why there are relatively few allusions to Joyce in Beckett's allusion-packed texts.

Avoidance is an active and conscious method of dealing with the starting point Joyce, and indeed it is widely agreed upon in Beckett scholarship that in the early 1930s Beckett is spite of his admiration for Joyce deliberately seized every opportunity to counterbalance Joyce's influence. Beckett parodied the last lines of Joyce's "The Dead" in his own Dubliners' story "A Wet Night," for example, and, much more important, he

---

Beckett: From Epiphany to Anti-Epiphany," Phyllis Carey and Ed Jewinski (eds.), *Re: Joyce'n Beckett* (New York: Fordham University Press, 1992), pp. 160-74, pp. 166 f.

4    Samuel Beckett, "Dante ... Bruno . Vico .. Joyce," *Disjecta*, pp. 19-33, p. 21.

wrote a book on Joyce's rival Marcel Proust. Proust himself became a strong influence on Beckett's work afterwards, but the difficulties to deal with Proust and yet achieve artistic independence were much smaller than the difficulties in independently dealing with Joyce. Proust could be kept at bay by simply radicalizing and reversing his achievement: Proust taught Beckett that repetition and ritualization obliterate and destroy life's vividness; Beckett concluded that repetition and ritualization are the only means to free oneself from the pains of living.

As far as Joyce was concerned, there was no simple way out by radicalizing or reversing anything: Joyce himself had been his own utmost radicalization and offered nothing for reversement. If Beckett did not want simply to become a second hand replica of Joyce he had, firstly, to admit that Joyce had already reached the end of his own course and, secondly, to pursue a course directly opposite to the Joycean one.

Beckett's course, then, was the outcome of Beckett's anxiety to pursue the Joycean course; the radicalism of Joyce's stepping in the one direction caused the radicalism of Beckett's stepping in the opposing direction. Thus we may have to agree with David Hayman: "The question of Beckett in relation to Joyce could be a fine test case for Harold Bloom's theory about the anxiety of influence and creative misreading."[5] It might be necessary, however, to distinguish between the terms involved here: 'anxiety of influence' and 'creative misreading' both come from Harold Blooms influential study on poetical influence, of course, but the term 'misreading' clearly means an incapability of continuation while the 'anxiety of influence' may also designate an unwillingness to continue. I believe that in the Joyce / Beckett relationship only the latter is the case.

In order to illustrate my argument I would like to compare Beckett's reactions to Joyce to that of the German novelist Arno Schmidt. Schmidt, born in 1914, did not read Joyce before the end of 1956, e.g., when Schmidt was nearly 43 years of age. Both *Ulysses* and *Finnegans Wake* had considerable effects on Arno Schmidt's prose as well as his artistic theory (Schmidt wrote several essays on Joyce, and his own works of the 60s are studded with Joycean quotations, allusions and puns) but it seems that Schmidt was never in danger to lose control and independence. He was anxious to do so, though, and some aspects of his utilization of Joyce bear witness of his more or less unconscious efforts to keep Joyce at a distance by various techniques of deliberate distortion; these distortions nevertheless reveal at the same time a remarkable incapability to understand what Joyce had been doing in *Finnegans Wake*. Arno Schmidt in relation to Joyce is one of the best possible examples for Bloom's 'creative misreading' process.

In the early 1950s, when Arno Schmidt's first books were published, there were critics already who found Schmidt to be a writer mimicking Joyce's techniques and mannerisms. The truth was that Schmidt had never read Joyce and had instead invented his own modernism, so to speak. When Schmidt at last did read *Ulysses*, he hastened to declare that Joyce was a great man but that not the slightest similarity existed between

---

[5]    David Hayman, "Joyce → Beckett / Joyce," *Journal of Beckett Studies* 7 (Spring 1982), pp. 101-7, p. 101; also printed in Bernard Benstock (ed.), *The Seventh of Joyce* (Bloomington: Indiana University Press, 1982), pp. 37-43, p. 37.

Joyce and himself. It is obvious that Schmidt tried to put Joyce at a distance, but at the same time he was so impressed that finally Schmidt in his text "Caliban upon Setebos" (1963) remodelled the old myth of Orpheus in a way quite similar to Joyce's remodelling of Homer's *Odyssey* in *Ulysses*.

When in 1957 Schmidt's publisher presented him with a copy of *Finnegans Wake*, Schmidt tried to reject this book on the grounds that it would threaten to divert him from his own work. Schmidt indeed resisted the temptation offered by *Finnegans Wake* for years, and when he finally read the *Wake* he was fascinated and frustrated at the same time: fascinated, because the techniques of creative misspelling invented by Joyce offered Schmidt something that he had been looking for in his own work, and frustrated, because Schmidt's first impression seems to have been that Joyce had already achieved long ago what Schmidt was still struggling to achieve in his own writings. In reaction to this, Schmidt started to say rather silly things about Joyce, denouncing him not only for his egocentrism but also for his alcoholism, his love of garlic, and his deficient personal hygiene, for example. Moreover, Schmidt wrote a number of essays in which he tried to keep the threatening influence of *Finnegans Wake* at bay by super-imposing rather misleading readings on Joyce's novel. Finally, Schmidt's coping with Joyce (and also with Sigmund Freud) lead to the writing of *Zettel's Traum*, Schmidt's large-format supernovel which on the surface looks like language gone mad quite in the manner of *Finnegans Wake*.

There is one question evolving from these observations: why does Beckett, understanding and admiring Joyce's aims and instruments so well, turn away from Joyce's work while Arno Schmidt, misreading fundamental principles of Joyce's work and disliking some of its vital features, turns more and more towards Joyce and as a result improves several features of his own writing?

At least in part the answer is contained in Schmidt's statement in an interview after completion of his monster novel *Zettel's Traum* in 1970: "I only got to know Joyce when I was in my early forties. That is, I was practically Arno Schmidt already."[6] Arno Schmidt was old enough to be equipped with consistent and full-fledged artistic conceptions of his own; he was the author of a series of genuinely and unmistakably independent short stories and novels; his style and technique had grown so steadfast that portions from all of world literature could be incorporated without altering the course of his prose. Contrary to this, Beckett had not been Samuel Beckett already when he got to know Joyce in Paris: Beckett was unable to incorporate facets of Joyce into his own work simply because there was no own work at all. Beckett had no alternative but either to substitute Joyce's work for his own or to strive after a work of his own by avoiding that of Joyce. Moreover, as one of Joyce's most understanding helpers (and the only one that was born to be a poet himself) he had not the least chance to misread anything. From some of Beckett's earliest texts (namely "Sedendo et quiescendo" and

---

6      Arno Schmidt as quoted by Gunar Ortlepp, "APROPOS: AH!; PRO=POE," *Der Spiegel* 17 (20 April, 1970), pp. 225-35, p. 228; my translation.

"Text") we may judge that Beckett might have been capable to imitate *Finnegans Wake* more or less accurately; Beckett nevertheless preferred genius to congeniality.

Beckett's relationship to Joyce is therefore marked by strategies of avoidance, denial, revocation, falsification, negativity. Beckett's works in a way negate the existence of Joyce's work; Beckett falsifies the Joycean omnipotence of the word; he revokes the accumulative Joycean strategies and thus denies being a follower of Joyce. And, oddly enough, these very modes of dealing with his predominant forefather – negativity, falsification, revocation, denial – subsequently become fundamental features of Beckett's creativeness in general. The whole of Beckett's works from *Watt* up to "what is the word"– e.g., from Joyce's death to Beckett's death – spring from an impulse to go on by denying any possibility to go on, an impulse to define reality by falsifying given portions of reality. From this we may well conclude that the modes of reaction Beckett had to develop in order to overcome Joyce's influence are the origin of all of Beckett's work.

Examples for negativity, falsification and revocation in Beckett's works are uncountable indeed and it seems unnecessary to give a long list here, particularly since several Beckett studies deal with these modes under various aspects. One of the scholars dealing with negativity is Wolfgang Iser who nevertheless does not link up Beckett's negativity with the Joyce connection: he discusses Beckett's techniques of negation in terms of reader response. All the more remarkable it may be that Iser's starting point seems to fit my argument surprisingly well. Iser founds his essay "Die Figur der Negativität in Becketts Prosa" on Jean-Paul Sartre's remark that negativity in literature is "a concrete negativity, which keeps to itself what it denies and is coloured by it entirely."[7] Isn't the seeming absence of Joycean influence from Beckett's work a concrete negativity in this sense – Joyce's influence as Beckett's starting point remaining completely under cover, being denied by the surface of Beckett's work which nevertheless is coloured in its entirety by the traces of the disengagement process? Elsewhere Iser quotes another of Sartre's remarks on negativity: "the object as conception is a *defined deficiency*; it emerges as a concave mould."[8] In this sense Joyce's work is to Beckett's like a mould is to the filling.

Beckett's work is a succession of revocations, of revocations of revocations and of revocations of revocations of revocations; let us quote *The Unnamable* as an example:

> he [Worm] often desires to, if when speaking of him one may speak of desire, and one may not, one should not, but there it is, that is the way to speak of him, that

---

[7]     Jean-Paul Sartre, *Was ist Literatur?* trans. Hans Georg Brenner (Hamburg: Rowohlt, 1958), p. 45, quoted by Wolfgang Iser, "Die Figur der Negativität in Becketts Prosa," Hans Mayer and Uwe Johnson (eds.), *Das Werk von Samuel Beckett: Berliner Colloquium* (Frankfurt am Main: Suhrkamp, 1975), pp. 54-68, p. 54; my translation.

[8]     Jean-Paul Sartre, *Das Imaginäre: Phänomenologische Psychologie der Einbildungskraft*, trans. Hans Schöneberg (Reinbek: Rowohlt, 1971), p. 207, quoted by Wolfgang Iser, *Der Akt des Lesens: Theorie ästhetischer Wirkung* (Munich: Fink, 1976), p. 329; my translation.

is the way to speak to him, as if he were alive, as if he could understand, as if he could desire, even if it serves no purpose, and it serves none.[9]

The first and initial of Beckett's revocations was his revocation of Joyce, thus turning Beckett's revocativeness, which cut off the Joycean influence, into an indirect Joycean influence itself. Beckett pushed his work ahead by systematically reducing his possibilities to go on: "you must go on, I can't go on, you must go on, I'll go on"[10]; the first and initial instance of cutting off possibilities was the necessity to cut off all Joycean possibilities; thus Beckett's method to cut off all possibilities to express and nevertheless face "the obligation to express"[11] is a direct offspring from his artistic obligation to face and at the same time reject the Joycean influence.

In facing and evading the maximizer Joyce; Beckett had to become the great minimizer: "the principle (minimum) of one contrary takes its movement from the principle (maximum) of one another." Beckett is the contrary of Joyce, exactly; but Giordano Bruno's identity of opposites principle tells us what this means: in principle, Beckett is Joyce.

## II: But what is the Principle?

So far I have discussed Beckett's conception of the identity of opposites principle in "Dante ... Bruno . Vico .. Joyce" as a metaphor for the Joyce / Beckett connection only, but Bruno's principle is a key to analogies in substance in Joyce's as well as Beckett's works, too. Strictly speaking, we even have to regard "Dante ... Bruno . Vico .. Joyce" as an instance of both writers' works overlapping each other: the essay is part of Beckett's creative work, of course, but in a way it is also part of Joyce's in so far as it not only deals with *Finnegans Wake* but also has been written at Joyce's suggestion and under Joycean supervision. This nevertheless does not mean that Beckett himself did not believe in the principle propagated in his essay: in a letter on Joyce written in 1955 Beckett insists on the fact that the way "the form of judgement" in Joyce "more and more devoured its gist and the saying of all the saying of anything" must be regarded as being "consistent with Bruno's identification of contraries"[12]. As for Joyce's own conception of Bruno's principle, we may quote a letter, too: in a letter written on 27 January 1925, Joyce informs Harriet Shaw Weaver of "Bruno Nolano (of Nola) another great southern Italian": "His philosophy is a kind of dualism – every power in nature most evolve an opposite in order to realize itself and opposition brings reunion etc. etc."[13]

---

9    Samuel Beckett, *The Unnamable, The Beckett Trilogy* (London: Pan / Picador, 1979), pp. 265-382, p. 329.

10   Ibid., p. 381.

11   Samuel Beckett, *Three Dialogues, Disjecta*, pp. 138-45, p. 139.

12   Samuel Beckett, Letter of 1955, quoted by David Hayman, "A Prefatory Note," *James Joyce Quarterly* 8.4 (Summer 1971), pp. 275-77, p. 276.

13   *Letters of James Joyce* [vol. I], ed. Stuart Gilbert (New York: Viking Press, 1957), p. 224.

In *Finnegans Wake*, Bruno's principle is present everywhere: in the constellation of Shem and Shaun the unequal brothers' always interchanging aspects of their respective personalities and being united in HCE the father; in connecting funeral and re-awakening; and explicitly in passages like the following:

> The hilariohoot of Pegger's Windup cumjustled as neatly with the tristitone of the Wet Pinter's as were they *isce et ille* equals of opposites, evolved by a onesame power of nature or of spirit, *iste*, as the sole condition and means of its himundher manifestation and polarised for reunion by the symphysis of their antipathies.[14]

Or:

> When himupon Nola Bruno monopolises his egobruno most unwillingly seses by the mortal powers alionola equal and opposite brunoipso, *id est*, eternally provoking alio opposite equally as provoked as Bruno at being eternally opposed by Nola.[15]

Even more important are the consequences of Bruno's principle concerning Joyce's ambiguous and multivalent use of language in the *Wake*: the sentences here always tend to contradict themselves and often contain their own countersentences. To state just one example I'd like to quote the description of the Ondt as "a weltall fellow" being "bynear saw altitudinous wee a schelling in kopfers"[16]: here the Ondt's height, loftiness and spaciousness are expressed in terms like 'altitude' and "weltall" (German for the universe), but at the same time the sentence says that this fellow 'fell low' and that he is but a wee bit of a man that can only be seen when being near at hand.

Traces of the identity of opposites principle in Beckett have been hinted at by David Hayman, who made a brief effort to connect Joyce and Beckett in his "Some writers in the wake of the *Wake*":

> By discovering this principle in Joyce, perhaps at Joyce's prompting, Beckett unwittingly disclosed one of the central and recurring themes of his own gestating work. The theme of the identity of opposites is almost everywhere. Murphy, for example, is in search of the ultimate or cosmic chaos which for him is order. He finds sanity among the insane, virtue in a whore named Celia (heavenly).[17]

More examples can be easily found everywhere in Beckett's works from the 30s through to the 80s, and I would like to quote just a few. An untitled poem written in 1937 reads thus:

---

[14]  James Joyce, *Finnegans Wake* (London: Faber, 1975), 92.6-11.

[15]  Ibid., 488.7-11.

[16]  Ibid., 416.3-4.

[17]  David Hayman, "Some Writers in the Wake of the *Wake*," David Hayman and Elliott Anderson (eds.), *In the Wake of the Wake* (Madison: University of Wisconsin Press, 1978), pp. 3-38, p. 15.

they come
different and the same
with each it is different and the same
with each the absence of love is different
with each the absence of love is the same[18]

In *A Piece of Monologue* we find this paradoxical contradiction: "None now. No. No such thing as none."[19] *Worstward Ho*, written in 1981, includes numberless passages like this one: "The say? The said? Same thing. Same nothing. Same all but nothing."[20] And one more example, this time from *The Unnamable* again: "one could multiply the examples, it would even be an excellent idea, but there it is, one can't."[21]

The reader may have noticed that contrary to Joyce Beckett uses the identity of opposites principle in terms of negativity: love is absent, things are nothing, possibilities are impossible. A negative relationship between all identical opposites is indeed the crucial point in Beckett's application of Bruno's principle; in "The Calmative" he notes that "All I say cancels out, I'll have said nothing."[22] The question arises as to what may be the differences between Joyce's and Beckett's respective application of Bruno.

David Hayman argues:

> Like Joyce, Beckett reproduces the universal in the trivial, though with important differences. Where Joyce finds glimmers of hope in small things, discloses a microcosm for universal order, and nourishes us on a revivifying humor, Beckett seems unremittingly faced with comic-cosmic despair which he sees mirrored both in the human condition and in the systems we have created to mask that condition, to paper over the flaws. Where Joyce chooses the little man, the norm, as his paradigm of grandeur [...] Beckett chooses the outcast, the clown, [...] turning him [...] into a quester after meaningless goals, magnifying squalor.[23]

Quite right so – but this doesn't explain where the differences come from and how they are connected with the identity of opposites principle itself. I think we have to go one step further by examining the conclusions that are possible from Bruno's principle.

If differences are identical, on the one hand this means that by taking up any single part of reality we also gain its opposite and by uniting both opposites and heaping pairs of opposites onto pairs of opposites we are able to accumulate a whole world; this of course is what Joyce is doing in *Finnegans Wake*. On the other hand if differences are identical, this also means that if we want to get rid of a certain part of reality we can

---

18    Samuel Beckett, "they come," *Collected Poems 1930-78* (London: John Calder, 1984), p. 41.
19    Samuel Beckett, *A Piece of Monologue*, *The Complete Dramatic Works* (London: Faber, 1986), pp. 423-29, p. 426.
20    Samuel Beckett, *Worstward Ho* (London: John Calder, 1983), p. 37.
21    Beckett, *The Unnamable*, p. 343.
22    Samuel Beckett, "The Calmative," *Collected Shorter Prose 1945-1980* (London: John Calder, 1984), pp. 35-49, p. 36.
23    Hayman, "Some Writers in the Wake of the *Wake*," p. 15.

never succeed by simply turning to its opposite: we are trapped, and the only way out is to oscillate between two given opposites and search for a gateway to what is behind or beyond; this is Beckett's situation while he is seeking to "bore one hole after another in the veil of language, until what lurks behind it – be it something or nothing – begins to seep through"[24], as he put it in his German letter of 1937. Having to face a given set of opposites, Joyce includes both into his art in order to include the whole range of possibilities that lie in between (just like Shakespeare did by putting diametrically different characters on one and the same stage), while Beckett in the same situation tries to exclude both opposites from his writing and approach to some unseizable portion of reality that can only be expressed in terms of denial. Thus the same principle – that of Bruno – lies behind the opposition worked out by Ruby Cohn, for example: that of "Joyce attempting to embrace all knowledge, all experience, all language" and of Beckett doubting all knowledge, all experience, all language and "even the cartesian tradition of doubt"[25].

Joyce's embracing strategy in using the identity of opposites principle could be labeled a strategy of 'not only but also": including one thing as well as the other. Beckett's strategy is that of saying 'neither': including neither one thing nor the other. Interestingly enough, the short text Beckett wrote in 1976 to be set to music by Morton Feldman bears the title "neither," and this poem is one of Beckett's most explicit comments on his conclusion from Bruno's principle:

> to and fro in shadow from inner to outer shadow
>
> from impenetrable self to impenetrable unself
> by way of neither
>
> as between two lit refuges whose doors once neared
> gently close, once turned away from
> gently part again
>
> beckoned back and forth and turned away
>
> heedless of the way, intent on the one gleam
> or the other
> unheard footfalls only sound
>
> till at last halt for good, absent for good
> from self and other
>
> then no sound
>
> then gently light fading on that unheeded
> neither

---

[24]   Beckett, "German Letter of 1937," p. 172.
[25]   Ruby Cohn, "Joyce and Beckett, Irish Cosmopolitans," *James Joyce Quarterly* 8.4 (Summer 1971), pp. 385-91, p. 391.

unspeakable home[26]

Here we have Beckett's striving in a nutshell: his striving for a state of betweenness, for a kind of no man's land between the identical opposites of light and darkness, self and unself, starting and stopping, life and death, language and silence. The unspeakable, unnamable state of 'neither' is Beckett's way to put the identity of opposites principle into his work: as a kind of gap or omission or deficiency. This gap can never be directly expressed in words, since it is a completely blank space the only definition of which is that it is neither something nor something's opposite. The only way to explore the gap – and this is the way tracked by the whole of Beckett's work – is to mark its unspeakable residua by constantly oscillating between given opposites, by defining an opposite's opposite's opposite and so on without end. The movement of Beckett's texts is a continuous to and fro movement like the one found in *Worstward Ho*:

> First the body. No. First the place. No. First both. Now either. Now the other. Sick of the either try the other. Sick of it back sick of the either. So on. Somehow on. Till sick of both. Throw up and go. Where neither. Till sick of there. Throw up and back. The body again. Where none. The place again. Where none. Try again. Fail again. Better again. Or better worse. Fail worse again. Still worse again. Till sick for good. Throw up for good. Go for good. Where neither for good. Good and all.[27]

This to and fro movement can be found even in some of Beckett's more or less critical writings such as his intense lyrical homage "For Avigdor Arikha":

> Siege laid again to the impregnable without. Eye and hand fevering after the unself. By the hand it unceasingly changes the eye unceasingly changed. Back and forth the gaze beating against unseeable and unmakable. Truce for a space and the marks of what it is to be and be in face of. Those deep marks to show.[28]

That this to and fro movement is in fact connected with the identity of opposites principle is indicated by one of the *Wake* passages I quoted above: in "the sole condition and means of its himundher manifestation and polarised for reunion by the symphysis of their antipathies"[29] the word "himundher" contains not only an equalization of 'him' and 'her' (e.g., of the opposed male and female principles) but also the German *hin und her* meaning 'to and fro.' Joyce nevertheless uses the to and fro movement positively to

---

26 Samuel Beckett, "neither," *Journal of Beckett Studies* 4 (Spring 1979), p. vii, completed with the word "neared" in line 4 – see editor's note in the *Journal of Beckett Studies* 5 (Autumn 1980), p. 6. The version printed in *As the Story was Told: Uncollected and Late Prose* (London: John Calder, 1990 and New York: Riverrun Press, 1990), pp. 108 f, is corrupt (as are other texts in that collection).

27 Beckett, *Worstward Ho*, p. 8.

28 Samuel Beckett, "For Avigdor Arikha," *Disjecta*, p. 152.

29 Joyce, *Finnegans Wake*, 92.9-11.

collect fragments of reality which are to be added up to establish a complete world, whereas Beckett uses this movement negatively to make room for the unspeakable between fragments of language that lose their correlation to any worldly reality.

This process of clearing space is possible because in Beckett speaking is no means to establish anything as it is in Joyce but a means to clear away and get rid of everything: Beckett has understood Proust's conception of habit and ritualization as murderers of immediacy and passion well enough to know that ritualization and repetition can be perfect means to hold the horrors of reality in check, that reality can be neutralized and overcome by being expressed in language. Malone recognizes that "my notes have a curious tendency, as I realize at last, to annihilate all they purport to record."[30] In order to annihilate the dictatorial presence of inner and outer reality, of self and unself, Beckett exploits strategies of weariness, of satiety: through repetitive expression of a thing and this thing's opposite he removes and can hope to go beyond both. The voice of the *Text for Nothing* no. 8 declares: "to have said so convinces me of the contrary"[31]; this statement in the original French version is followed by one that was cut out by Beckett in his English translation: "precisely this is the whole negative beauty of language, the negations of which unfortunately suffer the same fate, and precisely this is its ugliness."[32]

Beckett's negative, reductionist use of the to and fro movement, his willingness to accept neither the beauty of language nor its ugliness, is diametrically different from Joyce's willingness to accept both by positively, cumulatively using the to and fro movement, but both concepts arise from one and the same principle. We may well argue paradoxically that both Joyce's and Beckett's applying Giordano Bruno's identity of opposites principle in opposite ways while at the same time staying faithful to one and the same origin in themselves prove this principle to be true.

The identity of opposites principle, however, is always a principle of two elements, just like the to and fro movement is a movement between two poles. Where, then, does this leave us with the third element in our magic triangle? How does Arno Schmidt come into play?

## III: And Schmidt is Schmidt

Arno Schmidt's principle is always that of opposition, but never that of identities. Schmidt always knows if to say yes or no, he always knows how to decide, and he is always prepared to take sides. In all of Schmidt's oeuvre, I have found only one instance where a variation of the identity of opposites principle is present. The passage in question is to be found in Schmidt's early text "Dark Mirrors," written in 1951, at a time when Schmidt knew neither James Joyce nor Samuel Beckett.

---

[30]    Samuel Beckett, *Malone Dies*, *The Beckett Trilogy*, pp. 163-264, p. 238.
[31]    Samuel Beckett, *Texts for Nothing*, *Collected Shorter Prose 1945-1980*, pp. 71-115, p. 98.
[32]    Samuel Beckett, *Erzählungen und Texte um Nichts*, trans. [from the French] Elmar Tophoven (Frankfurt am Main: Suhrkamp, 1962), p. 142; my translation.

> *I awoke:* so hard was the moon staring through the side window into my mute face. Untiringly they came: day and night. One day I would lie there somewhere gasping (let's hope it goes quickly; and always keep a bullet in the colt as a free ticket for the trip into the blue somewhere). – I leaned against the wall, my knees in a crouch, and gazed thinking with owlish eyes into the slow shift of light.
>
> *Reciprocal radii* (and the notion fascinated me for 5 minutes). – Imagine the graphic representation of functions with complex variables, and in particular, the special case just mentioned: a most apt symbol of man in the universe (for he is the unit-scale circle in which All is mirrored and whirls and is reduced! Infinity becomes the deepest, internal center-point, and through it we cross our coordinates, our referential system and measure of things. Only the peripheral skin is equal to itself; the borderline between macro and micro. – In a unit-scale sphere you could indeed render the projection of an infinite three-dimensional space. – )
> Pretty and a clever little mind game; for 5 minutes.
>
> *The farther, then, that* the loved one moves away: the deeper she enters into us. And I pressed my brow to my knees and wove fingers through toes. [...]
>
> *My canteen?:* Yes! – (I've always drunk simply to augment the soul's power of vision; to loosen the flayed spirit from its earthly clogs; to widen the periphery of the unit-scale circle: reciprocal radii; so it does work!).[33]

From here, it is not too far a way to similarities between Beckett's work and Schmidt's work – similarities that can be seen in the role of the skull as a place where self and world confront each other, for example. Just like the characters in Beckett's postapocalyptic *Endgame* inhabit a stage which is dressed up like the interior of a human skull, the nameless protagonist in Schmidt's "Dark Mirrors" (set in a postnuclear world where the hero believes himself to be the last of mankind) enters a room which can be identified as an unobtrusive version of the skull with empty windows as eye sockets. Remarkably enough, in this room the protagonist discovers the skull and bones of his inventor – i.e., the skeleton of Arno Schmidt himself:

> *Across the vaporing meadow:* this time I entered the Mühlenhof from the rear; the window at the staircase fell out at me at the first rap (right: I've still got to pull out whole windows from somewhere and then reinstall them in my heath-home!), and I swung up inside: wretched furnishings: a bed on planks, no pillows or featherbed, just 5 blankets. An abraded desk, with twenty stray books in cardboard-box bookcases; a tiny cracked stove (well, it hadn't kept this big damp hole warm, that's for sure!), in recognition, I gave the cleft iron an appreciative tap, and looked glumly about. Paper in the drawers; manuscripts; "Massenbach Fights for Europe"; "The House on Holetschka Lane";

---

[33] Arno Schmidt, "Dark Mirrors," *Nobodaddy's Children*, trans. John E. Woods (Normal, IL: Dalkey Archive Press, 1995), pp. 177-236, pp. 190-92.

ergo, a literary starveling, cursed himself as Schmidt. But definitely long-boned: must have topped 6 foot at least. This then is life. I saluted the bony poet with my bottle (ought to take the skull along and set it up someplace); then I swung myself back through the fat window socket, and trudged uphill along the little gardens run wild.[34]

Both Beckett and Schmidt use mathematical, metaphorical and meta-philosophical systems in order to confront the self with the world and finally to establish what Joyce in *Finnegans Wake* calls a "selfmade world."[35] Arno Schmidt in his farce-like story "‹Piporakemes!›" (1962) rather ironically quotes this Joycean term[36], but it is Beckett who points out that art springs not from successfully and tracelessly transferring the world into the artist's skull but rather from his failure to do so. Art is not reality fixed by the artist's gaze or hand; true art consists of the traces of the failure to fix reality: "Those deep marks to show."[37]

The similarities between Beckett and Schmidt that can discovered by carefully examining the complex skull-versus-reality system in the works of both[38], however, have scarcely anything to do with Joyce: in a magic triangle, the problem is that whenever you stress the connection between two poles, the third pole tends to slip away.

---

[34]   Ibid., p. 196.

[35]   Joyce, *Finnegans Wake*, 252.26.

[36]   See Arno Schmidt, "‹Piporakemes!›," *The Collected Stories of Arno Schmidt*, trans. John E. Woods (Normal, IL: Dalkey Archive Press, 1996), pp. 189-207, p. 191: "tugged the hose one length farther across his selfmade world. (And the sprayed foliage rustled like the pages of bad, experimental novellas!)."

[37]   Beckett, "For Avigdor Arikha," p. 152.

[38]   For a more detailed investigation, see my book *Reziproke Radien: Arno Schmidt und Samuel Beckett* (Munich: edition text + kritik, 1990), esp. pp. 32-65. – It may be of some anecdotal interest to the reader that Arno Schmidt did not like Beckett's works (of which he probably knew only a few). See Arno Schmidt, *Zettel's Traum* (Stuttgart: Goverts Krüger Stahlberg, 1970), p. 221: "JOYCE is plentitude. BECKETT a spastic hen" (my translation). Beckett, on the other hand, when asked what he thought of Schmidt, replied: "I have no opinion on Arno Schmidt. Sorry." (Letter card to Friedhelm Rathjen, 26 June 1987.)

# TOTALITY.ZIP*
## How Melville, Joyce, and Beckett Unzip the World

In the modernist age, the increasing amount and complexity of knowledge about the world made it impossible to capture the whole of the world (or even one whole world) in a book of fiction. Any writer attempting to write a book of fiction had to in some way or other reduce the complexity of the world in its totality before being able to transfer any substantial parts of it into art. Taking my examples from works by Melville, Joyce, and Beckett, I'd like to illustrate three possible ways of reducing the world's complexitiy in modernist fiction.

**(1)    Radical subjectivity, i.e., employing a first person point of view – resulting, however, in the paradoxical finding that the self, the inside world, is even more complex than the outside world.**

The first chapter of Herman Melville's *Moby-Dick* begins with a sentence clearly underlining the narrator's subjectivity: "Call me Ishmael."[1] This is to say: 'I am a man with a name which will identify me as an individual, and everything I will tell you will be told from my individual point of view.' Ironically enough, exactly this is *not* what Melville's narrator does: instead, the narrator and his individual point of view are of no conceivable significance over vast parts of the novel, and Melville even makes his narrator tell us a lot of things which, following the rules of narrative probability, this narrator cannot know.

The narrative and the narrator's perspective begin to desintegrate in the very first paragraph of the novel proper already. After having told us to call him Ishmael, the narrator continues:

> Some years ago – never mind how long precisely – having little or no money in my purse, and nothing particular to interest me on shore, I thought I would sail a little and see the watery part of the world. It is a way I have of driving off the spleen, and regulating the circulation. Whenever I find myself growing grim about the mouth; whenever it is a damp, drizzly November in my soul; whenever I find myself involuntarily pausing before coffin warehouses, and bringing up the rear of every funeral I meet; and especially whenever my hypos get such an upper hand of me, that it requires a strong moral principle to prevent me from

*    First published as the article "TOTALITY.ZIP: How Melville, Joyce, and Beckett Unzip the World," by Friedhelm Rathjen, in *Papers on Joyce* No. 10/11, 2004-2005, pp. 197-208.

[1]    Herman Melville, *Moby-Dick or The Whale* (Evanston and Chicago: Northwestern University Press and The Newberry Library, 1988), p. 3.

deliberately stepping into the street, and methodically knocking people's hats off – then, I account it high time to get to sea as soon as I can.[2]

The self's point of view starts to disintegrate into a paratactical sentence pattern, and this reflects the fact that the world which surrounds the self is disintegrating from a well-ordered universe into a casual and coincidental conglomeration of mere details. Henceforth, in the narrator's mind information is organized by simply listing several things, naming one thing after the other without pretending to know the exact relationship between things. Melville's syntactical structures break down into paratactical listings of fragments, because perfect sentences cannot hold the world any more.

Like Melville, Joyce (in *Dubliners*) starts to narrate the world from a first person point of view, which, however, he soon gives up again. This tendency is explained by Stephen Dedalus (not a first person narrator, but the quite personal and subjective narrative point of view of a third person narrative) in *A Portrait of the Artist as a Young Man*:

> The narrative is no longer purely personal. The personality of the artist passes into the narration itself, flowing round and round the persons and the action like a vital sea. This progress you will see easily in that Old English ballad *Turpin Hero* which begins in the first person and ends in the third person.[3]

The artist "flowing round" persons and actions is an artist encompassing everything in his or her book: everything is conceived and told from a purely personal perspective – not the perspective of the author, of course, but the perspective of the narrative voice (even if this voice, like Stephen's in *A Portrait*, strictly speaking is not the narrator himself). This is a way out of the complexity of the modern world: if the narrator is telling everything from his or her own point of view, he or she is licensed to tell the world not in the complex state it really is (which would be beyond grasp and under-standing for any single person), but rather in the simplified and fragmentary form in which it is always perceived and witnessed by the individual. In order to increase this process of simplification and fragmentarization of the world even more, Joyce in *Ulysses* invents the technique of the interior monologue as a means to reduce narration to an extremely subjective, first person point of view again. Simplification means unification, but fragmentarization, on the other hand, means that in spite of the integrating first person point of view, the narrated world is disintegrating once more: in *Ulysses*, one subjectivity leads to another, and the relations between different points of view have somehow to be organized.

In the works of Samuel Beckett, the first person point of view is even more im-portant than it is in the works of Melville and Joyce. The most important artistic shift in the development of Beckett's fiction is the shift from third person narrative to first

---

2     Ibid.

3     James Joyce, *A Portrait of the Artist as a Young Man*, ed. Chester G. Anderson and Richard Ellmann (New York: Viking Press, 1966), p. 215.

person narrative we find in his stories and novels of the late 1940s. Again, however, the decision to reduce the world to what the self perceives of it does not really make matters simple enough to be narrated without difficulties. Beckett's short story "First Love" starts with the first person pronoun and the self's perception of the world, but this perception is marked by doubt and by the knowledge that the world beyond its grasp may be much more complex:

> I associate, rightly or wrongly, my marriage with the death of my father, in time. That other links exist, on other levels, between these two affairs, is not impossible. I have enough trouble as it is in trying to say what I think I know.[4]

This quite basic Beckettian gesture of saying "I" and reducing the world to simple statements, while at the same time the self becomes more and more insecure of itself and the most trivial facts of the world, is to be found again in the very first sentences of *Molloy*, the first part of Beckett's trilogy of novels: "I am in my mother's room. It's I who live there now. I don't know how I got there."[5] These sentences clearly show that the lack of knowledge is part of the first person situation, and this lack of knowledge (and of any kind of orientation in the world) is becoming increasingly more overwhelming in the course of Beckett's fiction writing. The very first sentences of *The Unnamable*, the third and final part of Beckett's trilogy, show that the narrative voice, in spite of being a highly subjective, self-related voice, is losing the world's seemingly simplest things out of its grips: "Where now? Why now? When now? Unquestioning. I, say I. Unbelieving. Questions, hypotheses, call them that."[6] The simplest questions about oneself become much to complex to be dealt with in any successful way. In order to successfully reduce the world's complexity, other narrative tricks have to be employed.

**(2)   Flight from overly complex, overdetermined territory (the self, home, modern society) into realms of the unknown, of something new, something trivial – resulting, however, in the necessity to explore the world at an ever-increasing speed.**

As the narrative voice soon finds out in the course of its unsuccessful attempts to find shelter in the realms of the self, the impossibility to deal with the world does not result from the vast amount of things which are unknown to the individual – it rather results from the complexity of all the things that are known but not understood. Melville's Ishmael therefore, after having told us about his problems with the reality of his inner self, lists several reasons for his flight into the vastness of the sea and onto the small space offered by a whaling ship:

---

[4]   Samuel Beckett, "First Love," *Collected Shorter Prosa 1945-1980* (London: John Calder, 1984), p. 1.
[5]   Samuel Beckett, *Molloy, The Beckett Trilogy* (London: Picador, 1979), p. 9.
[6]   Samuel Beckett, *The Unnamable*, ibid., p. 267.

By reason of these things, then, the whaling voyage was welcome; the great flood-gates of the wonder-world swung open, and in the wild conceits that swayed me to my purpose, two and two there floated into my inmost soul, endless processions of the whale, and, mid most of them all, one grand hooded phantom, like a snow hill in the air.[7]

Here, however, in the closing lines of Melville's first chapter, a new problem of all the self's attempts to get to grasp with the world emerges: one particular fragment of reality – the whale – is transforming itself into a series of phenomena, i.e., it is transforming itself into a whole world again which is too expansive to handle. Although in *Moby-Dick* the narrative world is reduced to nothing but a ship and a whaling voyage, this voyage soon becomes as all-embracing and complex as the world can be: the whaling voyage turns out to be a trip around the whole world, and the novel covering this voyage turns out to become a book of 135 chapters, a book with chapters about nearly everything conceivable in the world. On his one small whaling ship, Melville soon discovers gigantic masses of information which have to be somehow organized and narrated in order to make the readers understand his book.

And what Melville has to get to grasps with and organize in the body of his novel are bits of *information* indeed, whereas what Joyce has to organize in *Ulysses* are merely bits of *knowledge*. There is, as the basics of information theory tell us, a fundamental difference between information and knowledge: you can tell a person anything, but you can only inform this person of something he or she does not know already – information is knowledge which for the informed person is new. Melville in *Moby-Dick* tells us something that is new to us (virtually no one of his first-time readers had ever been on a whaling voyage, nor knew any of his readers much about whales and the complicated ways of hunting these creatures); Joyce, on the other hand, tells us something which every readers knows already. We are all quite familiar with what Joyce narrates in *Ulysses*: everyday life in the streets of an ordinary city. Leopold Bloom leaves his house in order to avoid a certain knowledge, so the problem here is not that so many things are unknown, the problem is that certain things are too well-known. Bloom wanders the streets of Dublin with attention to detail, but he always finds his own problems everywhere.

Like Bloom, Beckett's characters are wanderers. Beckett's first person narrators are expelled from home, they try to get away from somewhere or something, but they tend to become slower and slower in their progression, until they are barely able to move while lying on their back in the dark. A successful flight from the self and other things that are all too well-known, however, would quite contrarily to this mean that the wandering individual is able to gradually increase the speed of his or her flight, since the more you learn of the unknown world, the harder it becomes to still find worldly things that remain unknown and can distract you from yourself.

---

[7]     Melville, *Moby-Dick*, p. 7.

The wandering self is looking for the freedom to start anew from scratch, a freedom which can only begin after getting rid of all the overly complex burdens of the ever more complicated world one is carrying around in the form of ones material and immaterial belongings. In Beckett's novel *Malone Dies*, the narrator longs for this kind of freedom but knows that before being able to achieve it, he has to face what he calls his "pensum":

> Yes, I have a pensum to discharge, before I can be free, free to dribble, free to speak no more, listen no more, and I've forgotten what it is. There at last is a fair picture of my situation.[8]

Much earlier in the book, Malone attempts to make of catalogue of all his belongings, which seems quite a simple task to fulfill, but he never succeeds. At least one of the reasons is that in his wanderings (which now means: the wanderings of his mind) he cannot keep up with the speed in which his personal world is growing: "I disposed of things I loved but could no longer keep, because of new loves. And often I missed them. But I had hidden them so well that even I could never find them again."[9]

Even though Malone is not successful, he has at least discovered the last and perhaps most basic way of reducing the world's complexity: the decision to neglect all causal or other relationships (which always tend to make things more complicated), and instead just to list isolated fragments of the world one after the other.

(3)  **Reducing fiction to catalogues of arbitrary and accidental details of the world, neglecting the complex interdependencies that may exist between these details – resulting, however, in the fact that the more one includes, the more seems to remain excluded.**

In a way, much of Melville's *Moby-Dick* is sheer catalogue: having boiled down the world to the subject of the whale and its pursuit, Melville and his narrator want to tell us everything about this one and only subject, which is only possible by treating one sub-subject after the other. Soon a process starts which seems to be a never-ending one: if you tell your audience one thing, there are so many other things which remain to be told. Even Melville's chapter titles bear witness to this phenomenon. In chapter 55 of his book, for example, Melville finds eloquent words about the topic named by the title: "Of the Monstrous Pictures of Whales."[10] If there are "monstrous" pictures, however, there must be others as well, so Melville deals about these in chapter 56: "Of the Less Erroneous Pictures of Whales, and the True Pictures of Whaling Scenes."[11] This, however, cannot justifiably be the end of Melville's talking about pictorial representations of the whale, insofar as Melville still has to name all the "true pictures" in their

---

[8]  Samuel Beckett, *Malone Dies, The Beckett Trilogy*, p. 284.

[9]  Ibid., p. 228.

[10]  Melville, *Moby-Dick*, p. 260.

[11]  Ibid., p. 265.

wide-spread diversity, which he does in chapter 57, nicely entitled: "Of Whales in Paint; in Teeth; in Wood; in Sheet-Iron; in Stone; in Mountains; in Stars."[12]

We see here that Melville, although employing paratactical structures in order to submit catalogues of very concrete phenomena, sometimes falls victim to a tendency to lose hold of the particular and lose oneself in statements of a general nature. At least in part this is due to the fact that Melville tries to be all-inclusive: in his novel, he wants to capture the totality of his topic, and for this reason he sometimes transforms his inventories into a systematics with a tendency towards generalization. In his semi-scientific chapter on "Cetology," for example, he tries to get to grips with his complex subject matter in the following peculiar way:

> Already we are boldly launched upon the deep; but soon we shall be lost in its unshored, harborless immensities. Ere that come to pass; ere the Pequod's weedy hull rolls side by side with the barnacled hulls of the leviathan; at the outset it is but well to attend to a matter almost indispensable to a thorough appreciative understanding of the more special leviathanic revelations and allusions of all sorts which are to follow.
>
> It is some systematized exhibition of the whale in his broad genera, that I would now fain put before you. Yet it is no easy task. The classification of the constituents of a chaos, nothing less is here essayed.[13]

This passage shows a certain dilemma Melville in *Moby-Dick* faces again and again: he wants to tell a story, but there are so many strange and unknown details involved in the whalers' world, "indispensable to a thorough appreciative understanding" by the reader, that Melville either has to explain all these things "at the outset" when no reader knows why he or she should read such explanations, or has to constantly interrupt his narrative. The problems faced by Melville here are the problems of succession, the problems of a logical sequence: even if you are capable of telling the reader *everything* about a given topic, the question remains in what order all this should be best dealt with. If Melville decides to give a general description of some special procedure before his narrative reaches the point where the readers need this knowledge, Melville has to refer back from his linear narrative to the previous remarks: "That whale of Stubb's so dearly purchased, was duly brought to the Pequod's side, where all those cutting and hoisting operations previously detailed, were regularly gone through."[14]

The more complex the system of having to refer backwards and forwards becomes, the more obvious it also becomes that if you chose a linear narrative structure, the succession of details which to relate to the reader is becoming an endless one. In the first sentence of his 60th chapter, for example, entitled "The Line," Melville finds it high time to explain a certain device:

---

[12]   Ibid., p. 269.
[13]   Ibid., p. 134.
[14]   Ibid., p. 415.

With reference to the whaling scene shortly to be described, as well as for the better understanding of all similar scenes elsewhere presented, I have here to speak of the magical, sometimes horrible whale-line.[15]

In the next chapter ("Stubb Kills a Whale") Melville can continue his story, but then again, with the first sentence of chapter 62 ("The Dart"), he has to interrupt his narrative: "A word concerning an incident in the last chapter."[16] Now the harpooneers' most important dart is explained in every detail, but still this is not enough, for both the line and the dart cannot fully be understood without knowing another device, so Melville adds another chapter ("The Crotch"), which starts: "Out of the trunk, the branches grow; out of them, the twigs. So, in productive subjects, grow the chapters. / The crotch alluded to on a previous page deserves independent mention."[17] In this way, Melville starts a process which never really ends: each and every subject is "productive" in that it leads to some other subject which also deserves mention.

James Joyce in *Ulysses* (and later in *Finnegans Wake*) equally starts processes which never end: his novel consists of lists and catalogues which are ended only by the book's going into print. Out of the trunk, the branches grow, and out of Joyce's lists, his additions on the galley and page proofs grow. In the end, all these catalogues of fragments of the world are supplemented by (or even supplanted by) catalogues of ways in which to speak about fragments of the world (and perhaps about the world as a whole, after all). In *Finnegans Wake*, Joyce radicalizes this tendency even further: here he puts the fragments of the world not one after the other, but rather squeezes them into each other, and at the same time he squeezes different ways of speaking about the world into each other. Even in *Finnegans Wake*, Joyce cannot really achieve totality, of course, but here he finds ways of simulating a whole by collecting and integrating fragments.

Every whole consists of fragments, of particulars, but this unfortunately does not mean that if you get hold of the particulars, you also gain a whole at last. The narrator of Beckett's *Molloy* realizes:

> For the particulars, if you are interested in particulars, there is no need to despair, you may scrabble on the right door, in the right way, in the end. It's not for the whole there seems to be no spell.[18]

The problem is that if you name one aspect of the world, you lose hold of totality, and in order to regain totality, you would have to name *all* other aspects of the world, too, which of course is impossible, unless you reduce the world to a level on which all the world's aspects are limited to a manageable set of possibilities. This in a way is the Beckett principle: going back to basics, he looks out for fields of investigation where

---

[15]    Ibid., p. 278.
[16]    Ibid., p. 287.
[17]    Ibid., p. 289.
[18]    Beckett, *Molloy*, p. 27

everything can be boiled down to just a small set of possibilities. One example are the "twelve possibilities" that occur to Watt, the hero of the epinomous novel. Beckett lists all the possibilities which are theoretically conceivable, but exactly this theoretical approach marks the whole system as a non-adequate way of coping with the non-theoretical world:

> Twelve possibilities occurred to Watt, in this connexion:
> 1. Mr. Knott was responsible for the arrangement, and knew that he was responsible for the arrangement, and knew that such an arrangement existed, and was content.
> [...]
> 12. Mr. Knott was not responsible for the arrangement, but knew who was responsible for the arrangement, but did not know that any such arrangement existed, and was content.[19]

Beckett, however, does not leave it at such an only theoretically possible, practically absurd arrangement. He goes still one step further. After having listed what is a more than exhaustive catalogue of possibilities, he even adds: "Other possibilities occurred to Watt, in this connexion, but he put them aside, and quite out of his mind, as unworthy of serious consideration, for the time being."[20] This, if anything, is the Beckett principle, his way of going on to write in the face of the acknowledged failure to do so: Beckett invents and shapes arenas out of words, small worlds indeed, in which he can exhaust all possibilities – but after having done so, he looks out for and finds ways for still finding more (impossible) possibilites. This principle in a nutshell can be seen at work in his late dramatic piece *Quad*, a pantomime script describing four walkers walking an arena, following a neat system of constant motion. Beckett carefully makes sure that in various respects, all possibilities are covered:

> Together all four complete their courses. [...] Unbroken movement. [...] Four possible solos all given. Six possible duos all given (two twice). Four possible trios all given twice. [...] All possible light combinations given. [...] All possible percussion combinations given. [...] All possible costume combinations given. [...] *Players* As alike in build as possible. [...] Sex indifferent.[21]

Beckett here (and elsewhere) invents a closed system in a closed space, where everything is reduced to just a few possibilities, so that Beckett on the field of his invention can achieve totality indeed. At least so it seems – but then suddenly Beckett opens up the whole system again and thus contradicts totality. At the end of the *Quad* script, after all this detailing of 'all possibilities given,' we reed the following remark: "This original

---

[19]   Samuel Beckett, *Watt* (London: John Calder, 1970), pp. 86 f.
[20]   Ibid., p. 87.
[21]   Samuel Beckett, *Quad, The Complete Dramatic Works* (London: Faber, 1986), pp. 451-53.

scenario [...] was followed in the Stuttgart production by a variation"[22]! Where there is still room for the development of new variations, totality still cannot be wholly achieved.

So, to sum up our findings: where Melville is still looking for a logical sequence in which to arrange a never-ending (and therefore arbitrarily ended) catalogue of fragments, i.e., of particulars, Joyce tries to be virtually exhaustive by covering everything possible. Of course he cannot literally succeed to do so, however, and it is Beckett who really is exhaustive (and exhausted), because he drastically limits the scope of his world before cataloguing all possibilities. Beckett in his later works even tries to compose his works out of abstract concepts of the mind instead of arbitrary relics of the outer world, because only by abstraction any kind of totality can be achieved.

Totality is like a Pandora's box: once you open it, you can never hope to close the box again. The Joycean imperative is the "O tell me all" of *Finnegans Wake*'s "Anna Livia" chapter, but strictly speaking, telling anyone "all" about anything is only possible by simply saying 'All' or 'The Whole' or 'Cosmos' or 'One' – if you add 'two,' you cannot stop adding all other numbers, as soon as you specify what the 'whole' and the 'all' comprises, you lose hold of totality. This is the fundamental and unsolvable problem of all integrative approaches: once a process of integration is being started, there is also a counter-process of disintegration.

Totality is only possible as a ZIP file: TOTALITY.ZIP, so to speak. If you use modern personal computers you know what this means: everything is included in ZIP files, but you cannot read it and cannot work with it, unless you unzip it. As soon as you begin to unzip the world, however, the temptation arises to zip it again, to put everything back into the Pandora's box – but exactly this you can't.

It seems that the unique artistic quality of *Finnegans Wake* lies in the way in which this tricky book simulates totality, although totality cannot be achieved. Joyce here at the same time reduces and multiplies everything by always saying quite different (and indeed opposite) things at the same time. As a result, everybody, everything, every place and every time in *Finnegans Wake* is somebody else, something else, somewhere else and some other time. Each one thing is (or rather seems to be) everything, and thus Joyce makes the impossible possible by "Putting Allspace in a Notshall."[23]

A simulation of totality is attempted in *Moby-Dick* and *Ulysses*, too, but only by way of succession, of sequential catalogues. If Joyce in *Ulysses* employs a specific "art" and a specific style of writing for each chapter, this aims at totality by suggesting that all arts and all modes of style are presented – but this of course is not the case. We can always think of an "art" or a stylistic mode *not* present in the text. The same can be said of *Moby-Dick*, where Melville tries to say something about the whale from the points of view of quite diverse disciplines or fields of knowledge (the whale in the fine arts, in history, in the bible, in biology, in the law, in economics and so on), employing quite different modes of speaking (contemporary jargon, quasi-philosophical musings, the pathos of sermons, Shakespearean blank verse, different modes of pidgin or broken

---

22    Ibid., p. 453.
23    James Joyce, *Finnegans Wake* (London: Faber, 1975), p. 455.

English and so on), but still every reader could name certain disciplines or modes of style *not* to be found in the text. If you start to catalogue the world by naming one phenomenon after the other, you will never be able to get through with it. The only possible way out of this dilemma is to break down the principle of succession and make an inventory of the world by naming (or suggesting) all phenomena at the same time. In *Finnegans Wake*, the inventory of the world is not made finite by any kind of logical sequence (which would have to end somewhere) – in principle, the inventory is infinite, and the complete world is transferred into a never-ending book of fiction.

Of course the forgivable conception that everything is included in *Finnegans Wake* it is not really true: it is not hard to think of something *not* present in that book. Nevertheless the simulation of totality is there, even up to the point where readers, scholars and interpreters have in innumerable cases been able to 'find' or 'discover' something in the body of the text which, as could be proved by one way or other, could not have been in Joyce's mind while he was working on the book. So, even *Finnegans Wake* does not achieve totality in fiction, and even *Finnegans Wake* is incomplete; it sometimes even plays with incompleteness by cutting, abbreviating or pasting fragmented words, sentences or paragraphs onto or into each other. But *Finnegans Wake*, this novel which solves all questions of sequence and succession by saying different things at the same time and by bringing the incomplete last sentence full circle with the incomplete first one, in a way is a complete picture of incompleteness.

# Neitherways*
## Long Ways in Beckett's Shorts

If Beckett used a certain word, he did so quite consciously, and if he used it again in another text we can be fairly sure that the repetition is intentional and serves a purpose. At least in Beckett's later works this is even true with respect to rather inconspicuous and unsuspicious words such as "way," "always" and "away." A close examination of the appearance of these words in some highly condensed and concentrated later texts shows that the lexeme "way" usually occurs in clusters which establish a meaning significantly different from what is associated with these terms in everyday usage.

\*

This paper grew out of a close reading of "neither"[1], the short text Beckett wrote for Morton Feldman in 1976. "neither" can be seen as a developed and modified derivative of a poem in French Beckett wrote nearly thirty years earlier; his English translation of that poem begins with the line "my way is in the sand flowing," and the second of two stanzas reads thus:

> my peace is there in the receding mist
> when I may cease from treading these long shifting thresholds
> and live the space of a door
> that opens and shuts[2]

Both the "way" and the "door" reappear in "neither," although here the relation between both is quite different – the one "door" has become two, and the "way" now is located between those doors. Let me for clearness' sake quote the complete text, and please pay particular attention to the lexemes 'way' and 'heed':

> to and fro in shadow from inner to outer shadow
>
> from impenetrable self to impenetrable unself by way of neither

---

\*    First published as the article "Neitherways: Long Ways in Beckett's Shorts," by Friedhelm Rathjen, in *"All Sturm and no Drang": Beckett and Romanticism / Beckett at Reading 2006*, edited by Dirk Van Hulle and Mark Nixon (= *Samuel Beckett Today / Aujourd'hui* 18, Amsterdam / New York: Rodopi, 2007), pp. 161-172.

[1]    See Friedhelm Rathjen, "Distanzierende Annäherung: Von Versuchen, Samuel Becketts 'neither' zu setzen und zu übersetzen," Olaf Kutzmutz, Adrian La Salvia (eds.) *Halbe Sachen: Wolfenbütteler Übersetzergespräche IV-V: Erlanger Übersetzerwerkstatt I-II* (Wolfenbüttel: Bundesakademie für kulturelle Bildung, 2006), pp. 360-73; rpt. in Friedhelm Rathjen, *Quadratur des Kreises: Zum Übersetzen* (Scheeßel: Edition ReJoyce, 2009), pp. 155-69.

[2]    Samuel Beckett, *Poems 1930-1989* (London: Calder, 2002), p. 67.

as between two lit refuges whose doors once neared gently close, once turned
away from gently part again

beckoned back and forth and turned away

heedless of the way, intent on the one gleam or the other

unheard footfalls only sound

till at last halt for good, absent for good from self and other

then no sound

then gently light unfading on that unheeded neither

unspeakable home[3]

Obviously the term "unheeded" in section 9 refers back to the word "heedless" in
section 5; if, however, we connect "that unheeded neither" to "heedless of the way," it
seems that "the way" and "that [...] neither" are identical. By calling "that [...] neither" an
"unspeakable home" the textual voice affirms that the term "neither" designates a
location indeed; this location is not a fixed but rather a shifting place – a way. If the
text's motion in section 2 is described as being performed "by way of neither" we
should take the word "way" quite literally again: the way evoked by the text is a "way of
neither." In sections 3 and 4 the textual voice is twice "turned away" from the doors;
this process of being 'turned a-way' really means what it says: being constantly kept on
the way. The way is endless and permanent.

The "way of neither" evoked here is the way of Beckett's art: a way of constant
renewal by way of constant repetition. Being on this way means constantly moving
without ever changing locations; the location where Beckett's texts are performed is a
place of movement on the spot, a place where you constantly follow a way without ever
getting away. This Beckettian way is endless – perhaps not in space but definitely in
time, and this means that it is always there. The word 'always' does not appear on the
surface of Beckett's text "neither," but implicitly a concept of 'alwaysness' is present,
too. Alwaysness is endlessness, as Beckett emphasises in *That Time* by using the phrase
"always winter then endless winter"[4]. Beckett's texts often deal with the process of
ending but seldom or never with an actual end. People who criticize Beckett's works

---

3     As far as I can see, all available 'official' printings of "neither" are corrupt in one way or
other, so here I use a version based on the one printed in S. E. Gontarski's edition of
Beckett's short prose (*The Complete Short Prose, 1929-1989*, ed. S. E. Gontarski, New York:
Grove Press, 1995), but modified in the light of other versions. In the first section,
Gontarski has "from inner to outershadow" (258) which, however, seems justified by
neither interior nor manuscript evidence.

4     Samuel Beckett, *That Time, The Complete Dramatic Works* (London: Faber and Faber, 1986),
p. 393. – The phrase "always winter" occurs three times in *Not I* already (ibid., p. 382); ...
*but the clouds* ... includes the phrase "always night" (ibid., p. 421). In both works it is implied
that the winter / the night will never end.

because of their apparent hopelessness tend to miss this fundamental difference: as long as things are in the process of ending they have not yet ended (and perhaps never will). Beckett's endgames therefore tend to be endless games – 'alwaysgames,' so to speak. Beckett's ways (those endless 'ways of neither') are ways which may perhaps lead to something (may-be even an end) but never actually reach this something, be it an end or not.

Usually Beckett's ways are not defined by aims, goals or destinations but rather by initiations – Beckett's ways tend to be 'ways away from' rather than 'ways to.' The classic 'way away from' is the 'way out' which occasionally figures in Beckett's texts, but only as a vague hope and never as a reality. In *The Lost Ones* "by insensible degrees the way out transfers from the tunnel to the ceiling prior to never having been"[5]. In "Long Observation of the Ray," a text Beckett worked on in 1975 and 1976 but never completed, the textual voice hopes for a device "Which once found and set in action would afford way out and/or in. Assuming for no avowable reason search to be afoot. Search for such a thing. Search for anything"[6]. "If of way in and/or out no trace has yet appeared some perhaps may yet to some eye to come if any"[7]. Like here, Beckett's characters usually try to keep their hopes with the help of a very subtle trick: they increase or at least preserve the chances that a way out exists by decreasing the chances that this way out can be found or reached. The longer Beckett's ways are the longer some hope remains that perhaps these ways turn into ways out.[8] Therefore these ways gradually turn into endless ways on which Beckett's characters or textual voices march away in order to always keep going.

'Way,' 'away,' 'always' – these are the three main and most frequent words which embed the lexeme 'way' in Beckett's texts. Given the fact that Samuel Beckett always wrote with outmost attention to detail and that if he used or repeated a certain word he did so quite consciously and with a certain purpose in mind, we should assume that even rather inconspicuous and unsuspicious words such as 'way,' 'always' and 'away' in Beckett's highly condensed and concentrated texts from his late period are able to establish a meaning significantly different from what is associated with these terms in everyday usage. Let's have a look at the shortest of all Beckett texts, a one-line poem he wrote for the magazine *Orange Export Ltd.* in 1981: "away dream all away"[9]. A surface reading would surely take "dream" as a verb and interpret the text as an invocation to dream everything away. It is also possible, however, to read "dream" as a noun, and if in addition to this we admit that "away" may include a half-hidden 'way,' the poem unfurls

---

[5]    Samuel Beckett, *The Lost Ones, The Complete Short Prose, 1929-1989*, p. 207.

[6]    Samuel Beckett, "Long Observation of the Ray": UoR MSS 2909 i-vi, Beckett Manuscript Collection, University of Reading (1977), p. ii.

[7]    Ibid., p. iv, deleted.

[8]    A "Way out through the grey rift in dark" (*The Complete Dramatic Works*, p. 429) is also hoped for in *A Piece of Monologue* where the lexeme 'way' is present mainly in the word "away" occurring five times.

[9]    Samuel Beckett, *Dikter*, trans. and ed. Magnus Hedlund (Viborg: Albert Bonniers Förlag, 2001), p. 157.

a wide range of possible meanings: 'away-dream – all away'; 'a way – dream all – a way'; 'a way – dream – all a way'; even 'a way-dream – all a way' etc. Of course this is an extreme case; surely not each and every use of the terms 'away' and 'always' in Beckett's texts is as ambivalent as this one. At least whenever these terms and the noun 'way' appear in close vicinity, however, 'away' and 'always' get loaded with an additional meaning which cannot be ignored.

Often in Beckett's later texts the lexeme 'way' and its derivatives occur in clusters. A survey limited to Beckett's works originally written in English after 1965 yields the following results: we find all three words "way," "always" and "away" in *Eh Joe, Not I, That Time*, "Heard in the Dark 1," *Company* and *Worstward Ho* (with an additional "halfway" in "Heard in the Dark 1" and *Company*, and a "highway" and the plural form "ways" in *Company*, too); both "way" and "away" occur in "As the story was told" (which also has a "doorway"), "Sounds," "neither," "Long Observation of the Ray" and *A Piece of Monologue*; "way" plus "always" can be found in "Still" (which also has "midways"), *Footfalls, ... but the clouds ...*, "The Voice" (which includes an additional "wayfarer"), "The Way" (which also has "midway," "one-way," "crossways" and the plural form "ways") and *Stirrings Still*; both "always" and "away" are present in "Still 3." Apart from "away dream all away," there are only three texts where we find just one of the terms in question here: in *Ohio Impromptu* Beckett uses "away" only, and only once; in *What where* he again uses "away," but four times; in the four-line poem "Go where never before" we find "always" twice.

Limitations of space prevent me from discussing each and every usage of the terms in question; instead, I'd like to concentrate on a few chosen cases where we find variations of the 'way' lexeme in very close vicinity. In "As the story was told," we come across "a small hut in a grove some hundred yards away, a distance even the loudest cry could not carry, but must die on the way"[10]. Here "the way" clearly refers back to the adjective "away," both terms designating both a distance and the possibility or impossibility of bridging this distance in one way or other.[11] The adjective "away" recurs on the next page when the textual voice sees "a hand" appearing "in the doorway" and holding out "a sheet of writing. I took and read it, then tore it in four and put the pieces in the waiting hand to take away"[12]. This is one of several instances in Beckett's work where an enforced act of producing text is described with the help of the word "away": either an unwilling 'confessor' is 'taken away' against his will (like in *What where*: "Take him away and give him the works until he confesses"[13]) or what has been 'confessed' is 'taken away' from the 'confessor' like in the passage quoted from "As the story was told." Contrary to customary usage, the term 'away' seems to designate not the end of

---

10      Samuel Beckett, "As the story was told," *The Complete Short Prose, 1929-1989*, p. 255.
11      See also a similar passage in "Sounds," a preliminary version of "Still": "air [...] too still for even the lightest leaf to carry the brief way here and not die the sound not die on the brief way the wave not die away" (ibid., p. 267).
12      Beckett, "As the story was told," p. 256.
13      Samuel Beckett, *What where, The Complete Dramatic Works*, p. 473, 475.

something but rather something (speech, for example) being made durable. The act of 'awaying' at least in some of Beckett's texts seems to be an act of making utterance permanent.

This is not as bizarre or obscure as might appear. Admittedly in everyday usage the term 'always' refers to a concept of duration and the term 'away' to a concept of termination, which nearly turns these words into contraries. This is not valid for all uses, however. According to the *Oxford English Dictionary*, the adjective 'away' originally meant: "On (his or one's) way; onward, on, along. Hence used also with *come*, as still in north. Eng. and Sc., where 'Come away' = 'come along, come on,' without reference to place left"[14]. Derived from this archaic sense is a modern sense of 'away' still in use: "Onward in time, on, continuously, constantly; with idea of continuance of action and progress; e.g. *to work away* = to go on working"[15]. Beckett frequently uses 'away' in this sense of continuity, as when Joe in *Eh Joe* is told to "squeeze away"[16], when Mouth in *Not I* talks about "the brain ... raving away on its own"[17] and "flickering away"[18] while the woman is "waiting to be led away"[19], or when in *That Time* voices and forms from the past are not only "drowsing away" but also "muttering away" and "drooling away"[20]. If we bear this sense of continuity in mind, other appearances of the term 'away' in Beckett's texts lose their apparent unambiguousness. Let's take *Ohio Impromptu,* for example, where it is said of a reader: "So from time to time unheralded he would appear to read the sad tale through again and the long night away"[21]. Does this mean that the night is made to disappear, or does it mean that the night is stretched continuously?[22] Shortly after, first there is "no sound of reawakening"[23], and then there is the "sound of reawakening"[24]. Keen ears will be able to hear both a 'way' and an 'away' in "reawakening," but what, then, does 're-away' mean?

So it appears that both termination and duration can be involved in the process of 'awaying.' 'Awayness' can be a permanent state, so to speak. 'Alwaysness' by comparison seems to be a more straightforward concept, but if we look at Beckett's use of the term 'always' this is not so clear either. It seems that 'alwaysness' can have its beginning and its end, or at least that 'alwaysness' can be conceived as once having begun and once

14  *Oxford English Dictionary*, Second Edition, Complete Text Reproduced Micrographically (London: BCA 1994), "away" lemma, I.1.
15  Ibid., II.7.
16  Samuel Beckett, *Eh Joe, The Complete Dramatic Works*, p. 365.
17  Samuel Beckett, *Not I*, ibid., p. 380.
18  Ibid., pp. 381, 382.
19  Ibid., p. 381.
20  Beckett, *That Time*, p. 393.
21  Samuel Beckett, *Ohio Impromptu*, ibid., p. 447.
22  A comparably complicated case can be found in Samuel Beckett, *Worstward Ho* (London: Calder, 1983), p. 44, where – after the word "Away" has been used three times in the temporal sense of 'gone' – we read: "Stare away to child and worsen same."
23  Beckett, *Ohio Impromptu*, p. 447.
24  Ibid., p. 448.

having to end. In the poem "Go where never before" there is this seemingly contra-
dictory line: "No sooner there than there always"[25], meaning that alwaysness has just
begun.[26] Here it also seems that alwaysness is a place where you can 'go' although having
been there "never before"; if you want to go somewhere, however, you usually use or
take a 'way.' We must conclude that there are ways which lead to alwaysness, and that at
the same time these ways can be ways into awayness.

If we bear this in mind, Beckett's texts enfold meanings which reach far beyond
the surface level. This is especially true for the short drama *That Time* where on just eight
pages of text "always" appears eleven times, "away" eight times and "way" six times in
different senses. At one point of the text voice A conjures up a scene from Beckett's
early years:

> none ever came but the child on the stone among the giant nettles with the light
> coming in where the wall had crumbled away poring on his book well on into the
> night some moods the moonlight and they all out on the roads looking for him or
> making up talk breaking up two or more talking to himself being together that
> way where none ever came

Then voice C takes over: "always winter then endless winter year after year as if it
couldn't end"[27]. This last phrase "always winter then endless winter" – a variation of the
earlier "always winter then always raining"[28] – stresses again that alwaysness equals
endlessness, but even more significant is Beckett's use of "away" in "the wall had
crumbled away" and of "way" in "being together that way." The boy here is at rest in
what seems to be Barrington's tower, while his people are looking for him "on the
roads." Literally speaking, these people outside are 'on the way,' while the tower as the
place "where none ever came" seems to be a locality where no ways lead to – out of the
way, so to speak. Beckett, however, avoids the lexeme 'way' when speaking of the world
outside while repeatedly using it in quite different senses when speaking of the durable,
motionless and unmoving world inside the tower. Beckett's 'way' is not a path or road
which leads from some place to another; Beckett's 'way' instead is a place or realm of
unceasing or constantly repeated 'alwaysness.'

About the same time when writing *That Time* Beckett composed the French prose
text "Pour finir encore." When translating this piece into English as "For to end yet
again" he took advantage of the fact that quite different French terms like 'se detacher,'

---

[25]  Samuel Beckett, "Go where never before," *Poems 1930-1989*, p. 46.

[26]  The concept of an alwaysness that comes with time is also implied in a passage in Samuel
Beckett, *Company* (London: Calder, 1980), p. 51, also included in Samuel Beckett, "Heard in
the Dark 1," *The Complete Short Prose, 1929-1989*, p. 248: "You are no more tired now than
you always were. Not because of age. You are no older now than you always were. And yet
you halt as never before."

[27]  Beckett, *That Time*, p. 393.

[28]  Ibid., pp. 388, 392.

'ouvrir la march,' 'toujours' and 'parcours'[29] can be transferred into variants of the 'way' lexeme. At one point the English version speaks of "a fragment" which "comes away from mother ruin"[30] (1995, 245), thus reminding us of "the wall" that "had crumbled away" in *That Time*, and on the next page all three variants of the 'way' lexeme appear in close vicinity:

> Sepulchral skull is this then its last state all set for always litter and dwarfs ruins and little body grey cloudless sky glutted dust verge upon verge hell air not a breath? And dream of a way in a space with neither here nor there where all the footsteps ever fell can never fare nearer to anywhere nor from anywhere further away?[31]

The "Sepulchral skull" here seems to be a reduced and abstracted version of the tower in *That Time*, and again the "way in a space" conceptualised here does not lead from somewhere to somewhere but remains a realm apart from anything else. It surely is not coincidental that in this context Beckett uses the phrase "neither here nor there," thus anticipating the text "neither" written shortly afterwards. Another text Beckett was working on at that time is the unpublished "Long Observation of the Ray" where again he stresses that the Beckettian way is not a way out but rather a way of restlessly staying the same: "Scarcely at rest or at most a matter of seconds later when away to the next and thence in the same way."[32] In still another unpublished text from this period, "The Voice," Beckett even introduces a "wayfarer out since dawn plodding forward in the failing light through the gloaming"[33] in order to create what could be labelled the unchanging changeability of walking a way. First it is said that the sounds of the "boots meeting the ground one after the other" are the "sole sounds for they change from one tread to the next," but after the wayfarer "listens to each one and adds it in his mind to the ever increasing sum of those that went before"[34] we finally have to accept that the change of sound "from one tread to the next" does not really make a difference: "Always the same flat tone"[35]. It seems that in "The Voice" the Beckettian 'way' forms the rhythm to which the 'voice' subjoins a melody, thus walking and talking adding up to a closed audio-world.

---

[29]   See Samuel Beckett, "Pour finir encore," *Um abermals zu enden und anderes Durchgefallenes: Prosadichtungen in drei Sprachen* (Frankfurt am Main: Suhrkamp, 1978), pp. 130-36.

[30]   Samuel Beckett, "For to end yet again," *The Complete Short Prose, 1929-1989*, p. 245.

[31]   Ibid., p. 246.

[32]   Beckett, "Long Observation of the Ray," p. iii. In a later version Beckett deletes the word "away" from this passage: "Scarcely at rest on any given blank or at most some seconds later when this leap to another and thence in the same way to yet another. As well on the same of those countless hemispheres as among its antipodes" (p. iv).

[33]   Samuel Beckett, "The Voice": UoR MS 2910, Beckett Manuscript Collection, University of Reading (1977), p. 2.

[34]   Ibid., pp. 2 f.

[35]   Ibid., pp. 3 f.

A passage right from the centre of *Company* has been published separately as "Heard in the Dark 1," and in this passage again all three main variants of the 'way' lexeme appear in close vicinity:

> You lie in the dark with closed eyes and see yourself there as described making ready to strike out and away across the expanse of light. You hear again the click of the door pulled gently to and the silence before the steps can start. Next thing you are on your way across the white pasture afrolic with lambs in spring and strewn with red placentae. You take the course you always take which is a beeline for the gap or ragged point in the quickset that forms the western fringe.[36]

As in "neither," here a "door" comes into play, although this time the textual voice is situated not "between two [...] doors" but between just one door and a gap; at the end "Heard in the Dark 1" will stop "Halfway across the pasture on your beeline to the gap"[37]. The way trodden is marked by an endless continuity again, for the steps "number each day the same. Average day in day out the same. The way being always the same"[38]. Two lines later, however, we read:

> Your father's shade is not with you any more. It fell out long ago. You do not hear your footfalls any more. Unhearing unseeing you go your way. Day after day. The same way. As if there were no other any more. For you there is no other any more.[39]

Strictly speaking, these lines are self-contradictory, for if something is "not [...] any more" what it was or like it was, it seems wrong to say that this something is "always the same." If Beckett nonetheless does say so, we must conclude that sameness can change – a way which is always the same may still alter or even die away.

This surprising fact that a way's alwaysness can end and that its unchangeability can change is confirmed by a short two-part text Beckett wrote in 1981 but never consented to publish; this text's title is "The Way." Beckett here describes a path running up and down a hill in the shape of the figure 8 (or the infinity symbol):

> The way wound up from foot to top and thence another way. On back down. The ways crossed midway more and less. A little more and less than midway up and down. The ways were one-way. No retracing the way up back down nor back up the way down. Neither in whole from top or foot nor in part from on the way. The one way back was on and on was always back. [...] Gait down as up same plod always. [...] So from foot and top to crossways could the seconds have been numbered then height known and depth. [...] Thorns hemmed the way. The ways.

---

36      Beckett, "Heard in the Dark 1," p. 247.
37      Ibid., p. 249.
38      Ibid., p. 248.
39      Ibid.

Same mist always. [.../] Forth and back across a barren same winding one-way way. [...] Through emptiness the beaten ways as fixed as if enclosed. [...][40]

By accurately describing this 8-shaped way, Beckett shows that "on" can at the same time mean "back," that a singular "way" can be identical with plural "ways," that a "one-way way" can lead "Forth and back" and meet itself at a "crossways" – and that progression does not necessarily mean progress, that a way can be walked endlessly without ever leading anywhere.

The text "The Way" is the grand finale but not the end of Beckett's ways. The lexeme 'way' re-appears – if less frequently than before – in Beckett's works from the 1980s. In the first part of *Stirrings Still*, someone is "Seen always from behind whither-soever he went" apparently "seeking the way out. A way out. To the roads. The back roads"[41]. In the second part of *Stirrings Still*, this concrete "way out" is turned into an abstract "in the way"[42] and "some way"[43] in the sense of a mode or manner; in the third part the lexeme 'way' is completely absent, everything is "stayed," and the character is looking for a "missing word" and has "no danger or hope as the case might be of his ever getting out"[44] – it seems that finally all ways have ended. The last appearance of the lexeme 'way' in Beckett's oeuvre can be found in "what is the word" (the English translation of the original French "comment dire") where there is a last glimpse "afaint afar away over there what –"[45]. Several readers (myself included) have independent of each other here heard an echo of the last sentence of Joyce's *Finnegans Wake*, "A way a lone a last a loved a long the"[46], which is an incomplete sentence running into the novel's very first line again.[47] *Finnegans Wake*, therefore, never ends for good but always starts anew. Joyce's cyclic novel is an extremely eloquent and detailed version of the rather bare and reduced neitherways in Beckett's later works, those ways without beginning or end which seemingly never change, ways in progression without progress.

Beckett's most refined versions of this way date from the 1970s, when he experimented with abstract forms of sense perception and utterance. I believe that at least in Beckett's works of the 70s there is an extremely important triad formed by the eye, the voice and the way – or in other words, by seeing, saying and walking. I'd like to connect this triad to another, much more basic triad which elsewhere I have tried to

---

[40]    Samuel Beckett, "The Way," typescript III, facsimilized in Carlton Lake (ed.), *No Symbols Where None Intended: A Catalogue of Books, Manuscripts, and Other Material Relating to Samuel Beckett in the Collections of the Humanities Research Center* (Austin: Humanities Research Center, 1984), p. 173.

[41]    Samuel Beckett, *Stirrings Still, The Complete Short Prose, 1929-1989*, p. 260.

[42]    Ibid., p. 262.

[43]    Ibid., p. 263.

[44]    Ibid., p. 264.

[45]    Samuel Beckett, "what is the word," *Poems 1930-1989*, p. 115.

[46]    James Joyce, *Finnegans Wake* (London: Faber and Faber, 1975), p. 628.

[47]    See Phyllis Carey, "Ireland, Island of Saints and Searchers," Friedhelm Rathjen (ed.), *In Principle, Beckett is Joyce* (Edinburgh: Split Pea P, 1994), p. 91.

show being at work in Beckett's oeuvre as a whole and particularly in his two prose trilogies, namely the triad of perception, expression and imagination[48]. Perception and expression surely form one of Beckett's characteristic dualities; usually Beckett's voices and characters are trapped in binary structures, even more so if the respective duality includes identical opposites which often figure in Beckett's works[49]. The "two lit refuges" in the text "neither" can be conceived as such. If for Beckett's textual voices there is no way out of these binary structures, however, what is left is a way in between. This is the way which does not lead anywhere and which does not change anything but which when being walked is a way to get away from utter hopelessness. As long as Beckett's characters are in motion, even if this is a motion in a closed place or womb-tomb enclosure and even if the walkers walk an the spot, they are able at least temporarily to transport themselves elsewhere – in their imagination. Even if there is no way out they may thus get away; even if there is an overwhelming alwaysness it is not impossible to look for neitherways.

Artistic neitherways are what Beckett himself is always looking for. In the face of the strong binary structures to be found in his works Beckett is constantly striving to go beyond two given poles or modes or directions and to expand binary into triple structures by some kind of movement or motion. In other words: he is always trying to find new ways, ways away from the acceptance of limitations.

---

[48] See Friedhelm Rathjen, *Beckett zur Einführung* (Hamburg: Junius, 1995), pp. 43-146; new and enlarged edition as *Beckett: Eine Einführung ins Werk* (Scheeßel: Edition ReJoyce, 2007), pp. 41-132.

[49] See Friedhelm Rathjen, "Maximal Joyce is a State of Beckett: Joyce, Beckett, and Bruno's *Coincidentia Oppositorum,*" Friedhelm Rathjen (ed.), *In Principle, Beckett is Joyce* (Edinburgh: Split Pea Press, 1994), pp. 99-112, pp. 105-8; Friedhelm Rathjen, "The Magic Triangle: James Joyce, Samuel Beckett, Arno Schmidt," Angela Moorjani and Carola Veit (eds.), *Samuel Beckett: Endlessness in the Year 2000 / Samuel Beckett: Fin sans fin en l'an 2000* (= *Samuel Beckett Today / Aujourd'hui* 11, Amsterdam / New York: Rodopi, 2002), pp. 92-99, pp. 95 f.; both essays merged into "In Principle, Beckett is Joyce (and Schmidt is Schmidt): The Magic Triangle and Giordano Bruno's *Coincidentia Oppositorum*" in the present collection, pp. 107-19, pp. 113-16.

# III: Getting back

# "The ashplant is Stephen's Bloom-ing rod"*
## Stephen, Bloom, and Seamus Heaney on Sandymount Strand

for jörg drews

My starting point is a short poem by Seamus Heaney, entitled "The Strand":

> The dotted line my father's ashplant made
> On Sandymount Strand
> Is something else the tide won't wash away.[1]

These eighteen words in three lines make up the sum total of Heaney's text, and nobody familiar with James Joyce's *Ulysses* (consisting of eighteen episodes in three parts) will fail to see a connection between Heaney's poem and Joyce's novel. In order fully to establish the Joycean sub-text of "The Strand," we may first try to identify the poem's three major constituents: the father, the ashplant, and the strand.

Easiest to identify is the place: it's the same beach Stephen Dedalus is walking in the third episode of *Ulysses* and the same beach where Bloom is resting in the thirteenth episode. Not quite so easy to identify is the father in Heaney's poem. At least in part this father-figure incorporates the poet's corporeal father. In a radio interview Heaney has revealed the biographical germ-cell of his brief text:

> I remember when my father and mother came down to Dublin in the late 1970s or early '80s, just after we bought our house in Sandymount. My father went out walking on the strand, and he had an ash-plant with him, but of course he had no sense of James Joyce's Stephen Dedalus walking into eternity across Sandymount Strand carrying an ash-plant. Then, after my father died, I remembered him like that, making a dotted line across the strand. [...] In one hundred years time I would like a few dots to be on the strand, and in those dots would be a poem or two – something, as the poem says, that 'the tide won't wash away'.[2]

It would be inappropriate, however, to conclude from this (quite unguarded and simplifying) statement of the poet that "The Strand" is just the poetic description of a biographical incident. In pairing and blending his father with Joyce's autobiographical hero, Heaney transcends the father-figure in order to include other fathers – non-

---

*     Previously unpublished.

[1]     Seamus Heaney, "The Strand," *The Spirit Level* (New York: Farrar, Straus and Giroux, 1996), p. 73.

[2]     "Seamus Heaney," *Reading the Future: Irish writers in conversation with Mike Murphy*, ed. Clíodhna Ní Anluain (Dublin: The Lilliput Press, 2000), pp. 81-97, p. 96.

corporeal ones. The fatherhood which "the tide won't wash away" is something which includes but is not limited to 'real-life' progenitors. At least equally important is the artistic father-figure.

Although Joyce and Heaney work in seemingly different genres (Joyce the novelist having produced a novel in eighteen episodes, Heaney the poet producing the poem in eighteen words), Heaney is able to conceive and use Joyce as a father. In his earlier (and longer) poem "Station Island" he unmistakably makes him appear as a father "in the flesh":

> Then I knew him in the flesh
> [...]
> His voice eddying with the vowels of all rivers
> came back to me, though he did not speak yet,
> a voice like a prosecutor's or a singer's,
> [...] Old father, mother's son[3]

Joyce can be a father to Heaney because Heaney conceives the novelist as a poet, too: "The great poetry of the opening chapter of *Ulysses*, for example, amplifies and rhapsodises the world with an unlooked-for accuracy and transport."[4] In this sense, Joyce evolves as a father-poet to Heaney.

The significance of the "ashplant" in Heaney's "The Strand" largely depends on the Joycean sub-text established by the place and the multi-layered father-figure. This is not the only instance where an ashplant appears in Heaney's poetry, but when in "The Harvest Bow" Heaney speaks of "[h]ands that aged round ashplants and cane sticks"[5] this has nothing to do with Joyce, although these hands seem to belong to a father figure, too. In "The Harvest Bow," ashplants are farmers' instruments and not poets' weapons, which the ashplant clearly becomes in the hands of Stephen Dedalus. In order to clarify the special and specific rôle played by the ashplant as soon as it is present on Sandymount Strand, it is necessary to have a look at similar or comparable instruments as they appear in Joyce's novels.

Morris Beja in an early contribution to the *James Joyce Quarterly* was able to demonstrate that there are several sticks, clubs, canes and other more or less phallic weapons in

---

3    Seamus Heaney, "Station Island," *Station Island* (New York: Farrar, Straus and Giroux, 1985), pp. 92 f. On Joyce in "Station Island," see Darcy O'Brien, "Piety and Modernism: Seamus Heaney's 'Station Island'," *James Joyce Quarterly* 26.1 (Fall 1988), pp. 51-65. See also Lucy McDiarmid, "Joyce, Heaney, and 'that subject people stuff'," Diana A. Ben-Merre, Maureen Murphy (eds.), *James Joyce and His Contemporaries* (New York et. al.: Greenwood Press, 1989), p. 131: "The poem ["Station Island"] is an example of that quintessentially Joycean event, the discovery of the true father, but with this wrinkle: the father tells the son not to look for fathers."

4    Seamus Heaney, "Joyce's Poetry," *James Joyce: Bloomsday Magazine 2002* (Dublin: James Joyce Centre, 2002), p. 35.

5    Seamus Heaney, "The Harvest Bow," *Field Work* (New York: Farrar, Straus and Giroux, 1981), p. 58.

Joyce's works. In many cases these phallic weapons are connected with acts of violence, and in all these cases a special kind of fixed gaze or stare is involved: either the aggressor stares with perverse eyes, or the victim begs with pleading eyes not to continue.[6] Eyes can be cast upwards or downwards, just as a stick can be directed up into the sky (this is the phallic weapon) or down to the ground (this is the tool that can produce a "dotted line"). In both cases, the stick or prick or cudgel or rod is an instrument of paternity, something which can generate or procreate.

Stephen's ashplant makes his first appearance in *A Portrait of the Artist as a Young Man* when Stephen tries to come to terms with his own Daedalean nature while watching birds in front of the National Library: "What birds were they? He stood on the steps of the library to look at them, leaning wearily on his ashplant."[7] Here Stephen apparently is gazing upwards, but his stick is pointing downwards and anchored in the ground, otherwise Stephen would not be able to lean on it. He's still leaning on it on the next page of the novel: "The colonnade above him made him think vaguely of an ancient temple and the ashplant on which he leaned wearily of the curved stick of an augur."[8] Here it becomes even clearer than before than Stephen's eyes (and thoughts) on the one hand and Stephen's ashplant on the other hand are pointing into quite different directions. Stephen is watching the sky in an augury, which means that he is trying to read in the sky; his ashplant, however, is pointing downwards as if a writing instrument. The fact that Stephen is able to lean on it, however, shows that the ashplant is motionless: Stephen does not write anything with it yet.

The ashplant reappears in the opening episode of *Ulysses* when Stephen leaves the Martello Tower and goes down to the sea with Buck Mulligan and Haines: "He walked on, waiting to be spoken to, trailing his ashplant by his side. Its ferrule followed lightly on the path, squealing at his heels. My familiar, after me, calling Steeeeeeeeeeeephen! A wavering line along the path."[9] In this scene, the ashplant is not motionless anymore; by being moved along the ground it produces speech ("Steeeeeeeeeeeephen") and a "wavering line" which as such resembles writing. This "wavering line" produced by Stephen's ashplant resembles the "dotted line" the father's ashplant in Heaney's "The Strand" produces, but with a difference: the "dotted line" is created by the ashplant's being lifted up and sinking down again several times, but Stephen apparently does not lift his ashplant from the ground, not even for a short moment. His "wavering line" is a continuous line, and his ashplant is even more earthbound than the stick carried by Heaney's father, although the poet in the interview quoted before calls his father a man

6   See Morris Beja, "The Wooden Sword: Threatener and Threatened in the Fiction of James Joyce," *James Joyce Quarterly* 2.1 (Fall 1964), pp. 33-41.

7   James Joyce, *A Portrait of the Artist as a Young Man*, ed. Chester G. Anderson and Richard Ellmann (New York: Viking Press, 1966), p. 224.

8   Ibid., p. 225.

9   James Joyce, *Ulysses: The Corrected Text*, ed. Hans Walter Gabler (Harmondsworth: Penguin, 1986 [Student's Edition], 1.627-9.

"than whom no more earthbound creature could be imagined"[10] – it seems that lofty Stephen Dedalus has indeed crashed to the ground.

If this is a humbled Stephen, he apparently still acts very humbly in the third episode of *Ulysses* while walking along Sandymount Strand. He is "resting his ashplant in a grike"[11], and he tends to be frightened and anxious: "My ashplant will float away"[12]. Even when using his ashplant as a weapon he does so with a certain softness, and the weapon is blunt: "He took the hilt of his ashplant, lunging with it softly, dallying still"[13]. Later in the day, in the library, Stephen appears to be more offensive, but still he uses his stick rather softly and defensively: "Stephen [...] hung on his ashplanthandle over his knee. My casque and sword. Touch lightly with two index fingers."[14] A "casque" is a protective and not an aggressive weapon, so still the use Stephen makes of his ashplant emphasizes a certain passivity and even limpness in his behaviour. Up to this point, Stephen's ashplant is not phallic at all.

This only changes in the Nighttown episode when Stephen overcomes his passivity for a moment. While he is *"flourishing the ashplant in his left hand"*[15] the ashplant becomes erect, phallic, procreative, and the verb *"flourishing"* indicates that it turns into a plant indeed – a flower beginning to grow and to bloom. (It should be noted that etymologically speaking, an ash-'plant' is not a dead twig or branch but rather the living shoot or cutting of an ashtree.) By being lifted over the owner's head, the ashplant finally turns into the weapon of an aggressor: "*Nothung!* [...] *He lifts his ashplant high with both hands and smashes the chandelier*"[16]. This is the one and only phallic use of the ashplant indeed that we ever come across in Joyce's works, but it does not generate or procreate – instead it destroys. Stephen is not a father, and he does not become a father by using his ashplant in a phallic way. Instead he has to lose his ashplant (and the ashplant has to lose its phallic significance again) in order to find a new father himself. The moment when Leopold Bloom takes over the rôle of Stephen's protector is exactly the moment when Bloom picks up Stephen's ashplant: "*Bloom, holding in his hand Stephen's hat* [...] *and ashplant, stands irresolute. Then he bends to him and shakes him by the shoulder.*"[17] Bloom takes up the phallic instrument, but he is careful not to act phallic himself; at first he bends down to Stephen, and even after straightening himself he keeps his eyelids drooped: "*Bloom, holding the hat and ashplant, stands erect.* [...] *He looks down on Stephen's face and form.*"[18] This is the moment when the ghost of Bloom's real (but dead) son Rudy appears;

---

10      *Reading the Future: Irish writers in conversation with Mike Murphy*, p. 89.
11      Joyce, *Ulysses*, 3.284-5.
12      Ibid., 3.454.
13      Ibid., 3.489.
14      Ibid., 9.295-7.
15      Ibid., 15.73.
16      Ibid., 15.4242-4.
17      Ibid., 15.4920-3.
18      Ibid., 15.4944-7.

Bloom takes up the rôle as Stephen's father, using the ashplant as a kind of wonderbat[19] but strictly not as a phallus.

So, the ashplant is not one of the phallic sticks, clubs, and canes to be found in Joyce's works – the ashplant is not a shillelagh. It has been suggested that the 'ash' Stephen's weapon is made of may actually have been a 'mountain ash', which is a common Anglo-Irish name for the rowan-tree[20], but of course Joyce is quite aware of the term 'rowan' – he names one of the characters in his play *Exiles* Rowan, after all, and in the tree wedding passage of *Ulysses*, he includes one "Mrs Rowan Greene" as well as one "Mrs Poll Ash"[21] –, so we should take the ash as an ash indeed. As such, it refers to the ash-tree Yggdrasil, the universal tree of life of Norse mythology, which with its branches reaches up high to sky and heaven, but which at the same time is rooted deep down in the earth. These two diametrically opposite directions of movement – up and down – are equally inherent in the ashplant's wonderbat-like potency.

Eyes can be cast up to the skies like in an augury, which means reading the future, but they can also be cast also down for the purpose of reading (and writing down) the past or the present. When pointing downwards, Stephen's ashplant can turn into a writing instrument. As such, it acts like a procreative tree: the ashplant is a tree's derivative, but the letters it can produce may also be trees, as we are told in Seamus Heaney's poem "Alphabets" where the poet remembers how as a young pupil he learned

> Of new calligraphy that felt like home.
> The letters of this alphabet were trees.
> The capitals were orchards in full bloom,
> The lines of script like briars coiled in ditches.[22]

The alphabet alluded to by Heaney here is the Celtic ogham alphabet, an alphabet made up quite literally of trees: each of the twenty letters of this alphabet is associated with and referred to by the name of a tree (the ash stands for the letter *n* or *nion*, the rowan-tree for the letter *l* or *luis*).[23] The association of alphabetical units with trees (or

---

[19]   See Sandra Manoogian Pearce, "Stephen's Ashplant as Bloom's Wonderbat in 'Circe''s Harlequinade," *James Joyce Quarterly* 35.4 / 36.1 (Summer / Fall 1998), pp. 866-72.

[20]   See Ruth Bauerle, "Some *Mots* on a Quickbeam in Joyce's Eye," *James Joyce Quarterly* 10.3 (Spring 1973), pp. 346-48; John Garvin, *James Joyce's Disunited Kingdom and the Irish Dimension* (Dublin: Gill and Macmillan, 1976), pp. 27-32.

[21]   Joyce, *Ulysses*, 1269-71. – See Brigitte L. Sandquist, "The Tree Wedding in 'Cyclops' and the Ramification of Cata-logic," *James Joyce Quarterly* 33.2 (Winter 1996), pp. 195-209.

[22]   Seamus Heaney, "Alphabets," *The Haw Lantern* (New York: Farrar, Straus and Giroux, 1987), p. 2.

[23]   For details as to the ogham alphabet, see Curtis Clark, "Natural history of the trees of the Celtic Ogham," *Circle Network News* 56 (Summer 1995), pp. 12 f.; see also Friedhelm Rathjen, "Was bleibt?: Eine Fährtensuche am Strand von Sandymount," Sabine Kyora, Axel Dunker, Dirk Sangmeister (eds.), *Literatur ohne Kompromisse: ein buch für jörg drews* (Bielefeld:

derivatives of trees), however, is not restricted to the ogham alphabet; the German word for 'letter', for example, is *Buchstabe* which literally translates as 'book-stick'. These 'book-sticks' form the "lines of script" Heaney speaks of in "Alphabets" and in a way also the "dotted line" produced by the stick of Heaney's father in "The Strand."

In *Ulysses*, Stephen Dedalus no longer attempts an augury; when at the end of the library episode he remembers his auguric aspirations from *A Portrait*, he has to realize that there are "[n]o birds" anymore, and he lowers his attention and directs it to "wide earth"[24]. When in *Ulysses* Stephen attempts to read, he does not do so in the sky but on earth, in the ground, on Sandymount Strand: "Signatures of all things I am here to read, seaspawn and seawrack, the nearing tide, that rusty boot. Snotgreen, bluesilver, rust: coloured signs. [...] Shut your eyes and see."[25] Shutting his eyes, Stephen tries to read in the sand, but he also writes in the sand with his ashplant, which is a magical rod of a special kind – not a phallic prick or pole, but rather a downcast stick, a pencil. With this ashplant-pencil, Stephen produces a "dotted line" which leaves vacant bits, spaces of uncertainty which have to be filled up by later readers such as Seamus Heaney or our-selves.

But can such a message in the sand be durable, can it hope for eternity? Literally speaking, of course it cannot; in order to endure, the message should rather be carved in stone like the ogham writings of old, which still today can be found elsewhere in Ireland. The ogham alphabet is a writing system consisting of horizontal or slanting strokes carved around the edge of a pole or standing stone – a "dotted line," so to speak. Only when carved in stone those messages have survived though the centuries.

Strictly speaking, however, not the messages as such have survived; it's only the material which survives: stone. A few years ago, I took a photograph of an ogham stone found at Derrynane Bay, Co. Kerry, because it looked so picturesque; I did not and do not know what its carvings mean. But what if the message read "here I was on April 13, 939"? I am quite sure it doesn't, but if it did this message would have become a lie, because the ogham stone is not standing anymore where it was found: it was found farther out in the bay, under the waterline, and subsequently re-erected in solid ground.

Surprisingly the "dotted line" Stephen produces with his penis pointing down and peeing in the sand is more dependable. It cannot be carried away and placed elsewhere: as long as you can see this dotted line it is where it has been produced. Later in the day, Leopold Bloom on the same strand produces something with his erected penis, but this does not leave a "dotted line" – it happens in his trousers. Nevertheless Bloom, too, leaves a message, and he does so with a "[b]it of stick" he finds, not a phallus:

> Mr Bloom with his stick gently vexed the thick sand at his foot. Write a message for her. Might remain. What?

---

Aisthesis, 2004), pp. 287-89, rpt. in Friedhelm Rathjen, *Flußgefließe: Aufsätze zu James Joyce* (Scheeßel: Edition ReJoyce, 2008), pp. 33-46.

[24]   Joyce, *Ulysses*, 9.1218-21.
[25]   Ibid., 3.2-9.

I.

Some flatfoot tramp on it in the morning. Useless. Washed away. Tide comes here. Saw a pool near her foot. Bend, see my face there, dark mirror, breathe on it, stirs. All these rocks with lines and scars and letters. O, those transparent! Besides they don't know. What is the meaning of that other world. I called you naughty boy because I do not like.

AM. A.

No room. Let it go.

Mr Bloom effaced the letters with his slow boot. Hopeless thing sand. Nothing grows in it. All fades.[26]

Paradoxically, Bloom's cryptic message is something "the tide won't wash away": by effacing the message with his feet, Bloom himself prevents the tide from washing away anything – and at the same time he makes his message durable, if only because his act of writing and effacing happens in a book.

Blooms "[b]it of stick" produces something that 'sticks'; and it sticks because the stick is pointed downwards, down to earth. Blooms also knows about the two directions the eyes and an ashplant can be turned to: "Up like a rocket, down like a stick."[27] The rocket may be more impressive, but it's glory is quite transitory: the rocket has to vanish, it leaves no traces, no signs, no scripture. The stick or prick of Bloom's body is so excited by Gertie MacDowell that it goes up like a rocket, but this is not an act of durability, and there's no fatherhood in it.

After finishing his phallic but non-procreative act, Bloom learns about Gertie what he has not realized before: "She's lame! [...] Mr Bloom watched her as she limped away. Poor girl!"[28] The verb "limped" suggests the adjective 'limp', too. As a father Bloom is truly limp – not erect, but "down like a stick," as we can see at the end of the "Lotuseaters" episode: "the dark tangled curls of his bush floating, floating hair of the stream around the limp father of thousands, a languid floating flower."[29] In a way, this "flower" is the "flourishing" ashplant.

Only fatherhood of a limp kind sticks, because this is an immaterial kind of fatherhood. Material traces can be washed away by the tide, by time and its forces of destruction; only immaterial traces and signs can survive and endure and procreate: as language, as text. The act of producing text does not resemble rockets flying high into the sky or weapons erected in order to kill and destroy, it rather resembles the workings of sticks in the sand, of tools in the ground. Hence Seamus Heaney's metaphors for the writing process are: digging, field work, groundwork. This is dirty work. The "tide" which this work is threatened by is connected with Gertie's dreams of tidiness, so to speak. Dublin in places is tidied up today, as if the city planned to run in the Irish "tidy

---

[26]     Ibid., 13.1252-67.
[27]     Ibid., 13.895.
[28]     Ibid., 13.771-2.
[29]     Ibid., 5.570-2.

town" competition, but Joyce's Dublin is always and necessarily "dear dirty Dublin." This is a Dublin which, strictly speaking, has vanished already – it did not endure except in Joyce's book.

This is the point where I have to contradict what I said at the beginning. Materially speaking, Seamus Heaney's Sandymount Strand is <u>not</u> the same anymore that it is in *Ulysses*: since 1904, Sandymount Strand has been built over, and part of the bay has become mainland, so today the beach is somewhere else from where it was in Joyce's time. Materially, Joyce's Sandymount Strand has not survived. If nevertheless the stretch of coastline where Stephen pees and Bloom masturbates are made durable and will exist in eternity, this is an immaterial kind of durability – the durability of text or scripture which can still generate and procreate other texts, which can still transport the reader or memorizer to Joyce's original places. In his poem "Vitruviana," Seamus Heaney indicates this generative potentiality:

> On Sandymount Strand I can connect
> Some bits and pieces. My seaside whirligig.
> The cardinal points. The grey matter of sand
> And sky. And a light that is down to earth
> Beginning to fan out and open up.[30]

In this respect, Heaney's "Strand" is still identical with Joyce's "Sandymount Strand" – as can be other beaches, coastlines, or any place where you read or remember these texts. And moreover, Heaney's "Strand" not only receives something from Joyce's "Sandymount Strand," it is even able to have an effect on Joyce's "Sandymount Strand" and on our readings of its script. Reading Heaney's poems about Sandymount Strand can shed new light on what Stephen and Bloom are doing there, especially on the way Stephen is behaving. His light, quite contrary to what we have read in *A Portrait*, now "is down to earth" indeed. Stephen's approach to reading and writing reality in *Ulysses* is not the same any longer that it was in *A Portrait*, and Stephen himself in *Ulysses* is no longer the Stephen of *A Portrait*. When I pointed this out to Seamus Heaney in order to thank him for the insights gained from reading his poems, Heaney even went so far as to suggest that in *Ulysses*, Stephen becomes Bloom: "The ashplant is Stephen's Bloom-ing rod."[31]

---

30    Seamus Heaney, "Vitruviana," *Electric Light* (New York: Farrar, Straus and Giroux, 1991), p. 64.

31    Seamus Heaney, personal communication to Friedhelm Rathjen, Newman House, Dublin, 16 June 2004.

# Silence, Migration, and Cunning*
## Joyce and Rushdie in Flight

There are several Joycean allusions in Salman Rushdie's *The Satanic Verses*: Finn MacCool and *Finnegans Wake* are named explicitly, once a Martello tower occurs in the text, and a police inspector is called Stephen Kinch. The most vital of these allusions, however, is to be found in the description of the Imam at the beginning of chapter IV:

> Who is he? An exile. Which must not be confused with, allowed to run into, all the other words that people throw around: émigré, expatriate, refugee, immigrant, silence, cunning.[1]

At first glance, Rushdie here seems to link Joyce with the Imam, but if we read on we should see that Joyce and the Imam are rather opposed to each other. The exile, Rushdie tells us, dreams of a glorious return home; his vision is that of a revolution: Elba instead of St Helena. He never stops looking back, hoping for some kind of restoration. The state of exile in the narrower sense of the word is a state that is always involuntary and never accepted; this is not the kind of exile that Joyce did experience. On February 28, 1905, he wrote to his brother Stanislaus: "I have come to accept my present situation as a voluntary exile – is it not so?"[2]

Salman Rushdie, as he sees himself, is not an exile but rather a migrant. Migration means that there is no return: paradise is lost, and this is accepted as a matter of fact, albeit painfully. Migrants are uprooted and injured, but they take this as a starting point for exploring new worlds and for freeing themselves from the bonds of repression and dogmatism. This, of course, is what Stephen Dedalus is talking about when he names "silence, exile, and cunning"[3] as being his only weapons, and if we are to follow Salman Rushdie's distinction between exile and migration, we should rephrase Stephen's words as 'silence, migration, and cunning'.

Salman Rushdie, a migrant from two countries (India and Pakistan), holds that the migrant's major advantage is that he "is obliged to find new ways of describing

---

\*  First published as the article "Silence, Migration, and Cunning: Joyce and Rushdie in Flight," by Friedhelm Rathjen, in *James Joyce Quarterly*, Volume 39, no. 3, Spring 2002, pp. 553-58. Copyright © 2003 by the James Joyce Quarterly, Tulsa, Oklahoma. All rights reserved.

1   Salman Rushdie, *The Satanic Verses* (London: Viking, 1988), p. 205.

2   James Joyce, *Letters of James Joyce*, vol. II, ed. Richard Ellmann (New York: Viking Press, 1966), pp. 83 f.

3   James Joyce, *A Portrait of the Artist as a Young Man*, ed. Chester G. Anderson and Richard Ellmann (New York: Viking Press, 1966), p. 247.

himself, new ways of being human."[4] "Migrants may well become mutants, but it is out of such hybridization that newness can emerge."[5] Newness can emerge, because migrants have left behind not only cities and countries but also the notion that reality and truth are static concepts: "The migrant suspects reality: having experienced several ways of being, he understands their illusory nature. To see things plainly, you have to cross a frontier."[6] In communicating himself, the migrant overcomes "the dread syntax of ethnic purity"[7] and gains a syntax of emancipation and metamorphosis that basically is the syntax of art (as opposed to the syntax of religion and ideology). "Stasis," Rushdie tells us, "the dream of eternity, of a fixed order of human affairs, is the favoured myth of tyrants; metamorphosis, the knowledge that *nothing holds its form*, is the driving force of art."[8]

Salman Rushdie believes that from "the very experience of uprooting, disjuncture and metamorphosis [...] that is the migrant condition [...], can be derived a metaphor for all humanity."[9] In his second novel, *Shame*, Rushdie uses a very Joycean concept to rename this metaphor of migration, a concept that we all know from *A Portrait of the Artist as a Young Man*: the concept of flight. Of himself and his fellow-migrants, Rushdie says:

> We have performed the act of which all men anciently dream, the thing for which they envy the birds; that is to say, we have flown.
>
> I am comparing gravity with belonging. Both phenomena observably exist: my feet stay on the ground, an I have never been angrier than I was on the day my father told me he had sold my childhood home in Bombay. But neither is understood. We know the force of gravity, but not its origins; and to explain why we become attached to our birthplaces we pretend that we are trees and speak of roots. Look under your feet. You will not find gnarled growths sprouting through the soles. Roots, I sometimes think, are a conservative myth, designed to keep us in our places.
>
> The anti-myths of gravity and of belonging bear the same name: flight. [...] To fly and to flee: both are ways of seeking freedom ...[10]

Seeking freedom: this is exactly what Stephen Dedalus is doing throughout *A Portrait*, and throughout *A Portrait* this notion is connected with the motif of birds and of flight, as has been shown by Anthony Burgess in his *Here Comes Everybody*, for example.[11]

---

[4]   Salman Rushdie, "Günter Grass," *Imaginary Homelands: Essays and Criticism 1981-1991* (London: Granta / Penguin 1992), pp. 273-81, p. 278.

[5]   Salman Rushdie, "John Berger," *Imaginary Homelands*, pp. 209-11, p. 210.

[6]   Salman Rushdie, "The Location of *Brazil*," *Imaginary Homelands*, pp. 118-25, p. 125.

[7]   Salman Rushdie, "Siegfried Lenz," *Imaginary Homelands*, pp. 285-87, p. 285.

[8]   Salman Rushdie, "Christoph Ransmayr," *Imaginary Homelands*, pp. 291-93, p. 291.

[9]   Salman Rushdie, "In Good Faith," *Imaginary Homelands*, pp. 393-414, p. 394.

[10]   Salman Rushdie, *Shame* (London: Pan / Picador, 1984), pp. 85 f.

[11]   See Anthony Burgess, *Here Comes Everybody: An introduction to James Joyce for the ordinary reader* (London: Faber, 1969), pp. 50-67.

"When the soul of a man is born in this country," Stephen tells his friend Davin, "there are nets flung at it to hold it back from flight. You talk to me of nationality, language, religion. I shall try to fly by those nets."[12] The flight metaphor, moreover, is included already in Stephen's strange and unfamiliar last name.

Stephen Dedalus, however, is the only one of Joyce's main characters who is not (or not yet) a migrant in the narrower and non-metaphorical sense of the word. H. C. Earwicker has got Scandinavian blood in his veins, Leopold Bloom is of Hungarian Jewish and Molly Bloom of British and Spanish stock, but Stephen Dedalus is Irish through and through. Nevertheless the theme of migration, of the wanderer between worlds, is present in Stephen, too. First of all, he is about to go into exile (or rather migration) at the end of *A Portrait*; and secondly, he is kind of a migrant from one cultural background into another: from Celtic Ireland into Anglo-Ireland. Stephen uses the English language as if it were his own, but he knows that it is not. "My ancestors threw off their language and took another"[13], Stephen tells Davin, but he knows all too well that for him, the English language will always remain an acquired language, as his silent musings about the dean of studies and himself reveal:

> – The language in which we are speaking is his before it is mine. How different are the words *home, Christ, ale, master*, on his lips and on mine! I cannot speak or write these words without unrest of spirit. His language, so familiar and so foreign, will always be for me an acquired speech. I have not made or accepted its words. My voice holds them at bay. My soul frets in the shadow of his language.[14]

Salman Rushdie, too, suffers from this special aspect of homelessness, from having lost one language but not quite gained another one. Rushdie speaks of the English language as being "this peculiar language tainted by wrong concepts and the accumulated detritus of its owners' unrepented past, this Angrezi in which I am forced to write, and so for ever alter what is written ..."[15] Exactly this fact of his being forced to alter language and concepts and reality, however, is the point where the migrant (and especially the migrant as artist) gains something new out of the loss and the pains that he has experienced. The migrant has to translate words and worlds, and he himself is translated from one context into another. "I [...] am a translated man," Salman Rushdie writes in his novel *Shame*. "I have been *borne across*. It is generally believed that something is always lost in translation; I cling to the notion [...] that something can also be gained."[16]

---

[12] Joyce, *A Portrait of the Artist as a Young Man*, 203.
[13] Ibid., 203.
[14] Ibid., 189.
[15] Salman Rushdie, *Shame*, p. 38.
[16] Ibid., p. 29. See also Salman Rushdie, "Imaginary Homelands," *Imaginary Homelands*, p. 17: "The word 'translation' comes, etymologically, from the Latin for 'bearing across'. Having been borne across the world, we are translated men. It is normally supposed that something always gets lost in translation; I cling, obstinately, to the notion that something can also be gained."

This fact that by losing something or leaving behind something something else can be gained in return to a certain degree underlies even the language of *Finnegans Wake*. In the language of the *Wake*, Joyce translates himself out of the boundaries of the English language; he gains freedom by voluntarily losing the familiarity of a mother tongue. As early as 1915, in a conversation with the Austrian writer Stefan Zweig, Joyce remarked: "I'd like a language which is above all languages, a language to which all will do service. I cannot express myself in English without enclosing myself in a tradition."[17] Enclosure means bondage as well as belonging; Joyce had to overcome both in the process of losing home and gaining something new.

This something that is (or can be) gained in translation and migration, however, is not a new home – at least not a new home that can be traced on maps and charts. The artist in exile has lost an isle but not gained another one; the migrant has gained something that lies beyond all isles: what he has gained is nowhere, no place – utopia. Salman Rushdie calls this "imaginary homelands"; and he also calls it fiction: the writer in exile migrates into realms of reality that cannot be defined in positive terms but rather work like an open and unfulfillable gap of experience – a kind of longing that is paired with the knowledge that it can never be stilled.

Joyce, then, as an exiled artist is not an Irish writer but definitely an ex-Irish writer, and the Irish Tourist Board's attempts to repatriate Joyce will always be in vain. Neither is the Dublin of Joyce's novels simply a replica of the historical city of Dublin that Joyce has grown up in. In the process of migration, Joyce takes Dublin along with him, and the city itself migrates into exile. "Exiles, refugees, migrants have carried many cities in their bedrolls in this century of wandering," Salman Rushdie writes in one of his essays, and he names "Kundera's Prague, Joyce's Dublin, Grass's Danzig" as examples.[18] The utopian and imaginary character of these cities lies in the fact that to a certain degree they are restored in the writings of these exiled authors but that at the same time these cities testify the fact that their authors' longings towards things past must necessarily remain unfulfilled forever. Thus real cities and countries are translated into 'imaginary homelands'. In a way, Joyce's Dublin has got more in common with Rushdie's Bombay than it has with non-fictional Dublin.

There is no real restoration in the writings of both Joyce and Rushdie; instead both writers prefer modes of hybridization and bastardization. The following is Salman Rushdie's own characterization of his novel *The Satanic Verses*, but I believe that it is also a fair description of what is going on in *Ulysses* and *Finnegans Wake*:

> Those who oppose the novel most vociferously today are of the opinion that intermingling with a different culture will inevitably weaken and ruin their own. I am of the opposite opinion. *The Satanic Verses* celebrates hybridity, impurity, intermingling, the transformation that comes of new and unexpected

17    Stefan Zweig, *The World of Yesterday* (New York, 1943), p. 275, quoted by Richard Ellmann, *James Joyce*, rev. ed. (New York: Oxford University Press, 1982), p. 397.
18    Salman Rushdie, "Günter Grass," p. 277.

combinations of human beings, cultures, ideas, politics, movies, songs. It rejoices in mongrelization and fears the absolutism of the Pure. *Mélange*, hotchpotch, a bit of this and a bit of that is *how newness enters the world*. It is the great possibility that mass migration gives the world, and I have tried to embrace it. *The Satanic Verses* is for change-by-fusion, change-by-conjoining. It is a love-song to our mongrel selves. [...] *The Satanic Verses* is, I profoundly hope, a work of radical dissent and questioning and re-imagining.[19]

Reimagining of the world and radical dissent from all kinds of absolutism and dogmatism – this is what we find not only in the transformative language of the *Wake* but also in *Ulysses*. *Ulysses* is a bastard that combines topographical realism with archetypal universalism. The Dublin of 1904 migrates into literature, where to a certain degree it can stand for other, 'imaginary homelands', and into this new, fictionalized Dublin still more realms of experience are able to migrate: Odysseus migrates into Joyce's Dublin after having already assumed the bastardized Latin form Ulysses; Daidalos migrates into early 20th century; uncountable details from history, philosophy, literature migrate from given contexts into new ones, sometimes transformed, sometimes translated, sometimes bastardized. Allusions and quotations, especially garbled quotations, are modes of a literature of migration, just like translations are.

The newness that enters the world in *Ulysses* feeds itself on set pieces of old: songs and concepts and images which belong to a world that Joyce was struggling hard to leave behind. Joyce's radical modernism is no weightless modernism; Joyce's flight is charged with the burden of things past, with the handicapping force of gravity that, when finally overcome, sets free conflicting artistic energies of the highest potency. Cunningly, the artist in exile wrests his fuel from his very losses and injuries: migration and silence. The silence, Juan Goytisolo, still another exiled novelist, writes in his memoirs *Forbidden Territory* –

> the silence, alienation, and emptiness that envelop me and several others, far from saddening me, convinces me that the opposition loyalty / rootlessness in relation to language and country of origin is the best indicator of aesthetic and moral value fortunately beyond the reach of the organizers of Homages. Freedom and isolation will be the reward of the creator immersed to his eyebrows in a multiple, frontierless culture, able to migrate as he pleases to the pasture that suits him and without becoming attached to any.[20]

This description of Goytisolo's, however, depicts not the reality of the artist as migrant but rather his utopia. He is not really able to feel at home anywhere "as he pleases," and nowhere in the world he will find any place "that suits him": nowhere but in the "imaginary homelands" that transcend and transform and translate the purity that he has lost forever into the intense creative impurities of art.

---

[19]  Salman Rushdie, "In Good Faith," pp. 394 f.
[20]  Juan Goytisolo, *Forbidden Territory: The Memoirs of Juan Goytisolo 1931-1956*, trans. Peter Bush (San Francisco: North Point Press, 1989), p. 29.

# Joyce in Galsworthy[*]

John Galsworthy is not a name which usually springs to one's mind if thinking about the traces James Joyce left in his fellow writers' works. The standard opinion about Galsworthy and his best-remembered effort, the *Forsyte Saga* trilogy, is something like Charles Osborne's summary in the *Penguin Companion to Literature*: "The cycle is notable more for its painstaking completeness than for any speci.c literary virtues."[1] If high modernist novelists condescend to comment anything on Galsworthy at all, the outcome usually sounds like Arno Schmidt's remarks in his 1951 novella "Brand's Heath": "*Greasylivered Galsworthy!*: [...] I mean, talk about selfmade problems (as if English society itself were one! [...])."[2] In a way, Galsworthy stands for the whole late victorian culture and aesthetics that was thrown overboard by Joyce and other modernist writers and artists.

It should not be forgotten, however, that Galsworthy (1867-1933) and Joyce were contemporaries. It is true that nowhere in Joyce's writings have any traces of Galsworthy's extremely popular works been discovered so far (nor does it seem likely that any will ever be discovered), but Joyce must have been aware of the tremendous commercial success of the *Forsyte Saga*, which was completed by the third part of the trilogy, *To Let*, in 1921, just one year before Joyce published his *Ulysses*.When in 1926 Joyce (assisted by Ludwig Lewisohn and Archibald MacLeish) assembled an international phalanx of 167 writers to sign a public letter of protest against Samuel Roth's piracy of *Ulysses*, Galsworthy was one of the signers (which of course does not necessarily mean that Galsworthy took any interest in the pirated book).[3] A few years later, in December 1931, Joyce in a letter to Harriet Shaw Weaver expressed his suspicion that Galsworthy had his hands in an attempt to prevent Harold Nicholson from lecturing on Joyce on BBC radio[4]. Apart from these two very minute details, not the least cross-connections between Joyce and Galsworthy (who in 1932 was awarded the Nobel Prize) have been discovered by anyone inside or outside the Joyce industry.

All the more interesting it seems that in one of his later novels, Galsworthy alludes to the circumstances of the publication of *Ulysses* in Paris. Chapter XXXI of

---

[*]  First published as the article "Joyce in Galsworthy," by Friedhelm Rathjen, in *Joyce Studies Annual* Volume 2001, pp. 176-78. Copyright © 2001 by the University of Texas Press. All rights reserved.

[1]  CO [Charles Osborne], "John Galsworthy," David Daiches (ed.), *The Penguin Companion to Literature* Vol. I: Britain and the Commonwealth (Harmondsworth: Penguin Books, 1971), 201.

[2]  Arno Schmidt, "Brand's Heath," *Nobodaddy's Children*, trans. John E. Woods (Normal, IL: Dalkey Archive Press, 1995), 147.

[3]  Richard Ellmann, *James Joyce*, rev. ed. (New York: Oxford University Press, 1982), 586.

[4]  James Joyce, *Letters of James Joyce*, Vol. I, ed. Stuart Gilbert, rev. ed. (New York: The Viking Press, 1966), p. 307.

*Maid in Waiting*, a novel set in amid-1920s London and published in 1931, includes the following piece of ladies' conversation, incited by Dinny Conway, the novel's heroine:

> "It would be delicious if you could work up a scandal. [...] Uncle Lawrence would love it."
>
> Lady Mont seemed to go into a sort of coma. . . .
>
> "[...]He's been readin' me Gulliver's Travels, Dinny. The man was coarse, you know."
>
> "Not so coarse as Rabelais, or even as Voltaire."
>
> "Do you read coarse books?"
>
> "Oh! well, those are classics."
>
> "They say there was a book – Achilles, or something; your Uncle bought it in Paris; and they took it away from him at Dover. Have you read that?"
>
> "No," said Dinny.
>
> "I have," said Clare.
>
> "From what your Uncle tells me, you oughtn't to."
>
> "Oh! one reads anything now, Auntie, it never makes any difference."
>
> Lady Mont looked from one niece to the other.
>
> "Well," she said, cryptically, "there's the Bible. [...]"[5]

There can be no doubt that in this scene, the ladies confuse one classic hero with another: instead of Achilles, the reference is meant to be to Ulysses. Joyce's novel, then, is included in the list of "coarse books" – but it seems that in *Maid in Waiting*, *Ulysses* has already begun its conversion from obscene book into classic masterpiece. Finally, John Galsworthy had to admit that the Victorian world of his previous novels was gone for good, and that James Joyce played a major role in the new world that was emerging. So perhaps Joyce may even be one of the reasons why there is quite a bit of "miserable Starkey"[6] in Galsworthy's novel – modest attempts at incorporating bits of cockney, slang expressions and strong language in the soft bottom of the conventional novel. Joyce was acknowledged by Galsworthy as the new voice in literature, and rightly so.

---

[5]  John Galsworthy, *Maid in Waiting* (London: William Heinemann, 1931), 275 f.

[6]  Ibid., p. 16.

# Edward Thomas / James Joyce*
## Inventing a Connection

Perhaps I should first of all invent Edward Thomas for those of you who don't know much about him. He is best known today as a poet – Alistair Stead quite rightly told me that "most of the poetry [...] is pure gold."[1] But Thomas did not begin to write poetry until 2 ½ years before his early death, urged to do so by his friend Robert Frost, and not before he was dead where his poems published under his own name. So, today I'd like to speak not about Edward Thomas the poet but Thomas in three other capacities: Thomas the reviewer; Thomas the hack-writer; and finally Thomas the writer of fiction.

Born in 1878, Edward Thomas was an exact contemporary of James Joyce, if only up to his death in 1917 when he was killed by German troops in France. In a first attempt to establish a connection, I therefore looked out for acquaintances they shared. My first candidate was William Butler Yeats; between 1902 and 1913 Thomas wrote more than a dozen reviews on books by Yeats, but unfortunately he apparently never met him in person or corresponded with him. A second candidate could be Padraic Colum; Thomas corresponded with him in September 1906[2], which, however, was a time when Colum and Joyce apparently had no contact. My third candidate is less apparent but proves more fruitful. One of Thomas's closest literary friends was the critic Edward Garnett, who indeed played a role in Joyce's career when in late 1915 as a reader for Duckworth he rejected *A Portrait of the Artist as a Young Man* on the grounds that the novel had "many 'longueurs'" and needed to be "pulled into shape" and turned into "a more finished piece of work"[3]; Joyce himself, however, had no contact with Garnett. In London, Garnett for long years presided at a weekly meeting of literati which included Edward Thomas, Joseph Conrad and Ford Madox Hueffer, better known today as Ford Madox Ford; so Ford was another one of Thomas's literary acquaintances in London, but up to 1914 Hueffer apparently did not know Joyce or Joyce's work.

It seems like Joyce and Thomas lived in two separate literary worlds. Once, however, these separate worlds intersected; this happened in 1904 when Joyce and Thomas both contributed to the 1905 number of *The Venture: An Annual of Art and Literature*. Joyce on 12 July 1904 was asked to contribute by the editor John Baillie who had heard about him from Arthur Symons. On 23 July Baillie acknowledged receipt of

---

*     Previously unpublished.
[1]     Alistair Stead, email to Friedhelm Rathjen, 22 July 2004.
[2]     See *Letters from Edward Thomas to Gordon Bottomley*, ed. R. George Thomas (London: Oxford University Press, 1968), p 123.
[3]     Richard Ellmann, *James Joyce*, New and Revised Edition (New York: Oxford University Press, 1983), pp. 403 f.

"two notes and the poems" from Joyce; he printed the "Two Songs" which were to become nos. XII and XXVI of *Chamber Music*.[4] Thomas's contribution was the story "The Skeleton," written between March and August 1904 and then submitted to Baillie, perhaps on order.[5] Strangely enough, the name "Holinshed" appears both in the Thomas story and in the second one of the Joyce poems[6], but of course this is purely coincidental, and as far as I know, Joyce did never comment on Thomas's contribution and Thomas not on Joyce's.

The main thing Joyce and Thomas had in common is that they both for long years struggled hard and without much success to make a living for themselves and their young families. One of the many differences is that Thomas did much of his travelling on foot; he walked up to 50 miles a day, a feat we surely wouldn't expect from Joyce. Even more impressive, however, was Thomas's pensum as a book **reviewer**; in 15 years he wrote about 1900 reviews, an average of three per week; sometimes he reviewed up to 13 books a week, mainly poetry, and his production for newspapers sums up to a mass of text thrice as long as *Ulysses*. Among these 1900 reviews there are one and a half dealing with Joyce. On 31 August 1907, *The Daily Chronicle* printed an unsigned review by Thomas which seems to be completely unknown to the Joyce community, so let me quote a few sections. Thomas starts by saying: "In these four books there is the too common contrast between fairly accomplished but rather empty verses and strong feeling expressed with fatal imperfection." Then follow remarks on Francis P.B. Osmaston's *Springfield and Concord*, Oswald Harcourt Davis's *Town Moods*, and Arthur Dillon's *Orpheus*; all three are dismissed rather harshly. The rest of the review reads thus:

> In most of his thirty-six short poems Mr. Joyce, too, has only the negative merits of purity and lucidity, so that it is all the more pleasant to come upon the two or three where the purity and lucidity have something positive to support, as in:
>
> > O sweetheart, hear you
> >     Your lover's tale;
> > A man shall have sorrow
> >     When friends him fail.
> >
> > For he shall know then
> >     Friends be untrue
> > And a little ashes
> >     Their words come to.

---

4  See Robert E. Scholes (Hg.), *The Cornell Joyce Collection: A Catalogue* (Ithaca, NY: Cornell University Press, 1961), p. 70 (letters no. 407-9).

5  See *Letters from Edward Thomas to Gordon Bottomley*, pp. 53-58, 60, 63.

6  See Edward Thomas, "The Skeleton," John Baillie (ed.), *The Venture: An Annual of Art and Literature* (London: John Baillie, 1905), pp. 17-26, p. 18: "I am the fond Holinshed of his story, and cannot translate out of silence"; James Joyce, "Two Songs," ibid., p. 92: "And all for some strange name he read / in Purchas or in Holinshed."

## II.—Some New Singers.

In these four books there is the too common contrast between fairly accomplished but rather empty verses and strong feeling expressed with fatal imperfection. Mr. Osmaston's book, indeed, we only mention because we feel bound to acknowledge the impassioned love of freedom and desire for equality in his "Ode on the Death of President Lincoln," "A Black Man's Appeal," "A Voice from West Africa," "The Burden of the Black Folk," &c., in none of which is it possible to get over the singularly tame or inchoate language. Mr. Davis, a cleverer writer, is hardly more successful, because his power of saying facile, smooth, vaguely beautiful things almost invariably obscures, though it cannot hide, a really deep emotion in the presence of London and its suburbs. Even his style is not impeccable, as may be seen in the fourth line of this, his best passage :

For the God of Earth is a lavish Lord,
An importunate giver of good.
And evil shall perish. Nought shall prevail
Save a life sheer loveliness.

Mr. Dillon we have praised before, for poetry rather remote from any kind of life, but in its own thin altitudes exceptionally good. But a long poem on Orpheus that is merely fluent and well-rhymed and has no originality except in such details as crediting Cerberus with mange, is bound to be tedious. Probably there are not more than fifty men now living who could write as good a poem on the subject, but ten years hence it will appear as dead and conventional as the stiffest of eighteenth-century eclogues. Its best passage is this picture, to which the words do little justice :—

Wine-flown, Silenus who all tipsy went,
In Bacchus' cup the purple clusters crushed.
On Bacchus' breast a panting Mœnad leant
Despoiled of raiment, sumptuous, and flushed,
Who in her right hand held a sickle bent
Like a new moon ; from her red locks unbrushed,
She drew a hair across the edge, and proved
Its cutting. Orpheus gazed, and gazed unmoved.

The new moon has so often been compared with a sickle that it is but a feeble originality to compare a sickle with the new moon.

In most of his thirty-six short poems Mr. Joyce, too, has only the negative merits of purity and lucidity, so that it is all the more pleasant to come upon the two or three where the purity and lucidity have something positive to support, as in :

O sweetheart, hear you
Your lover's tale ;
A man shall have sorrow
When friends him fail.

For he shall know then
Friends be untrue
And a little ashes
Their words come to.

But one unto him
Will softly move
And softly woo him
In ways of love.

His hand is under
Her smooth round breast ;
So he who has sorrow
Shall have rest.

If he can do as well as that in every thirty-six poems the more he writes the better.

But one unto him
    Will softly move
And softly woo him
    In ways of love.

His hand is under
    Her smooth round breast;
So he who has sorrow
    Shall have rest.

If he can do as well as that in every thirty-six poems the more he writes the better.[7]

The best possible comment on this review is what Bill Brockman wrote to me in an email: "I think that Thomas himself does a better job in the areas of 'purity and lucidity' than his subject – but how was he to know in 1907 that JJ would spend a career bemoaning his 'untrue' friends?"[8]

So this was in 1907; seven years later Thomas reviewed the *Des Imagistes* anthology edited by Ezra Pound and including Joyce's poem "I hear an army" from *Chamber Music*. Pound really comes closest to an acquaintance shared by Thomas and Joyce. In Edward Thomas criticism you usually find the assertion that Thomas was one of the first reviewers who realised and acknowledged Pound's talent; if you check these reviews, however, you'll find that Thomas's praise for Pound was never too enthusiastic, and even less so where his remarks on Pound in private. At any rate, Pound apparently never felt encouraged by Thomas and seems to have disliked him in person; R. George Thomas in his introduction to a volume of Thomas letters even states that "Ezra Pound continued a feud against him long after his death."[9] But let's have a look at Thomas's review of the *Imagistes* anthology, printed by *The New Weekly* on 9 May 1914:

There are in this book sixty-three pages, many of them only half-filled; yet it sticks out of the crowd like a tall marble monument. Whether it is real marble is unimportant except to posterity; the point is that it is conspicuous. Only Mr Ford Madox Hueffer, Miss Amy Lowell, and Mr James Joyce contribute pieces resembling ordinary poems. The rest, though divided into lines just like ordinary poems, are for the most part very different.

The rest of the review deals with the poems *not* resembling ordinary poetry, so Joyce is out of the game, and the best thing Thomas allows himself to say about Pound is that "Mr Pound [...] has seldom done better than here under the restraint imposed by

---

7    [Edward Thomas], „Some New Singers," *The Daily Chronicle*, 31 August 1907; used by kind permission of Cardiff University Library (Edward Thomas Archive), where a newspaper cutting dated in Thomas's hand is archived.

8    Bill Brockman, email to Friedhelm Rathjen, 27 February 2006.

9    R. George Thomas, "Introduction," *Letters from Edward Thomas to Gordon Bottomley*, pp. 1-19, p. S. 11

Chinese originals or models."[10] This was Thomas's public opinion on the Imagistes; in one of his letters written a few days later we find the private version: "What imbeciles the Imagistes are."[11]

Here ends the story of Edward Thomas the reviewer, as far as the Joyce connection is concerned; let's move on to **Thomas the hack-writer**. Thomas started his career very early as a writer of nature essays; later on he wrote books on topics like *The Heart of England*, *The South of England* or a cycling trip from London to the Bristol Channel. Usually Thomas began these works with a certain enthusiasm but soon grew weary of the project and managed to finish it off by inserting lengthy quotations or descriptions. From 1909 onwards he also published a number of critical and biographical studies which with few exceptions he also considered hack-writing, one of the most notable exceptions perhaps being the first of these books, *Richard Jefferies: His Life and Work*, a still very readable study of the English nature writer on whose essays Thomas had modelled his own early writings. Now, Jefferies is a writer who did not escape Joyce's attention, as Harald Beck discovered a few years ago and Alistair Stead reported in the *James Joyce Broadsheet*: in the library episode of *Ulysses*, we can find the phrases "In painted chambers loaded with tilebooks" and "mesial groove," which both are quotations from *The Story of My Heart*, the most interesting book by Jefferies.[12] But where did Joyce pick up these quotations? According to the catalogue *James Joyce's Trieste Library*, Joyce owned Thomas's study *Richard Jefferies: His Life and Work* – to be exact, a copy of the second edition printed in 1911.[13] The "mesial groove" quotation can be found in Thomas's book[14]; the "tilebooks" quotation, however, is nowhere in there, so Joyce must have had at least one other, additional source. There are some other details in Thomas's study of Jefferies may have had an influence on the text of *Ulysses*, but for reasons of space limitations I cannot discuss these here in full but only give an abbreviated list:

- A description of Coate reservoir: "It was reputed to have a whirlpool. [...] The south-west side has its now peninsulated island and many willows; then a gulf –

10    Edward Thomas, review of *Des Imagistes: An Anthology*, *The New Weekly*, 9 May 1914, rpt. in *A language not to be betrayed: Selected prose of Edward Thomas*, ed. Edna Longley (New York: Persea Books, 1981), pp. 123-25.

11    *Letters from Edward Thomas to Gordon Bottomley*, p. 233 (Thomas to Bottomley, 22 May 1914).

12    See [Harald Beck] / Alistair Stead, "Of Tilebooks and Mesial Grooves," *James Joyce Broadsheet* 61 (February 2002), p. 3.

13    Michael Patrick Gillespie / Erik Bradford Stocker (eds.), *James Joyce's Trieste Library: A Catalogue of Materials at the Harry Ransom Humanities Research Center / The University of Austin* (Austin: Harry Ransom Humanities Research Center, The University of Texas at Austin, 1986), pp. 237 f. (no. 499).

14    See Edward Thomas, *Richard Jefferies: His Life and Work* (London: Hutchinson, [²1911]), p. 204: "The lips and hair of Cytherea, 'Juno's wide back and mesial groove,' slake the same thirst."

The 'Fir-tree Gulf' of *Bevis* – shadowed by tall willows"[15] – see Joyce's allusion to whirlpool and gulf in the "Scylla and Charybdis" episode.

- A paraphrase of Jefferies's "Meadow Thoughts": "The thought comes to him amid the weariness of printed matter at the British Museum: the pigeons fleeting about the portico lure him again to the something beyond thought"[16]; and a quotation from "Sunlight in a London Square": "I stood under the portico of the National Gallery in the shade, looking southwards [...] I looked for the swifts, but they had gone, earliest of all to leave our sky for distant countries"[17] – see Stephen's augury in *A Portrait of the Artist as a Young Man*, remembered at the end of "Scylla and Charybdis."

- Several hints at Jefferies's fascination with Homer – "The first attraction of books for him was that of the unusual, the adventurous, the antique. 'Ulysses,' he says, 'was ever my pattern and model.'"[18]; "'Everything beautiful is Greek,' he writes; 'the greatest poet was a Greek – Homer. [...]'"[19]; quoting from *Amaryllis at the Fair*: "Homer is thought much of; now, his heroes are always eating. [...] Ulysses eats a good deal in the 'Odyssey'; Jupiter eats. They only did at Coombe Oaks as was done on Olympus"[20]; quoting "Nature in the Louvre" from *Field and Hedgerow*: "But imagination stops our ears against the song of the cold sirens on the rocks, and helps us to go on living as if for ever, to do and to be the greatest and most god-like things, making nothing of time or death. Thus, the contrast is not between imagination and reality, but between imagination and death"[21].

- Another quotation from Jefferies: "Time's the great physician and Nature the best nurse"[22] – see a line in "Hades": "The great physician called him home."[23]

- Biographical information: "He mentions how he used to be afraid of thunder and lightning, but had the cowardice frightened out of him when lightning struck his aunt's house one day while he was there alone"[24] – see Joyce's fear of thunderstorms.

- A quotation from *The Gamekeeper*: "that's the real cause of these here rinderpests"[25] – see the *rinderpest* motif in *Ulysses*.

- Quoting Jefferies's widow: "'Almost his last intelligible words were: Yes, yes; that is so. [...]'"[26] – see the final "Yes" of *Ulysses*.

---

[15]  Thomas, *Richard Jefferies: His Life and Work*, p. 28.

[16]  Ibid., p. 221

[17]  Ibid., pp. 230 f.

[18]  Ibid., p. 54 (the quotation is from Jefferies's *The Amateur Poacher*).

[19]  Ibid., p. 72.

[20]  Ibid., p. 294.

[21]  Ibid., p. 316.

[22]  Ibid., p. 70.

[23]  James Joyce, *Ulysses: The Corrected Text*, ed. Hans Walter Gabler (Harmondsworth: Penguin, 1986 [Student's Edition], 6.942-3.

[24]  Thomas, *Richard Jefferies: His Life and Work*, p. 71.

[25]  Ibid., p. 135.

-   Quoting Walter Besant on Jefferies: "'[...] He was satisfied with the words of the great socialist and anti-sacerdotalist' (*i.e.* Jesus)"[27] – see Molly quoting Bloom: "the first socialist he said He was"[28].

The question whether or not some of these details from Edward Thomas's study of Jefferies may have had an influence on Joyce surely has to remain purely speculative.

So here ends the story of Edward Thomas the hack-writer, as far as the Joyce connection is concerned; let's finally move on to Thomas the **writer of fiction**. We have seen already that Thomas in 1904 wrote a story and contributed it to *The Venture*; fiction writing, however, was always far in the background of Thomas's work, so much so that Thomas uncharacteristically used an exclamation mark when in late October 1912 he wrote to a friend:

> [...] I have started a fiction! It is a loose affair held together if at all by an oldish suburban home, half memory, half fancy, and a Welsh family (mostly memory) inhabiting it & collecting a number of men & boys including some I knew when I was from ten to fifteen. The scheme allows me to use all memories up to the age of 20 & so far I have indulged myself freely. I feel however that it will be better than isolated essays & sketches, each helping the other, & the same characters reappearing; & more honest than the other pseudo-continuous books I have written. I hope it will get finished or drafted before the year is out.[29]

As you may expect from this description, Thomas's novel (which appeared as *The Happy-Go-Lucky Morgans* in 1913) has not much of a continuous plot but simply introduces the inhabitants and visitors of a suburban house by way of a combination of character sketches, stories, and fantasies. The twenty rather heterogeneous chapters include a fairy tale ("Green and Scarlet"), a Celtic legend ("The Wild Swans"), a Norse saga

---

26    Ibid., p. 322 f.
27    Ibid., p. 323.
28    Joyce, *Ulysses*, 18.178.
29    *Letters from Edward Thomas to Gordon Bottomley*, pp. 223 f. (Thomas to Bottomley, 31 October 1912). – The impulse to write this novel apparently was much older. See ibid., p. 93 (Thomas to Bottomley, 15 September 1905): "No other form [than a projected volume entitled *Illusions: Ejaculations in Prose* which never came into existence] ever occurs to me, tho I see that I may come to stories of some kind – not plotty cathartics, but episodes ending suddenly & soon; & that a novel is possible, & fine on account of its difficulties. Once or twice, I have thought of a suburban novel to be called *A Suburban Education* but vaguely, & I don't like great blocks of autobiography. But stories & novels seem far off & what am I to do? I can't force myself as you can. For instance, I can't tell myself to do portraits & I dislike action and psychology." See also ibid., p. 66 (Thomas to Bottomley, 27 March 1907): "Then I do want to arrange my chiefly pathetic memories of the Suburbs – their grave charming old Annes now tumbling down at the feet of the villa-builder – their little bits of waste ground – my own special memories – a little girl, the first whose sex I dimly knew (when I was 7 or 8) – the quite new houses so difficult to like & yet to be liked. But of course not 100 people want such a book."

("Philip and the Outlaws of the Island"), the biographical and critical portrait of a Welsh poet ("Ned of Glamorgan"), a patriotic hymn to England ("Mr Stodham Speaks for England – Fog Supervenes"), a nature diary (interspersed with poetry) in the romantic manner of Jefferies and Thomas's own early writings ("The Poet's Spring at Lydiard Constantine"), the story of a recluse given to ecstatic behaviour ("Morgan"), and other styles and modes of prose. What I find most fascinating in the Thomas-Joyce non-connection is that both writers at more or less the same time started writing a novel marked by considerable stylistic and narrative inconsistencies but turning these incon-sistencies into virtues rather than weaknesses. Of course there's no direct connection, Thomas could not have known about *Ulysses* and I don't think that Joyce ever took notice of *The Happy-Go-Lucky Morgans*, but it could be argued that Thomas (in chapter 7 entitled "Wool-Gathering and Lydiard Constantine") even demonstrated how a stream of consciousness works: the participants of a rambling conversation at a certain point try to analyse the coincidental turns this "wool-gathering" conversation has made and reveal what they have been thinking about all this time, and the narrator adds a list of the "dozen things at once"[30] he has been going through in his mind meanwhile. If there's no direct connection between *Ulysses* and *The Happy-Go-Lucky Morgans*, perhaps we can find an indirect one, either by suspecting that writing novels in an inconsistent, multi-stylistic way may have been in the air at that time (although at least 99 per cent of all authors writing novels in 1913 seem to have breathed quite another air), or by looking for a common precursor. If we have a look at older writers preferred by Edward Thomas on the one hand and Joyce on the other, there seems to be only one who was a major influence on both, namely Laurence Sterne. Perhaps the digressive techniques of Sterne indeed stimulated both Thomas's "wool-gatherings" and Joyce's interior mono-logues. There may, however, have been other (and quite unexpected) stimulators or inspirers as well. In his study of Richard Jefferies, Thomas quotes from Jefferies's early novel *The Scarlet Shawl* a passage foretasting *The Story of my Heart* and adds the following comments:

> The unconscious cerebration which had been going on in his mind [...] forced itself forward, and he grasped at it as the readiest and best means of showing his worth. He could no more have written down that stream of unconscious thought than he could have turned sensation itself into material shape; but he conceived the ideal of doing so....[31]

Unfortunately *The Happy-Go-Lucky Morgans* (which sold even worse than Thomas's other books) remained his one and only novel. His other books of fiction comprise two slight collections of stories and sketches, a children's book with stories based on English proverbs, and two books for use at school containing rewritten versions of *Norse Tales* and *Celtic Stories*. It is hard to find anything in Thomas's *Celtic Stories* which could be fruitfully connected with the Celtic material in *Finnegans Wake*, but

---

30    Edward Thomas, *The Happy-Go-Lucky Morgans* (Woodbridge: Boydell, 1983), p. 49.
31    Thomas, *Richard Jefferies: His Life and Work*, p. 101.

in his short afterword Thomas says: "The date of Finn's death is given in an old Irish book, called *The Annals of the Four Masters*, as A.D. 283."[32] If you're good in algebra, you'll see at once that this number is related to *Finnegans Wake*: 4 times 283 is 1132; 1132 divided into prime numbers is 2 x 2 x 283. If the number 1132 in the *Wake* can be explained by Joyce's plan to cover Irish history from B.C. 566 up to A.D. 566, which makes 1132 years, A.D. 283 would mark the end of the third part of the four-part-cycle spanning the *Wake*'s 1132 years.[33] Of course Thomas was not Joyce's source for all this, but apparently Thomas and Joyce used the same source, most probably Kuno Meyer whose *Selections from Ancient Irish Poetry* were reviewed by Thomas in *The Daily Chronicle* in 1911.[34]

Another source for Thomas mentioned in his afterword were "Professor Rhys' Hibbert Lectures"[35]; it seems that Joyce knew these lectures, too, for on p. 388 of *Finnegans Wake* we can spot "the grandest gloriaspanquost universal howldmouther-hibbert lectures"[36]. Immediately after having mentioned the lectures, Thomas goes on by saying: "So Finn, again, is 'the counterpart of the Welsh god Gwyn, king of the fairies and the dead', and both of them are shown to have learnt wisdom by sucking their thumbs."[37] Well, here we find a proof that the phrase "Finn, again" had been invented by Edward Thomas more than 25 years before Joyce re-invented it on the very last page of *Finnegans Wake* as an apt symbol of the Finn/Finnegan connection.

---

[32]   Edward Thomas, "Note on Sources," *Celtic Stories* (Oxford: Clarendon Press, 1911), p. 127.

[33]   See James MacKillop, *Fionn mac Cumhaill: Celtic Myth in English Literature* (New York: Syracuse University Press, 1986), p. 17. According to MacKillop, Fionn's death in A.D. 283 was recorded in the *Annals of Tigernach* and "inter-leafed" in the *Annals of the Four Masters* in the 17th century; the exact source he gives is *Annals of the Four Masters*, 2nd ed., edited by John O'Donovan, Dublin: Hodges, Smith, and Co., 1856, vol. I, p. 119. According to MacKillop (ibid., p. 30), of the two versions of Fionn's death the one recorded by Tigernach and the Four Masters is the one which is least well-known "in romance"; it can be found as "The Violent Death of Finn" in Standish Hayes O'Grady, *Silva Gadelica: A Collection of Tales in Irish With Extracts Illustrating Persons and Places: Edited from MSS*, London: Williams and Norgate, 1892, vol. II, pp. 96-99, and is discussed by Kuno Meyer, "The Death of Finn MacCumaill," *Zeitschrift für celtische Philologie* 1 (1897), pp. 426-65.

[34]   Review by Edward Thomas, printed in *The Daily Chronicle*, 4 August 1911; see *Letters from Edward Thomas to Gordon Bottomley*, pp. 230 (note 1), 231 (Thomas to Bottomley, 2 August 1913: Thomas sends Bottomley Meyer's book as a gift).

[35]   Thomas, "Note on Sources," p. 128.

[36]   James Joyce, *Finnegans Wake* (London: Faber, 1939), p. 388.

[37]   Thomas, "Note on Sources," p. 128. – The source quoted by Edward Thomas here is John Rhys, *Lectures on the Origin and Growth of Religion as Illustrated by Celtic Heathendom: The Hibbert Lectures, 1886* (London: Williams and Norgate, 1887, ³1898). Rhys argues (and Edward Thomas repeats) that the "Elopement of Gráinne" was originally a solar myth: Gráinne is a goddess of the dawn, Diarmaid is a solar hero, and Fionn is the king of darkness and as such "the counterpart of the Welsh god Gwyn, king of the fairies and the dead" (1898 edition, p. 146; quoted by MacKillop, p. 145, and by Thomas, p. 128). Gwyn is clearly alluded to by Joyce in *Finnegans Wake*, p. 173: "Wynn's Hotel."

And I'm afraid that's all that I could find in my attempt to invent a Joyce / Thomas connection. After all, there is no connection at all. It's nothing. All invention. It's unbelievable. Damn it, I hardly could invent anything, I should never have mentioned it. Extraordinary how philology helps you to know yourself.

# Arnotations*
## Arno Schmidt annotates *Finnegans Wake*

It is quite a trivial fact that annotation depends on *for whom and why* it is done. Equally trivial, but sometimes forgotten is the fact that it also depends on *by whom and why* it is done. In the case of Arno Schmidt's annotations in the margins of his copy of *Finnegans Wake*[1] (and in particular of the *Wake*'s page 308) the authorship of the annotations is made quite clear by the fact that Schmidt signed several of his comments, using his shorthanded abbreviation "Sch." Arno Schmidt when annotating the *Wake* was definitely no scholar – he was a writer himself, which means that he was Joyce's competitor. The basic reason for his annotating Joyce's novel at all, therefore, is that Schmidt felt the need to somehow get to grips with *Finnegans Wake*, somehow to work his way through the whole of the text. Consequently, Schmidt's annotations to a certain extent are simply details of micro-understanding, e.g. the deciphering of "eneugh"[2] as both "anew" and "genug" (enough) or of "youlldied"[3] as "Yul=Tide." Slightly different is the case where Schmidt finds Shakespeare's Prospero in "preprosperousness"[4] or Annie Besant (an English theosophist and birth control activist) in "beyant"[5]. It is obvious here that Schmidt reads (and annotates) the text through a very personal lens: *The Tempest* was one of Schmidt's favourites among Shakespeare's plays, and Annie Besant had been praised by Schmidt in his novella "Dark Mirrors"[6], long before he read Joyce. This all means that Schmidt, while annotating the *Wake*, in a way translates this unknown text back into the world Schmidt already knows.

Not only on a metaphorical level, but also in a literal sense Schmidt was working on a translation of (parts of) the *Wake*. Some of his annotations are preparatory work for this: e.g., "*Pantocracy*"[7] is deciphered as "Hosen=Verrückt" in the margin, and this is

---

[*]    First published as the article "Arnotations: Arno Schmidt Annotates *Finnegans Wake*," by Friedhelm Rathjen, in *An Occasional: Bulletin of the Friends of the Zürich James Joyce Foundation* No 1, January 2002, pp. 13 f.

[1]    Published in full-colour facsimile form as *Arno Schmidts Arbeitsexemplar von Finnegans Wake by James Joyce* (Zurich: Haffmans, 1984); all my quotations are from p. 308 of this edition or from Schmidt's translation of the same page (supplement to the *Arbeitsexemplar*).

[2]    James Joyce, *Finnegans Wake* (London: Faber, 1975), 308.2.

[3]    Ibid., 308.17.

[4]    Ibid., 308.19.

[5]    Ibid., 308.19.

[6]    See Arno Schmidt, "Dark Mirrors," *Nobodaddy's Children*, trans. John E. Woods (Normal, IL: Dalkey Archive Press, 1995), pp. 177-236, p. 208: „if only they had listened to Malthus and Annie Besant; but by 1950 things had gone so far that the earth grew by 100,000 every day: one hundred thousand!!"

[7]    Joyce, *Finnegans Wake*, 308.11.

a first step on the way to Schmidt's final translation "Hosen=Wildheit." Surprisingly enough, Schmidt's translation itself does not suffer from Schmidt's theory that *Finnegans Wake* is all about the war of brothers James and Stannie Joyce over Nora Barnacle – but while reading and annotating the book, Schmidt was of course looking out for details supporting this theory, and some of his findings surface in the 'variants and alternative readings' column that he added to his translation. Where Joyce's text counts from one to ten in garbled Gaelic[8], Schmidt even gives two versions in his translation: an honourable reading and an obscene reading.

Even before Schmidt read the *Wake* for the first time in 1960, he already knew how to understand the text, for Schmidt had found his theory concerning the 'real message' of *Finnegans Wake* while translating Stanislaus Joyce's *My Brother's Keeper* in 1959. Consequently, when reading the *Wake* Schmidt annotated textual details that could be linked to Stannie's books – Joyce's drawing at the bottom of the *Wake*'s page 308, for example, is linked by Schmidt's annotations to page 225 of *Meines Bruders Hüter* (Schmidt's translation) and to page 55 of the *Dublin Diary of Stanislaus Joyce*.

Schmidt, however, did not only annotate links to Stannie's books, he also recorded links to other passages in the *Wake* itself. It seems that Arno Schmidt could never bear the accidentality of textual details – everything had to be ordered and grounded in some kind of deeper reason. Lots of Schmidt's annotations to the *Wake* therefore can be seen as attempts to find the structure(s) hidden under the textual chaos of this book. Schmidt wanted to find the 'real key' to *Finnegans Wake* – for some time, he was planning to write a detailed non-mythological commentary, a 'diabolical key' as opposed to Campbell and Robinson's *Skeleton Key* which for Schmidt suffered from a tendency to find nothing but mystical mists in the *Wake*. The hard facts of a hidden superstructure were what Schmidt was looking for; in particular he noted numerous repetitions and variations in the text. Every hat and every stone in the text was noted by Schmidt and indicated in the margins ("Hut!"; "Stein!"); moreover, he found cross-references in abundance. To give just a few examples: Schmidt annotates "MAWMAW, LUK, YOUR BEEFTAY'S FIZZIN OVER"[9] as being repeated in "His Bouf Toe is Frozen Over"[10], "Boox and Coox"[11] as reappearing twice in the text[12] and "the free of my hand to him"[13] as finding an echo a dozen pages later ("the big bag of my hamd till hem"[14]). It seems that Schmidt had quite a good ear for all this, but obviously the flat pages of a book are not the best possible medium for marking such cross-references. Is not Hypertext the ideal medium for making the network that Schmidt was looking for visible? Where there are clusters of references from one piece of literature to other texts

---

[8]   Ibid., 308.5-14.

[9]   Ibid., 308.r1.

[10]  Ibid., 421.9.

[11]  Ibid., 308.l13.

[12]  See ibid., 409.35, 517.18.

[13]  Ibid., 308.n1.

[14]  Ibid., 320.8.

(say, from certain Schmidt texts to much-quoted *Wake* passages or from *Ulysses* to different versions of the *Odyssey*), Hypermedia editions could even include 'background texts' as a whole and introduce cross-connections that prepare a network for jumping from one textual level to another while at the same time enabling the user to discover something for him- or herself instead of telling him or her everything right away in an annotation – which either tends to narrow the reader's focus by giving just one short quotation or else tends to widen the reader's focus unduly by giving all too general explanations.

Of course every reader (Arno Schmidt is a good example) overstates what he or she discovers him- or herself. Surprisingly enough, Schmidt seems to have noted the questionable nature of many such discoveries, for there are lots of question marks in his handwritten annotations to the *Wake*. (Unfortunately there are no more question marks in Schmidt's translation script – it seems that as soon as annotations become public, all healthy self-doubts are forgotten.) Shouldn't it be vital to the usability of hypermedial annotations in particular that these 'question marks', that the questionable nature of certain suggestions is somehow communicated to the user? Annotations do not always define something once and forever – there is a certain suggestiveness to many annotations, which may even become free associations provoked by the text. It seems extremely important that annotators differentiate between established facts, tentative suggestions and mere possibilities, and maybe it is equally important that a good editorial apparatus should encourage the reader's own associations: after all, every reader deserves a chance to be a bit like Arno Schmidt.

# Arno Schmidt's Utilization of James Joyce[*]
## Some Basic Conditions

When discussing the work of Arno Schmidt in relation to that of James Joyce we tend to use the word 'influence' – and of course Schmidt was influenced by Joyce. Nevertheless influence suggests a conception of the relationship between two creative writers that seems hardly appropriate to describe what happened to Schmidt's work after he read James Joyce. The stimulus-response scheme of the influence process is inadequate in this case – and, indeed, in most (if not all) cases of literary kinship, as Harold Bloom indicated in his studies on the anxiety of influence. It would be rewarding to apply Bloom's theories to our particular problem. He talks about "creative correction"[1] and "poetic misreading"[2] and believes that weak writers produce weak misreadings and strong writers produce strong, creative misunderstandings[3]. Arno Schmidt as a writer was very strong indeed; moreover, he was a very conscious one with his creative consciousness being lopsided in some respects. Schmidt was aware of the natural resources that could be found in other writers, but he was at least equally conscious of the dangers resulting from incautiously harnessing these resources. The more he felt creatively involved with the work of another writer, the greater was his need to create literary devices by which this involvement could be overcome.

To apply this to the Joyce case: Schmidt's rather misleading readings of *Finnegans Wake* may have been half-conscious attempts to widen the distance between Joyce and himself, and he constantly harped on the less amiable and, to Schmidt, less applicable sides of Joyce's work and personality. For instance, in his novel *B/Moondocks* Schmidt allows the narrator Karl Richter to lament Joyce's love for garlic: "how could Joyce be so devoted to *garlick*?! Verily a bloth 'pon his otherwise not xseedingly admirubble character."[4] How, for goodness sake, could a man be followed – be it artistically only – who believed in the curative power of garlic? In this way, Schmidt again and again suggested the threatening power of Joyce's work be enumerating what Schmidt believed to be its author's defects: love for garlic, drunkenness, and deficient personal hygiene.

*Ulysses* and the *Wake* were stimulating for Schmidt, but not in a way that automatically results in an involuntary, uncontrollable response. There is a response, of

[*]  First published as the article "Arno Schmidt's Utilization of James Joyce: Some Basic Conditions," by Friedhelm Rathjen, in *James Joyce Quarterly*, Volume 30, no. 1, Fall 1992, pp. 85-90.

[1]  Harold Bloom, *The Anxiety of Influence: A Theory of Poetry* (New York: Oxford University Press, 1973), p. 30.

[2]  Ibid., p. 14.

[3]  See ibid., p. 5.

[4]  Arno Schmidt, *B/Moondocks, Two Novels*, trans. John E. Woods (Normal, IL: Dalkey Archive Press, 1997), pp. 155-416, p. 349.

course, but it is active, conscious, and emancipated, in one word: creative. Joyce's impact on Schmidt cannot be analyzed in a way similar to the stimulus-response concept connected with terms like "hypodermic needle model"[5] or "bullet theory"[6]. One of the most popular books following this conceptual paradigm is Vance Packard's *The Hidden Persuaders* which, among other things, deals with subthreshold effects in cinema advertising[7]; Packard's ideas were used by Arno Schmidt – slightly modified – in his *Sitara und der Weg dorthin*[8]. In his later works Schmidt liked to identify literary subthreshold effects in reader response to works by Karl May, Adalbert Stifter, and Edgar Allan Poe, and his analysis of all kinds of appeals to the readers' unconscious made Schmidt less likely to fall victim to any subthreshold stimulus himself.

Nevertheless mass media research is able to offer us a concept that may help us to describe some basic conditions of the Joyce / Schmidt relationship. The leading theorists in mass communications have for a long time given up the stimulus-response model. Its successor – and in many respects its opposite – is the so-called 'uses and gratifications approach', and the basic assumptions of this approach – although again lacking validity for all members of the mass media audience – seem appropriate to be applied to Schmidt's reactions to Joyce. According to Elihu Katz, et al., the main theoretical assumptions are the following:

1. The audience is conceived of as active, i.e., an important part of mass media use is assumed to be goal directed [...].
2. In the mass communication process much initiative in linking need gratification and media choice lies with the audience member [...].
3. The media compete with other sources of need satisfaction.[9]

Let us perceive Arno Schmidt as Joyce's audience and Joyce's works as mass media, as *Ulysses* and the *Wake* indeed are. Arno Schmidt, then, is an active respondent to Joyce; he takes the initiative against Joyce, so that in this – and not only this – respect Joyce is treated more as a victim than as a catalyst. Of course, Joyce also has to compete with rival sources that may satisfy Schmidt's need for creative misunderstanding; one of the strongest of these is Sigmund Freud, as I hope to show below.

---

[5]  Charles R. Wright, *Mass Communication* (New York: Random House, 1959), p. 50.
[6]  Wilbur Schramm, "The Nature of Communication between Humans," Wilbur Schramm and Donald F. Roberts (eds.), *The Process and Effects of Mass Communication* (Urbana: University of Illinois Press, 1971), pp. 4-53, p. 8.
[7]  See Vance Packard, *The Hidden Persuaders* (New York: McKay, 1957), pp. 42 f.
[8]  See Arno Schmidt, *Sitara und der Weg dorthin: Eine Studie über Wesen, Werk & Wirkung Karl Mays, Bargfelder Ausgabe*, vol. III/2 (Zurich: Haffmans, 1993), p. 160. For details of Schmidt's use of Packard, see my article "Der unheimliche Verführer: Zwei sorgsam ausgewählte Beispiele für Arno Schmidts polemischen Umgang mit Fakten," *Der Haide-Anzeiger*, 3 (1986), pp. 7-10, p. 7.
[9]  Elihu Katz, Jay G. Blumler, and Michael Gurevitch, "Uses of Mass Communication by the Individual," W. Phillips Davison and Frederick T.C. Yu (eds.), *Mass Communication Research: Major Issues and Future Directions* (New York: Praeger, 1974), pp. 11-35, pp. 15 f.

The important point for us to understand now is that Joyce's work, for Schmidt, shows itself to be of extremely high utility – utility being the cognitive branch of the uses and gratifications dichotomy. Schmidt does not emulate Joyce in the narrow sense of the word; he rather appropriates him, in that he makes use of Joyce in every respect.

Schmidt's story "Kundisches Geschirr" ("Tools by Kunde"), written in May 1962, is a simple example of his use and abuse of *Finnegans Wake*. In the story's second paragraph the narrator describes what he calls "The House and the Distance": a quiet rural scene at four o'clock in the morning. The passage reads:

> Ruhe faltet die Fluren aus: Stillst'n Dank, 1 τ! (Das muß ich übersetzen? ⟨1 τ = ein Tau = a dew = Adieu⟩: Sag' lang, Frau Nacht! Da Lord Sun die Augen öffnet. So viele, uns wunderlich untertane Buchstaben.) Und Weizenkätzchen harren atemlos. Kleinstes plappert. Staare mit Roßtäuscherpfiffen..[10]

In John E. Woods's translation, this passage reads:

> Quiet takes back her folded fields. Tranquille thanks, + U! (I have to translate that? ⟨+ U = add you = a dew = adieu⟩: Say long, Madame Night! As Lord Sun ope's his eyes. So many, marvelously submissive letters of the alphabet.) And wheaten bells bide breathless. Tiny tattling. Starlings whistle like horse traders.[11]

What (even in the English version) sounds like pure Arno Schmidt is, with few exceptions, James Joyce translated by Arno Schmidt. In this short paragraph we can identify half a dozen phrases from page 244 of the *Wake*, translated into German and used in a radio essay that Schmidt wrote in June 1961[12]. I give the original phrases as compared to Schmidt's versions (translation and story) as well as Woods's re-translations:

| | |
|---|---|
| *Wake*: | "Quiet takes back her folded fields. Tranquille thanks. Adew."[13] |
| Trans.: | "Und Ruhe faltet die Fluren aus. Stillst'n Dank. Adieu." |
| Story: | "Ruhe faltet die Fluren aus: Stillst'n Dank, 1 τ!" |
| Woods: | "Quiet takes back her folded fields. Tranquille thanks, + U!" |
| | |
| *Wake*: | "Say long, scielo!"[14] |
| Trans.: | "Sag lang, mein Himmel." |
| Story: | "Sag lang, Frau Nacht!" |
| Woods: | "Say long, Madame Night!" |

---

[10]  Arno Schmidt, "Kundisches Geschirr," *Bargfelder Ausgabe*, vol. I/3 (Zurich: Haffmans, 1987), pp. 369-98, p. 371.

[11]  Arno Schmidt, "Tools by Kunde," *The Collected Stories of Arno Schmidt*, trans. John E. Woods (Normal, IL: Dalkey Archive Press, 1996), pp. 164-88, p. 164.

[12]  See Arno Schmidt, "Der Triton mit dem Sonnenschirm (Überlegungen zu einer Lesbarmachung von FINNEGANS WAKE von James Joyce.)," *Bargfelder Ausgabe*, vol. II/3 (Zurich: Haffmans, 1991), pp. 31-70, p. 64 f. All subsequent quotations from Schmidt's *Wake* translation are from this passage.

[13]  James Joyce, *Finnegans Wake* (London: Faber, 1975), 244.28-9.

[14]  Ibid., 244.25.

| | |
|---|---|
| *Wake*: | "As Lord the Laohun is sheutseuyes."[15] |
| Trans.: | "Da Lord Leu die Augen geschlossen hält." |
| Story: | "Da Lord Sun die Augen öffnet." |
| Woods: | "As Lord Sun ope's his eyes." |
| | |
| *Wake*: | "And wheaten bells bide breathless."[16] |
| Trans.: | "Und Weizenkätzchen harren atemlos." |
| Story: | "Und Weizenkätzchen harren atemlos." |
| Woods: | "And wheaten bells bide breathless" |
| | |
| *Wake*: | "Tiny tattling!"[17] |
| Trans.: | "Kleinstes plappert." |
| Story: | "Kleinstes plappert." |
| Woods: | "Tiny tattling." |

Without going into the semantic and syntactical details, we can realize three important tendencies: 1. The sequence of the phrases in the story does not correspond to their sequence in the *Wake*; 2. The context in the story into which the *Wake* lines fit – and they do fit indeed – has not much in common with the original *Wake* context; 3. The phrases of Joycean origin are by no means marked as such. Therefore, it is only natural that, for example, John E. Woods in the first version of his accurate translation of the Schmidt story "Great Cain" did not identify the *Wake* scraps incorporated there – he turned "Weißer Nebelbogen überspannt. Den Arsch im Bette"[18] into "White arc of fog stretched above. Ass in bed"[19], whereas it should at least allude to Joyce's words "White fogbow spans. The arch embattled"[20]. (After I pointed out all Joycean sources to Woods, he changed this translation into "White fogbow stands. The arse embedded"[21] – the translator's difficulties here lie not so much in translating but rather in spotting the allusion.)

This example may show not only that Schmidt makes free use of Joycean texts in his own writings but also that Schmidt's *Wake* translations, too, are usages of Joyce. Schmidt uses the *Wake* as both framework and pretext to produce a prose piece in German. These translations are the connecting link between the patterns used – *Finnegans Wake* – and Schmidt's own creative texts; with the latter they share some aesthetic qualities – their language is more Schmidtian than Joycean – but the succession of syntactical units submits to Joyce's dictate.

Sometimes Schmidt even comments (albeit indirectly) on the way in which he makes use of Joyce through processes of translation. If we take the paragraph from

---

[15] Ibid., 244.31-2.
[16] Ibid., 244.22.
[17] Ibid., 244.1
[18] Arno Schmidt, "Großer Kain," *Bargfelder Ausgabe*, vol. I/3, pp. 351-67, p. 366.
[19] Arno Schmidt, "Great Cain," trans. John E. Woods, *The Review of Contemporary Fiction*, 8.1 (1988), pp. 38-52, p. 49.
[20] Joyce, *Finnegans Wake*, 403.6.
[21] Arno Schmidt, "Great Cain," *The Collected Stories of Arno Schmidt*, pp. 151-36, p. 163.

"Kundisches Geschirr" quoted above and leave out all phrases that can be traced back to *Finnegans Wake*, what is left is the following: "(I have to translate that? [...] So many, marvelously submissive letters of the alphabet.) [...] Starlings whistle like horse-traders." It becomes clear here that horse-trader Arno Schmidt responds to the marvelously submissive Joycean stimulus in quite an active and creative way.

When Schmidt uses elements of Joycean origin in his own creative texts, this is by no means unusual: it is the way he handles every bit of literature that is at his disposal. Schmidt, as a strong and conscious writer, makes every contribution to world literature his own according to the specific utility it bears for him. Even if he transforms Joycean figural constellations into his own texts – *Ulysses* characters A.E., Buck Mulligan, and John Eglinton, for instance, serve as unobtrusive foils to Ann'Ev', Bastard Marwenne, and Egg in his novel *Evening Edged in Gold*[22] – this is nothing unusual for Schmidt. What really is unusual is the enormous intensity, both in quality and quantity, of Schmidt's commitment to the work of Joyce. Why, then, was Joyce's utility for Arno Schmidt so seminal at a certain point of his artistic development?

Several answers are possible. I prefer and would like to propose one that is closely connected with the logic of this development itself. In 1960, when Arno Schmidt plunged into *Finnegans Wake*, he needed to overcome two separate artistic dilemmas. The way in which he did so was to connect them, one with the other, and such a device was quite in tune with his linkage of Sigmund Freud and James Joyce, as I will demonstrate.

One of Schmidt's foremost artistic aims throughout the 1950s was what he called "to generate in the reader the suggestive *illusion of personal recollection!* "[23] Although the way Schmidt confronts his readers "with the strangest verbal concentrates"[24] is very suggestive indeed, his wish to evoke personal recollections remains necessarily illusory as long as narrator recollections and reader recollections are not identical. What Schmidt needs, therefore, is a guide to a kind of collective memory, individual experience, yet one that is shared, and this is what he finds in Freud.

The second dilemma evolved from Schmidt's characteristic orthographic deformations which continually increased during the fifties. The impulse for these deformations may have been expressionistic experiments of the 1910s, which had strongly impressed Schmidt; nevertheless Schmidt's artistic credo could never accept pure experimentalism or even the handling of language as a plaything. So, when his somewhat playful orthographic deformations reached a point where they could hardly be described as mimetic phonetic spellings any longer, especially in Schmidt's 1960 novel *B/Moondocks*, the author had to look for a new legitimation which, again, he found

---

[22]  See the essay "Scylla & Charybdis in Klappendorf? Um eine Joycesche Figurenkonstellation in *Abend mit Goldrand*" in my book *Dublin → Bargfeld: Von James Joyce zu Arno Schmidt* (Frankfurt am Main: Bangert & Metzler, 1987), pp. 56-93, esp. pp. 68-71.

[23]  Arno Schmidt, "Calculations (I-III)," trans. F. Peter Ott, *The Review of Contemporary Fiction*, 8.1 (1988), pp. 53-75, p. 55.

[24]  Ibid.

in Freud. From this point on, every misspelling for Schmidt is mimetically legitimated by the hidden reality of the individual's unconscious and its struggle towards the surface.

This use of Freud solved both of Schmidt's major artistic dilemmas, and the process was accompanied and supported by his studying the *Wake* in details just after *B/Moondocks* was completed.[25] He used Freud's theories to outline a concept for the creative use of the individual's secret recollections by way of language deformation, and the word formation techniques of *Finnegans Wake* were adapted as models for the rich possibilities of pun and word games that Schmidt explored in his later prose. With the assistance of both Freud and Joyce, Schmidt was able to invoke stimulus-response processes of the unconscious in writing creatively, but at the same time he was consciously trying not to be a passive victim of the influence of James Joyce.

From the very beginning of his acquaintance with Joyce, Schmidt realized that Joyce was a very strong writer – the greatest of the century so far, and perhaps even greater and stronger than Schmidt himself. Therefore Schmidt had somehow to come to terms with him, and, in the final analysis, he did.

---

[25]   For chronological matters of Schmidt's Joyce reception, see my book „... *schlechte Augen"*: *James Joyce bei Arno Schmidt vor „Zettels Traum"*: *Ein annotierender Kommentar* (Munich: edition text + kritik, 1988), pp. 183-98; on *Finnegans Wake*, esp. pp. 188-90.

# 69 Ways To Play Sam Again*
## Beckettiana in Jürg Laederach's Works and Letters

In the 1980s and early 1990s, the Swiss writer Jürg Laederach (b. 1945) was generally regarded as one of the most interesting and important postmodern avant-garde writers in the German language, although conflicts with his former publisher and a general change in readers' attention means he has somewhat fallen victim to public neglect since. In his 1986-87 lectures on literature (published as *Der zweite Sinn oder Unsentimentale Reise durch ein Feld Literatur*), Laederach names James Joyce, Marcel Proust and Robert Musil as the "großen Drei [big three)"[1], calling Proust "der neben Musil größte Virtuose des diskursiven Stils [the greatest virtuoso of the discursive style besides Musil]"[2] and Joyce his own "Vater und Paternoster [father and paternoster]"[3]. Laederach's own work is dominated by bulky novels and large-scale maximalist texts, so the reliance on the three writers mentioned above is quite obvious. It is thus all the more exceptional that another writer mentioned and alluded to frequently, not only in Laederach's lectures but also in his fiction, is Samuel Beckett, the champion of literary minimalism. Beckett's important influence on Laederach can be detected not only in Laederach's own minimalist (yet rather talkative) pieces for theatre but also in his essays, stories and novels, where Beckett's works (especially *Waiting for Godot* and *Murphy*, but also lesser known texts) are steadily quoted and alluded to; in many ways, Beckett is identified as an important part of the general cultural horizon Laederach's works are set against.

Unfortunately, it is quite difficult to establish exactly when Beckettian influences first enter Laederach's works. As a writer, Laederach is always prepared to drop a bulk of literary names into his texts; in his first book, a collection of stories entitled *Einfall der Dämmerung*, there are references to Faulkner, Dante and Robert Walser[4], and one of the stories even includes a character named "Von Göthe"[5]. In his second book, the novel

---

[*] First published as the article "69 Ways To Play Sam Again: Beckettiana in Jürg Laederach's Works and Letters," by Friedhelm Rathjen, in *Beckett's Literary Legacies*, edited by Matthew Feldman and Mark Nixon (Newcastle: Cambridge Scholars Publishing, 2007), pp. 129-151.

[1] Jürg Laederach, *Der zweite Sinn oder Unsentimentale Reise durch ein Feld Literatur* (Frankfurt am Main: Suhrkamp, 1988), p. 161.

[2] Ibid., p. 180.

[3] Ibid., p. 255. – These and all subsequent translations from Laederach's works (with the exception of *69 Ways to Play the Blues*) are mine. I would like to thank Mark Nixon for checking and improving a few of my English translations.

[4] Jürg Laederach, *Einfall der Dämmerung: Erzählungen* (Frankfurt am Main: Suhrkamp, 1974), pp. 10, 152, 159.

[5] Ibid., pp. 62 f.

*Im Verlauf einer langen Erinnerung*, Laederach refers to "Moby Dick"[6] and the Austrian town Mürzzuschlag[7] which, during the First World War, played a role in the life of Joyce. In his next novel, *Das ganze Leben*, we spot Karl May, Arno Schmidt, Stanislaus Joyce and Joyce himself[8] – Beckett, however, is never alluded to in any discernible way in these three books. This does not necessarily mean, of course, that Beckett may not yet have been an important author for Laederach during the 1970s. Yet his first explicit appearance comes in Laederach's fourth book, a collection of six longer stories entitled *Das Buch der Klagen*, which includes not only a phalanx of characters' names from Joyce's *Ulysses*[9] but also a "Beckettbanane [beckettbanana]"[10] mentioned completely out of context. The reference is clearly to Beckett's one-act play *Krapp's Last Tape*, in which the title character devours bananas.

In all four books mentioned so far, Laederach explores a diversity of literary forms and writing modes which, in different ways, allow him to address questions of identity and non-identity, of reality and fictionality, of fictional probability (which Laederach usually mocks and refutes) and developmental incongruity (which Laederach stresses and willingly precipitates). The rules are already made clear in *Einfall der Dämmerung*: "Nie Logik. Nie Erkenntnisse. Nie Wahrnehmungen [Never logic. Never knowledge. Never perception]"[11]. Laederach's plots lead nowhere, they erode or decompose, and his characters more often than not suffer from all kinds of ailments, injuries and molestations which, to a certain degree, makes these texts vaguely comparable with Beckett's, the main difference being that the instability of plot and character usually leads to reduced languages, stillness and silence in Beckett's texts, whereas Laederach quite verbosely (and sometimes even garrulously) generates realms of hastiness, disquietude and extreme restlessness. In *Das ganze Leben*, for example, after having read more than 200 pages of restless prose, we are told: "Bis hierher alles erlogen; von hier aus alles wahr [Up to here all a lie; from here on everything true]"[12], a phrase frequently varied on subsequent pages[13], until we finally learn: "Bis hierher alles wahr; von hier an Versuch einer letzten Lüge [Up to here everything true; from here on attempt at a last lie]"[14].

Such reversals of credibility are reminiscent of certain features in Beckett's prose, especially the novels and stories written in the immediate postwar years: the narrator of

---

6    Jürg Laederach, *Im Verlauf einer langen Erinnerung: Roman* (Frankfurt am Main: Verlag, 1977), p. 194.
7    See ibid., pp. 49 f.
8    Jürg Laederach, *Das ganze Leben: Roman* (Frankfurt am Main: Suhrkamp, 1978), pp. 58, 59, 92.
9    Jürg Laederach, *Das Buch der Klagen: Sechs Erzählungen aus dem Technischen Zeitalter* (Frankfurt am Main: Suhrkamp, 1980), p. 230.
10   Ibid., p. 41.
11   Laederach, *Einfall der* Dämmerung, p. 10.
12   Laederach, *Das ganze Leben*, p. 216.
13   See ibid., pp. 224, 225, 262.
14   Ibid., p. 285.

'The End', for example, at a certain point of his story interjects: "That's all a pack of lies I feel"[15]; in a similar vein his predecessor in "First Love," after telling half of his story, sums up: "But I have always spoken, no doubt always shall, of things that never existed, or that existed if you insist, no doubt always will, but not with the existence I ascribe to them"[16]. Just before doing so, this Beckett narrator changes the name he uses for the woman with whom he lives, a prostitute he finally (quite unwittingly) makes pregnant: "Anyhow I'm sick and tired of this name Lulu, I'll give her another, more like her, Anna for example, it's not more like her but no matter"[17].

Interestingly enough, the narrator of Laederach's *Im Verlauf einer langen Erinnerung* calls his whore-like female companion Lulu and, at one point of the non-story, has to endure her disclosure: "Ich bin schwanger [I am pregnant]"[18]. It should be noted, however, that this is no positive proof of Beckett's influence on Laederach at this stage of his career; after all, the name Lulu for a prostitute is rather widespread. Consequently, the first Laederach book with a really verifiable Beckett connection is *Fahles Ende kleiner Begierden*, a collection of "four minimal plays" published in 1981. On the preliminary pages of this book, Laederach's own comments on the four plays are quoted:

> Ich versuche eine szenische Anwendung der Prinzipien zu finden, nach welchen minimale Komponisten wie Steve Reich, Phil Glass [...] verfahren. Die Ergebnisse dieser Sprachverknappung und des (im Großen) Statik wie (im Kleinen) Unruhe produzierenden Repetitionsprinzips lauten: Witz und Verzweiflung. Ich habe jedes Stück in eine Klassikertradition eingeschrieben. 'Japanische Spiele' ist ein unziemliches Nô-Spiel, 'Rost...' ist für zwei Karl Valentins, 'Nacht denken' denkt über Beckett nach, 'Han und Amin' ist eine Erinnerung an einen Abend bei Peter Handke.[19]

> [I try to find a scenic application for the principles with which minimal composers like Steve Reich, Phil Glass [...] work. The results of this scarcening of language and of the repetitive principle producing (on the macro-level) stasis and (on the micro-level) restlessness are: joke and despair. I have written each play into a classic's tradition. *Japanische Spiele* is an unseemly nô game, *Rost...* is for two Karl Valentins, *Nacht denken* thinks about Beckett, *Han und Amin* is the memory of an evening with Peter Handke.]

It seems that, in order to counter his typically rampant approach to writing, in the plays collected here (and in some of his later plays, too), Laederach tries to restrict himself by looking for orientation and examples in the working practice of other writers, among

15    Samuel Beckett, "The End," *The Complete Short Prose, 1929-1989*, ed. S. E. Gontarski (New York: Grove Press, 1995), p. 82.

16    Samuel Beckett, "First Love," ibid., p. 35.

17    Ibid., p. 34.

18    Laederach, *Im Verlauf einer langen Erinnerung*, p. 53.

19    Jürg Laederach, *Fahles Ende kleiner Begierden: Vier minimale Stücke* (Frankfurt am Main: Suhrkamp, 1981), p. 2.

whom Beckett figures prominently. *Nacht denken*, the play Laederach explicitly links to Beckett, begins with a preamble in the form of "45 theses" stating basic assumptions like: "Er existiert. / Sie weiß, was er weiß, aber keiner weiß das, also weiß es keiner von beiden [He exists. / She knows what he knows, but nobody knows this, so none of the two knows it]"[20]; "Er weiß, daß er nie in der Stadt ankommen wird [He knows that he will never arrive in the city]"[21]. The Beckettian quality which is traceable, at least in some of these statements, is born out by the rest of the play. Through fragmented speech, a smashed storyline is presented about someone on the way to a city who speaks of talking about "wanderlust"[22], a "Krückenlied [crutch's song]" and "Endmusik [end music]"[23], while suffering a "Stillstand hinter seiner Lenkstange [standstill behind his handlebar]"[24], all of which are reminiscent of *Molloy* and Beckett's postwar texts generally; other relics from the world of Beckett's fiction and plays include the idea of making love over the pit, waiting for the lovers' corpses.

If Laederach's utilisation of Beckettian props in *Nacht denken* sometimes achieves a quasi-parodistic quality, the same can be said of another play of the collection, *Han und Amin*, which includes numerous empty phrases in fast succession like these: "Schwinden wir nicht? / Das ist unsere Stunde. / Nahe dem Ende. / Wir sind am Aufhören / So schnell [Do we not dwindle? / This is our hour. / Near the end. / We are in the process of ending. / So fast]"[25]. This minimalist (and often redundant) talk about ending – perhaps echoing Beckett's *Endgame* or, more generally, Beckett's preoccupation with finality and non-finality – eventually leads to the statement "Aber er ist gekommen [But he has come]"[26], which sounds a bit like (but is not necessarily) an ironic comment on *Waiting for Godot*.

The next book Laederach published following *Fahles Ende kleiner Begierden*, another collection of stories entitled *Nach Einfall der Dämmerung* (combining a selection from the firstling *Einfall der Dämmerung* with numerous additional texts), again shows no discernable traces of a demonstrable Beckettian influence. Yet with *69 Arten den Blues zu spielen* (*69 Ways to Play the Blues*, published in 1984), Laederach's most successful book (and the only one to have had selections translated into English), the picture becomes much more animated. *69 Ways to Play the Blues* is a collection of (not 69, but 74) extremely short stories, several of which show evidence of Laederach's utilisation of Beckett. These stories deal with the tricky problems of proving a character's existence or non-existence[27], with a "Programm zur Ichverkleinerung [programme of self-reduction]"[28].

---

[20]   Ibid., p. 101.
[21]   Ibid., p. 102.
[22]   Ibid., p. 105.
[23]   Ibid., p. 112.
[24]   Ibid., p. 126.
[25]   Ibid., p. 166.
[26]   Ibid., p. 201.
[27]   See Jürg Laederach, *69 Arten den Blues zu spielen* (Frankfurt am Main: Suhrkamp, 1984), p. 63.
[28]   Ibid., p. 333.

The degree to which Laederach twists all acknowledged categories of life and ist representation by fiction may be demonstrated by a sentence found in the short text 'Vanitas': "Das Ende ist ein Zeugungsakt, aber er entzeugt [The end is a procreative act, but it de-procreates]"[29]. Even if the similarity of the underlying concept may well be purely coincidental, it seems worth pointing out that Beckett's early essay "Dante ... Bruno . Vico .. Joyce" illustrates Giordano Bruno's *coincidentia oppositorum*, declaring: "The maximum of corruption and the minimum of generation are identical: in principle, corruption is generation"[30].

If we cannot prove whether or not Laederach knew the above quotation when he wrote *69 Ways to Play the Blues*, we can at least demonstrate beyond doubt that he knew Beckett's *Murphy*. Towards the end of another piece in the book, 'Justus Liebig', Laederach alludes to the eponymous character and his rocking chair in the opening chapter of Beckett's novel:

> Alles, aber auch alles liegt jenseits unserer Fähigkeiten; Murphys Gesetz schaukelt gedörrt im Stuhl [...]. Wir können einfach nicht, es ist uns alles zuviel geworden, im Maß unserer Schrumpfung wächst es gen Himmel; und am meisten über-anstrengt uns das Sprechen darüber, das Springen und Tauchen in es hinein und, uff, püh, das quarkige Schreiben im einstimmigen Fröschechor aller.[31]

> [Everything, literally everything is beyond our capacities; Murphy's law is rocking dehydrated in the chair [...]. We really are incapable, it all became too much for us, in proportion to our shrinking it grows into the sky; and what over-exerts us the most is talking about it, plunging and diving into it and, ugh, pooh, writing croakily as a part of the unison frog's choir of all of us.]

If we take this passage as a first proof of Laederach's interest in Murphy and his rocking chair (and more evidence will follow), it becomes obvious that in a later piece of the same book, entitled 'Conversation', Laederach 'translates' that motif into his own new version – that text's narrator, before placing himself 'naked' in the bathtub ('naked' here meaning 'not undressed', since where everything is naked, the concept of 'nakedness' can only be enacted by dressing up), intentionally puts his telephone beyond reach (which Beckett's Murphy also did, but quite unintentionally). However, this is not enough to resist all temptation: "Ich muß mich in der Wanne anbinden, Lederschlaufen liegen unter Wasser bereit, der letzte Dorn kann mit den Zähnen durch die Fesselgurte getrieben werden. [I must bind myself to the tub, for which purpose, underwater straps lie ready; the tongue of the belt can now be drawn through the shackle with my

---

29  Ibid., p. 347.
30  Samuel Beckett, "Dante ... Bruno . Vico .. Joyce," *Disjecta: Miscellaneous Writings and a Dramatic Fragment*, ed. Ruby Cohn (London: John Calder, 1983), p. 21.
31  Laederach, *69 Arten den Blues zu spielen*, p. 86.

teeth]."[32] The leather straps used by Laederach's narrator in his bath, of course, take over the function of the "[s]even scarves" which Murphy uses to bind himself to the rocking chair[33]. It is quite instructive to see that what appears to interest Laederach most in Beckett's formally and stylistically least restrained novel is exactly this: a character restraining himself by putting himself into manacles.

At one point in his next novel, *Flugelmeyers Wahn*, Laederach literally makes use of one of Beckett's lesser-known titles. This novel, for the most part, consists of an interview with a writer called Georg Flugelmeyer, conducted by the journalist Ernst Jawosch. When Jawosch asks Flugelmeyer to help him end, Flugelmeyer replies by quoting the title of one of Beckett's shorter prose works: "Um abermals zu enden, ach [For to end yet again, alas]"[34]. Yet the Beckettian subtext developed thereafter is based not on Beckett's prose but on his best-known play, *Waiting for Godot*, perhaps owing to the fact that the interview structure provides Laederach's novel with a dialogue-oriented quality. A few pages after "For to end yet again" has been quoted, Flugelmeyer addresses the subject of silence: "Wer schweigt, hat nicht etwa keine Wörter mehr, sondern die Häufigkeit seiner Wortzwischenräume ist bedenklich gewachsen. [If someone is silent it's that he has got no words any more, but the frequency of his word-interstices has increased dramatically]"[35]. Twenty pages later, the Beckettian subtext resurfaces when Flugelmeyer says: "Oh Beckett: Du haben Kargheit des Vokabulars in Kargheit der Syntax übertragen. [Oh Beckett: you have transfered sparseness of vocabulary into sparseness of syntax]"[36]. Here, the context is a conversation on shoes and on waiting, thus clearly alluding to *Waiting for Godot*; the subject is concluded, for the moment at least, by Flugelmeyer, who remarks: "Kein Ende. Eine Flugelmeier-Einheit hat kein Ende. [No end. A Flugelmeyer unit has no end]"[37].

Much later in the novel, after various topics – including waiting: "Warten und dann sterben. Zwei existentielle Erlebnisse, so hab ich gelernt [To wait and then to die. Two existential experiences, so I have learnt]"[38] – have been discussed, Beckett is alluded to again through the relation of an anecdote about someone called Lucky, castigated by a certain Pozzo whom he tries to amuse; Pozzo wants (and indeed manages) to remain anonymous in his "Pozzowelt [pozzoworld]"[39], although he is clearly identified as being "ein holländischer Großgrund-Pozzo in Zandvoort [a Dutch

---

[32] Laederach, *69 Arten den Blues zu spielen*, p. 259; English version: Jürg Laederach, *69 Ways to Play the Blues*, pref. Walter Abish, trans. Peter Wortsman (New York: Semiotext(e), 1990), p. 28. (*69 Ways to Play the Blues* is a selection of 17 Stories from *69 Arten den Blues zu spielen*.)

[33] Samuel Beckett, *Murphy* (London: Calder & Boyars, 1977), p. 5.

[34] Jürg Laederach, *Flugelmeyers Wahn: Die letzten sieben Tage* (Frankfurt am Main: Suhrkamp, 1986), p. 74.

[35] Ibid., p. 78.

[36] Ibid., p. 97.

[37] Ibid., p. 100.

[38] Ibid., p. 148.

[39] Ibid., p. 195.

aristocratic Pozzo in Zandvoort]"[40]. The series of allusions to characters from *Waiting for Godot* in what gradually turns into a dialogue about jokes is expanded on the next page: "Witze kann man ewig quasseln, für Freud werden sie erst durchs Zuhören eines Dritten erwähnenswert. Darum hört Wladimir alles mit [Jokes can be yapped eternally, for Freud they only become worth mentioning when heard by a third person. Hence Vladimir overhears everything]"[41]. The one character from *Waiting for Godot* still missing from this discussion appears much later, when, in a completely different context, a manservant serves "Filet à la Estragon"[42]. All these fairly undisguised allusions to Beckett in general and *Waiting for Godot* in particular surely do not function as symptoms of a Beckettian influence on Laederach in any specifiable sense. Instead, they invoke a general cultural background shared by Laederach and his readers: by the 1980s (at least), Beckett's characters were sufficiently well-known to a culture-conscious audience to enable Laederach to use them as stock characters, to be introduced and remodelled into his fiction at will.

Unfortunately, the existence of such a cultural foil sometimes has its disadvantages, too: people tend to make connections all too willingly where they do not necessarily exist. When, in Autumn 1986, the play *Körper brennen*, which Laederach had written with Andres Müry, premiered during the "steirischer herbst" festival in Graz, Austria, at least one critic felt reminded of *Waiting for Godot*, describing the play in his festival report by constantly comparing it with Beckett's classic[43]. This putative connection is hardly justified by the text itself – if, in some parts of the play, two characters simply share a more or less barren stage, this is far from being a demonstrable 'legacy'. One could add that one of the characters, a professional soldier called "Sam Singer"[44], is constantly addressed only by his first name, yet although "Sam" is a widely known abbreviation for Beckett, any speculation about an intended link here must surely remain extremely tentative.

In the winter 1986/87, shortly after the publication of both *Flügelmeyers Wahn* and *Körper brennen*, Laederach held a series of lectures at Graz University in which he comprehensively explained his views on literature; these lectures where published afterwards as *Der zweite Sinn oder Unsentimentale Reise durch ein Feld Literatur*. Laederach's main concern here seems to be the strict avoidance of any fixed and determined concept: "Ich habe keinen festgefügten Ansatz, kein Prinzip, keine Kriterien [I have no fixed approach, no principle, no criteria]"[45], he declared right at the beginning, and then adds: "für mich ist Literatur nur erträglich, wenn ich alle Jahre wieder, oder spätestens alle zwei Jahre, das Gefühl haben darf, ich sei wieder an dem Punkt angelangt, wo ich nichts

---

[40]  Ibid., p. 196.
[41]  Ibid., pp. 196 f.
[42]  Ibid., p. 305.
[43]  See Peter von Becker, "Von Kathy Acker bis Kurt Waldheim: Graz verkehrt: Krieg und Lieben," *Theater heute* 11 (November 1986), pp. 6 f.
[44]  Jürg Laederach / Andres Müry, *Körper brennen*, *Theater heute* 11 (November 1986), p. 10.
[45]  Laederach, *Der zweite Sinn oder Unsentimentale Reise durch ein Feld Literatur*, p. 14.

mehr davon verstehe [for me, literature is only bearable if every new year, or at least every second year, I'm allowed to feel that I have returned to a point where I don't understand a bit of it]"[46]. On the other hand, the author assures us "daß ich immer alles mit allem zu vereinbaren trachte [that I always strive to unite everything with anything]"[47]. Laederach calls himself "ein zuvorkommender Chaos-Forscher [an obliging chaos-researcher]"[48] who "Chaos herstellen [will], selbst wenn ich dazu Ordnung schaffen muß [wants to create chaos, even if for this end I'll have to maintain order]"[49]; for him modernism is "der Idealzustand [the ideal state]"[50], which explains why he constantly refers to writers like Flaubert, Joyce, Musil, Proust, Nabokov, Pynchon – and, of course, Beckett.

At one point 'Bing [Ping]', one of Beckett's lesser-known prose pieces, is mentioned in Laederach's lectures[51], if only as part of a pun on onomatopoetic names; elsewhere *Mercier and Camier* is referred to in passing[52]; at another point Laederach asks himself (without giving an explicit answer): "War Becketts Inszenierung von »Warten auf Godot« die definitive? Sicher bietet die Tatsache, daß ein Text, einmal vollendet, nur von dem spricht, wovon er spricht, dem Autor die Möglichkeit, sich zu verbergen, so gut es geht [Was Beckett's production of *Waiting for Godot* the definitive one? Surely the fact that a text, as soon as it is finished, only speaks of that of which it speaks offers the author an opportunity to hide himself as far as possible]"[53]. Beckett's theatre work is also indirectly praised by juxtaposing it with Ionesco's:

> Daß Ionescos Stücke altern, ist ein Glücksfall für das Stadttheater. Es darf sodann sagen, die Stücke seien veraltet – und braucht sich nicht mehr mit ihnen zu beschäftigen. Was macht, inmitten dieser surrealistischen Tragödien, den Beckettschen Krapp, die Winnie, den Estragon, aber auch die beiden Stimmen vor dem Bewußtseins-Stau-Schieber in »Cascando« so unwiderstehlich?
> Ganz einfach: Chekhov was here. Beckett hat der Partei der Surrealisten, Absurden usw. nie sehr angehört. Ich darf, abschweifenderweise, auf das von ihm gehandhabte Freudsche Paarstimmenmodell in »Cascando« hinweisen. [...] Die Figuren haben Sprache, und unvermutet hat die Sprache die Figuren. Ein Innenwelt-Modell von höchstem Realitätsgehalt. Was andrerseits, gemäß meinen rezeptionsästhetischen Beobachtungen, mit sich bringt, daß kein Mensch sich darin erkennt oder erkennen will. Becketts Innenwelten, auch jene chronologisch auf verschiedenen Arbeitsschichten abgelagerte des Krapp, haben nichts Angenehmes an sich, kriegen also die gottverdammte Ähnlichkeit mit dem

---

[46]   Ibid., pp. 47 f.
[47]   Ibid., p. 92.
[48]   Ibid., p. 11.
[49]   Ibid., pp. 216 f.
[50]   Ibid., p. 176.
[51]   Ibid., p. 255.
[52]   Ibid., p. 97.
[53]   Ibid., p. 73.

gottverdammten Bewußtsein, dessen Darstellung man nicht ausgerechnet noch in der Literatur finden möchte. [...] Die Interna, sagen wir mal, vom »Letzten Band«, wären bei einem weniger virtuos geschriebenen Stück stets Anlaß zu Massenflucht. Beckett dämpft den vorhersehbaren Sturz unseres Affektbarometers tschechowsch milde ab. Wir kriegen nur eine leichte Depression. Die Innenwelt ging bei ihrer Darstellung unter – das Schicksal aller Innenwelten – aber sie tat es sanft. Der Tod kann nicht das Essen einer Banane sein, ihre fallende Schale nicht der fallende Stamm des Kirschgartens: Beckett, in seiner gnadenlosen Gnade, erlaubt unserem einfachen Gemüt das Gelächter. Wer Banane letal findet, hat es sich selbst zuzuschreiben.[54]

[The aging of Ionesco's plays is a stroke of luck for the municipal theatre. Now they can say the plays have aged – and don't have to deal with them any more. What, in the middle of these surrealist tragedies, makes Beckett's Krapp, Winnie, Estragon, but also the two voices in front of the consciousness-congestion-bolt in *Cascando* so irresistible? Simply this: Chekhov was here. Beckett never belonged to the party of the surrealists, absurds etc. May I, digressing, point out the Freudian model of pair voices used by him in *Cascando*. [...] The characters have language, and suddenly the language has the characters. An interior-worldmodel of the highest reality. Which, on the other hand, according to my observations on the aesthetics of effects, consequently leads to the fact that no human being recognizes him- or herself therein or wants to recognize him- or herself therein. Beckett's interior worlds, including Krapp's which is deposited chronologically on different working layers, don't have any pleasant qualities, therefore acquire a goddamn likeness to the goddamn consciousness, which under all circumstances you don't want to find depicted in literature. [...] The interna of, say, *Krapp's Last Tape*, would in a play written with less virtuosity cause a mass exodus. Beckett weakens the predictable crash of our emotional barometer with Chekhovian mildness. We only get a light depression. The interior world perished in the course of its depiction – the fate of all interior worlds – but it did so gently. Death cannot be the devouring of a banana, its falling peel not the orchard's cherry trunk toppling over: Beckett in his merciless mercy permits our simple mind to laugh. Whoever finds bananas lethal is to blame himself.]

What interests Laederach most, however, is not Beckett's drama but rather his prose fiction. He draws two separate lines from Chekhov to Proust, from Flaubert to Joyce, and then draws conclusions which end with Beckett:

Roman als Form nach hinten offen zum Tod, ein Enden ist grundsätzlich unmöglich, bis Arbiter Beckett in gewohnter Kühnheit die Prämisse umdreht: von nun an wird *nur noch* geendet. Das neue Postulat verfehlt seine Wirkung auf

---

[54]  Ibid., pp. 53 f.

die Hervorbringungen nicht. Die Romane werden kürzer, dafür nähert sich die Geltung der Kurzerzählung der des Romans.[55]

[The novel as a form on its backside exposed to death, ending is categorically impossible, until arbiter Beckett in his usual boldness reverses the premise: from now on there is *nothing but* ending. The new postulate does not fail to have its effects on the creations. The novels become shorter, whereas the validity of the short story approaches that of the novel.]

The single work which Laederach refers to most frequently is *Murphy*. While discussing what he calls the "Auslagern der Gefühle [evacuation of emotions]," that is to say, the flight from the here and the now, Laederach names examples: "Beckett schrieb seinen frühen Roman »Murphy« über Gerüsten des Präspinozisten Geulincx. Joyce versenkte sich tief ins Mittelalter, wie uns Umberto Eco in seiner aufschlußreichen Studie zum »Ulysses« nachweist [Beckett wrote his early novel *Murphy* on frameworks taken from the pre-Spinozist Geulincx. Joyce plunged deep down into the middle ages, as Umberto Eco proved us in his informative study on *Ulysses*]" (110). Much later in his book, Laederach again connects Joyce with Beckett, and in a lengthy passage – which includes long quotations both from Beckett's *Murphy* and from the philosophy of Geulincx – describes the step from Joyce's character Murphy (an eloquent old sailor in *Ulysses*) to Beckett's title character:

Es ist, als kämen in der divergierenden Behandlung der Murphy-Figur die entgegengesetzten Temperamente voll zum Zug: das Murphy-Sein wird zur Metapher für den jeweiligen Umgang mit Stil. Joyces Murphy, der Seefahrer, ist eine von vielen Parallelen zum ewigen Juden Bloom, geb. Virag, der auch Sindbad sein kann und doch eher auf einer Stufe mit engerem Horizont lebt [...] Aus dem saftigen Palaverer voll lügenhafter Seemannsgarne wird Becketts nach dem geulincxschen Modell erschaffener Trocken-Murphy. Kann der von Joyce sein Wasser nicht halten, sondern läßt es geräuschvoll schäumend vor dem Pub ab, so hat Becketts Murphy kaum mehr Nieren, ist ausgedörrt und verraucht wie ein altes Tabakblatt. Ebenso verhält es sich mit den wechselseitigen Humoren, die von alters her über den Feuchtigkeitsgrad einer Person Auskunft geben: Joyce läßt brüllend lachen und schaufelt Rabelais' Fleischeslust in die Wortlust hinüber, Beckett läßt kichern, wie Kekse es tun, wenn man sie rechtzeitig bricht.[56]

[It seems as if in the divergent handling of the Murphy character the contrary temperaments come into full swing: Murphy-ness is turned into a metaphor for the respective handling of style. Joyce's Murphy, the sailor, is one of many parallels of the wandering Jew Bloom, née Virag, who could also be Sindbad and yet lives on a level which has a narrow horizon [...] This juicy palaverer, full of

55   Ibid., p. 186.
56   Ibid., pp. 235 f. – I would like to acknowledge Volker Frick's help in locating this quotation.

untrue sailor's yarns, will be turned into a drained Murphy by Beckett according to Geulincx's model. Whereas Joyce's cannot hold his water, but lets it flow foaming noisily outside the pub, Beckett's Murphy has scarcely any kidneys left, is dried up and fumigated like an old tobacco leaf. It is the same with the mutual humours, which from time immemorial are the best indicators of a person's degree of humidity: Joyce causes roaring laughter and shovels Rabelais' carnal lust into verbal lusts, Beckett causes giggles like cookies giggle when cracked in time.]

If Laederach here talks about style and humour, we might point out that, while Laederach's own humour resembles Beckett's in many respects, the former's style (always extremely eloquent and somewhat whizzy) is much more Joycean than Beckettian. It should be added, however, that of all works Beckett published during his lifetime, *Murphy* is the novel approaching Joyce's style the most. Small wonder, then, that this is the book Laederach returns to again and again.

Traces of this preoccupation with *Murphy* also surface in Laederach's next book, a collection of stories entitled *Vor Schrecken starr*. In the story 'Weisman im Hund', a character called Van Heisig utters "etwas, das gekürzt und bearbeitet, zusammengefaßt in der Quintessenz lautete: ich muß dieses Kraut sofort haben, es geht um Leben und Tod [something which, abbreviated and edited, summarised in quintessence reads: I need this weed immediately, it's a matter of life and death]"[57]; Laederach thus quotes a formula used several times by Beckett in *Murphy*: "Celia's account, expurgated, accelerated, improved and reduced, of how she came to have to speak of Murphy, gives the following"[58]. In another story, 'Der Wanderbär im Schweizerbarock', we come across the term "des Syndroms Leben [the syndrome life]"[59]. Again, this is a formula from *Murphy*, where Beckett twice quotes the character Neary's fear that the "syndrome known as life is too diffuse to admit of palliation. For every symptom that is eased, another is made worse. The horse leech's daughter is a closed system. Her quantum of wantum cannot vary"[60]. This formula seems to please Laederach considerably, for he uses it again (if in misquoted form) in a letter written to his friend, the critic and writer Urs Allemann, on 27 December 1988: "Nun darf man Becketts Ökonomie des 'für jeden, der ... hört einer auf, der ...' durchaus zur Kenntnis nehmen. [Well, it really isn't forbidden to take note of Beckett's 'for everyone who ... someone else breaks off who ...']"[61]. In this period, it seems that Laederach is fascinated by Murphy's tragicomic attempts to pacify and sedate his own stirrings of emotion, even if pacification and sedation are obviously far from being Laederach's own aims – he always writes in order to stir and agitate the emotions of his characters as well as his readers. One of the

---

[57] Jürg Laederach, *Vor Schrecken starr: Fixierungen Stechblicke Obsessionen* (Frankfurt am Main: Suhrkamp, 1988), p. 95.
[58] Beckett, *Murphy*, p. 11.
[59] Laederach, *Vor Schrecken starr*, p. 263.
[60] Beckett, *Murphy*, pp. 36, 112.
[61] Urs Allemann / Jürg Laederach, "Das allmähliche Verschwinden des Lesens im Schreiben: Ein Briefwechsel," intro. Hermann Wallmann, *Schreibheft* 33 (May 1989), p. 146.

characters in *Vor Schrecken starr* thus quite characteristically talks of "die Beruhigung, eines meiner schlimmsten Leiden [the pacification, one of my worst sufferings]"[62].

In a review of Flann O'Brien's novel *At Swim-Two-Birds* published on 2 June 1989 by the weekly newspaper *Die Zeit* (and reprinted a few years later in the collection *Eccentric*), Laederach again uses *Murphy* (and in addition, the title of Beckett's later *Texts for Nothing*) in an attempt to describe the artistic consequences of Ireland's many centuries of poverty and foreign rule:

> Texte um Nichts: Dem öffentlich-realen pauperisierenden Zwangssystem ent-spricht eine Prosa, die mittellose Giganten hervorbringt. Ihre Wortgewalt wächst mit ihrer Bedürfnislosigkeit. Im Zustand absoluten und misogynen Bettlertums erreichen sie die höchste Stufe der Sprachbeherrschung. Zu erhaben – und zu spöttisch Blankvers sprechend – um äußere Zwänge auch nur wahrzunehmen, geruhen sie allenfalls, an den inneren zu scheitern. Zur Erinnerung: Bei Beckett, der diese ganzen Philosophien einen Zahn weiter gewendet hat, schützt sich der überall scheiternde Murphy vor weiterem Scheitern nicht etwa durch Anstreben von Erfolg, sondern durch Selbstfesselung an seinen Stuhl; damit muß er sich nicht mehr im Einzel-Scheitern verausgaben, sondern hat sich im Zeichen des Dauer-Scheiterns ruhiggestellt und kann nun in stiller Zufriedenheit leben und formulieren.[63]

> [Texts for Nothing: the public-real pauperising coercive system finds its equi-valent in a prose which produces destitute giants. Their power of expression rises in proportion with their frugality. In a state of absolute and misogynous pauperism they achieve the highest level of linguistic mastery. Much too noble – and speaking blank verse much too mockingly – to even perceive exterior coercion, they at the most condescend to be frustrated by interior ones. Just as a reminder: in Beckett, who turned all these philosophies one cog further, Murphy, failing everywhere, guards himself against further failures not by striving after success but by enchaining himself to his chair; henceforth he does not have to exhaust himself any more by singular acts of failing but has sedated himself under the banner of permanent failure and so can spend his life and language in silent contentedness.]

Consequently, Laederach conceives Flann O'Brien as a writer "der, Joycescher Erwei-terung und Beckettscher Verknappung so (platonisch) zugeneigt wie (real) abhold, im Schatten der beiden Extreme seinen eigenen, zu Unrecht verdeckten Weg ging [who, (platonically) inclined as well as (actually) averse to both Joycean expansion and

---

62  Laederach, *Vor Schrecken starr*, p. 349.

63  Jürg Laederach, *Eccentric: Kunst und Leben: Figuren der Seltsamkeit* (Frankfurt am Main: Suhr-kamp, 1995), p. 215.

Beckettian scarcity, in the shadow of both extremes went his own unjustly hidden way]"[64].

It seems that at this point in his artistic development, Laederach himself, although "(platonically) inclined" towards Beckett, decides to stay "(actually) averse" – from now on, references to Beckett occur considerably less frequently in Laederach's works. Although in the bulky novel *Emanuel* (which Laederach regarded as his *opus magnum*) "Belacqua Shuah, eine von Becketts ersten Figuren [Belacqua Shuah, one of Beckett's earliest characters]"[65] and the (apparently again *Murphy*-related) "dunklere Hälfte von Becketts Geist [darker half of Beckett's mind]"[66] are mentioned, there is no deeper-reaching involvement with Beckett here; the one possible exception being the ironic realisation "ÜBER etwas schreiben gibt mehr her, etwas schreiben ist einfältig, also schreibt man über das, was man gerade schreibt [writing ABOUT something makes more of a show, writing something is silly, hence one writes about that which one is just writing]"[67]. This may or may not be a comment on Beckett's early statement in his "Dante ... Bruno . Vico .. Joyce" that Joyce's "writing is not *about* something; *it is that something itself*"[68]. Furthermore, there are no discernable Beckettian traces in the 1993 novel *Passion*, the 1994 collection of stories *Schattenmänner*, nor Laederachs' second collection of "minimal plays" from 2003, *In Hackensack*. Such a silence may perhaps be due to the fact that in the early 1990s Laederach's attention shifted to less innovative writers, notably Harold Brodkey, with whom Laederach both collaborated as a translator and met with frequently during this period.

Laederach's shift of attention can be at least partly fathomed by reading *Eccentric*, his collection of reviews, portraits and essays from these years. In a portrait of Brodkey written presumably in late 1991, Laederach reports that Brodkey respects Joyce's *A Portrait of the Artist as a Young Man*, but not Joyce's later works, and definitely not Beckett:

> Brodkeys Ansichten sind denn auch eine Mischung. Er ist ein glühender Beckett-Gegner. Samuel Beckett wird als »Absolutist« beschimpft, der eine alternativlose Welt konstruiere, während er, Brodkey, mit dem, was er schreibe, niemals recht haben wolle, sondern nur eine Möglichkeit der Welt hinstelle, sich anderer Möglichkeiten immer bewußt sei, höflich auch an andere Weltauffassungen zumindest denke. Beckett lasse nicht von seinem moralischen Anspruch, verspüre geradezu eine Wut bei der Verkündung von Freude.[69]

> [Brodkey's opinions really are a curious mixture. He is a passionate adversary of Beckett's. Samuel Beckett is abused as being an 'absolutist' who constructs a

---

[64]  Ibid., p. 218.
[65]  Jürg Laederach, *Emanuel: Wörterbuch des hingerissenen Flaneurs* (Frankfurt am Main: Suhrkamp, 1990), p. 494.
[66]  Ibid., p. 498.
[67]  Ibid., p. 192.
[68]  Beckett, "Dante ... Bruno . Vico .. Joyce," p. 27.
[69]  Laederach, *Eccentric*, p. 274.

world without alternatives, while he, Brodkey, never wants to be right with what he's writing but merely suggests one possibility of the world, is always conscious of other possibilities, at least courteously thinks of other concepts of the world. Beckett, he says, does not desist from his moralistic pretension, indeed gets furious when announcing joy.]

This, however, should not be mistaken as being Laederach's own position – he still retains his admiration for Beckett, as other texts in the collection show. Laederach not only praises Beckett's self-handicapping techniques when working for the stage[70] and quotes the slogan at the end of *Watt*, "No symbols where none intended"[71], but also – on the occasion of a seemingly post-Beckettian novel by Kobo Abe – states that Beckett is "soviel besser [so much better]" than his younger inheritors[72].

Another book review, written after the completion of *Eccentric* and published in October 1995 in the theatre review *Theater heute*, is even more important – this is a review of Beckett's first (and only posthumously published) play *Eleutheria*; it is the only text by Laederach dealing exclusively with Beckett. Apart from a detailed retelling of the play's plot, Laederach (who explicitly mentions *Endgame, Stirrings Still, Waiting for Godot, Krapp's Last Tape* and Deirdre Bair's Beckett biography, if only in passing) sums up Beckett's career in an illuminating way:

> Zeitlebens schrieb Beckett nicht nur Texte, er erfand immer auch die Formen, in welche er die Texte goß; diesen Formfindungen haftete etwas Strenges, Diktiertes und nach außen Dikatorisches an. Die bevorzugten Schreibfarben zuerst probeweise und in grosser Menge auf einer Palette angerührt, dann folgerichtig kontrolliert, ausgeschieden, weggeworfen, einen Bruchteil davon zum Schluß verwendet. In dem Maße, wie seine Texte souveräner wurden, wurde sein Baukasten perfekter, aber, dies der Preis: fester eingerichtet, an Teilen knapper, Fortsetzungs-ärmer.[73]

> [All his life Beckett not only wrote texts but always also invented the forms into which to cast these texts; these forms were marked by something austere, dictated and – when seen from the outside – dictatorial. First by way of trial mixing the preferred colours of writing on the pallet, then consistently controlling, eliminating, throwing away, finally using just a fraction of these. In the same measure as his texts grew more sovereign, his building set grew more perfect, but, this being the price to pay: more fixedly arranged, with fewer parts, sequel-poorer.]

On the basis of this conception of Beckett's *oeuvre* as a whole, Laederach, after being confronted with *Eleutheria*, asks the following question: "Gibt es das? Einen form-

---

70  See ibid., pp. 37 f.
71  Ibid., p. 248.
72  Ibid., p. 62.
73  Jürg Laederach, "Salonkomödie und Säurebad: Über Samuel Becketts nachgelassenes Stück 'Eleutheria'," *Theater heute* 10 (October 1995), p. 1.

vergessenen, gleichsam urschreienden Beckett als Master of Chaos? Großartige Steigerung bei Ultimo (das erste Stück gedacht als letztes Stück) oder nur zersetzendes Säurebad eines Alptraums? [Is this possible? A form-forgetful, quasi primalscreaming Beckett as master of chaos? Grandiose cumulation at ultimo (the first play conceived as the last play) or just the decomposing acid bath of a nightmare?]"[74]. Laederach implies that this is exactly what we find in *Eleutheria*: a non-Beckettian Beckett – and Laederach apparently likes this idea very much. He summarises what he conceives as the main achievement of Beckett's premature play: "Becketts Kunst setzt dem bürgerlichen Leben die Segnungen absoluten und schmutzigsten Elends sowie die entflammte Begierde nach ebendiesem Elend entgegen [Beckett's art confronts bourgeois life with the benedictions of absolute and filthiest squalor as well as the inflamed desire for exactly this squalor]"[75].

With these words of praise ends the story of Laederach's public comments on Beckett – this, however, is primarily due to the fact that after 1995 (caused by his decision to leave his publishing house and also by a series of severe health problems) Laederach has published next to nothing, except for translations of works by writers such as Walter Abish, John Hawkes and Maurice Blanchot.

As can be seen from the inventory of references to Beckett given above, the climax of Laederach's literary reactions to Beckett was reached in the late 1980s. By favourable coincidence, this was the time when Laederach began an extensive correspondence with me, prompted by my first two reviews of his books.[76] Since Beckett was a topic in many of the letters exchanged between us, I would like to briefly detail at least some of Laederach's remarks, which shed further light on his view of Beckett. It should be noted that, in most cases, Laederach's comments were occasioned by topics first addressed in my own letters (I frequently talked about my own work on Beckett, or sent Laederach my Beckett-related publications), so the focus of attention is not necessarily always defined by Laederach's own interests.

On 2 June 1988, for example, after I had disclosed my own fascination with Beckett, Laederach mentioned Deirdre Bair's life of Beckett, judging: "Fand ich sehr spannend wegen der guten Dokumentation, auch wenn's in der Textanalyse meist unhaltbar war. Wird wohl nie auf Deutsch erscheinen, da's möglicherweise Old Sam nervte. [Found it very thrilling because of the good documentation, although mostly untenable in textual analysis. Will probably never come out in German, since it possibly annoyed Old Sam]." On 26 June, after having been told about Beckett's remarks on "Mrs Bair's flights of

---

[74] Ibid., p. 5.

[75] Ibid.

[76] Friedhelm Rathjen, "Literatur-Recycling: 'Flugelmeyers Wahn': Roman von Jürg Laederach," *Frankfurter Rundschau* 227 (1 October 1986), literary supplement, p. 4; and Friedhelm Rathjen, "Dozentur des Chaos-Forschers: Jürg Laederachs Poetik-Vorlesung 'Der zweite Sinn'," *Frankfurter Rundschau* 73 (26 March 1988), p. 2; both reviews rpt. as parts of "Alle Tasten im Schrank: Jürg Laederach," *Das war's. Strandfunde am Meer des Lesens: Rezensionen zur deutschsprachigen Literatur 1984-2007* (Scheeßel: Edition ReJoyce, 2009), pp. 65-84, pp. 65-69.

fancy"[77], Laederach added: "das Buch ist schwachsinnig, das fand ich bereits heraus. Sam Beckett will eben selber Mythos sein und keine Zweit-Mythologin ranlassen. Dabei fand ich ihren Abschnitt über das Exil im Roussillon glänzend. Eigentlich genügt Becketts SoWarEsNicht nicht [the book is moronic, this much I've found out already. Of course Sam Beckett wants to be a myth himself and not let a second-hand mythologess enter the game. For all that, I found her section on his exile in Roussillon brilliant. Actually Beckett's ItWasNotSo does not really suffice]." At this time, Laederach apparently enjoyed reading about literary lives; he repeatedly recommended Richard Ellmann's biography of Oscar Wilde to me, explaining in a letter of 12 September 1988 that, although Wilde's *oeuvre* is fairly mediocre, his life is absorbing:

> Wir wollen doch aber keine Sekunde mit Beckett vergleichen, das ergibt rein nichts, Beckett kann ja schreiben, und Bair fand ich ungeheuer. Ich warte noch immer auf den Regietitan, der uns die paar Seitelchen von 'Ohio Improptu' formvollendet auf die Bühne legt. Aber eben da kneifense alle. Es ist bei Sam sowiewo furchtbar, wie viel grösseren Mehrwert die Stücke in der reinen Notation entfalten als aufgeführt. Die Prosa ist dem Theater rücksichtslos überlegen, aber ich sitze da und hoffe trotzdem.

> [Not even for a second, though, dare we compare with Beckett, this leads to nothing, Beckett can write, after all, and I found Bair monstrous. I'm still waiting for the giant director who will present us the few pages of *Ohio Impromptu* perfect in form on stage. This, however, is where they all dodge. With Sam the dreadful thing anyway is that the plays unfurl so much more surplus value in pure notation than they do when staged. The prose is inconsiderately superior to the theatre, but here I sit and go on hoping all the same.]

Apart from Bair's biography (and my own publications, of course), no secondary sources on Beckett are ever mentioned in Laederach's letters. The range of Beckett's works referred to by Laederach, on the other hand, is quite wide, and includes *Stirrings Still* (19 March 1989, 20 April 1989), *More Pricks than Kicks* (12 June 1989), *Cascando* (6 October 1989), *Worstward Ho* (6 November 1989, 24 June 1992) and *Eleutheria* (12 July 1995, 17 December 1995). Generally, Laederach seems to be more interested in Beckett the prose writer than in Beckett the dramatist; the one instance where he finds mildly critical words for Beckett concerns his opposition to unfaithful stage productions:

> Schade dass Sam es nimmer played again. Becketts Verstummen dürfte zwar das werk-logischste der Literaturgeschichte sein, allein ich könnt ihn ewig reden hören. Sein Regieanweisungs-Fimmel ist etwas museal, das muss man zugeben, und die Stücke werden, einmal davon befreit, ihre enorme fantasiezeugende Kraft entfalten: wohl auch wieder nicht immer zum eignen Vorteil. Aber in dubio pro

---

[77]    Samuel Beckett, Letter to Friedhelm Rathjen, 19 April 1986.

theatro: man muss die Bühnenfritzen wohl eher machen lassen, als dass man sie in Korsette zwängt.

[It's a pity that Sam never played it again. Although Beckett's becoming silent seems inherent in his work and thus to be the most logical in the history of literature, I could hear him talk on forever. His illiberal stagedirectorial craze is somewhat antediluvian, this we have to admit, and the plays will, as soon as they are liberated from it, enfold their enormous imagination-creating power: probably not always only to their own advantage. But in dubio pro theatro: it seems you should let the stageguys do their thing instead of forcing them into corsets.][78]

After having received and read my comparative study on Beckett and Arno Schmidt, Laederach emphasised the differences between both writers:

Der frappanteste Unterschied zwischen Schmidt und Beckett liegt dann in den Zitaten. Du behandelst sie als vergleichbar. Wenn man aber die Auszüge von dem einen konfrontiert sieht mit jenen vom anderen, dann greift man sich an den Schädel und fragt sich, wie weit denn Texte überhaupt auseinanderliegen können. Ich denke ja, dass diese Zugehörigkeit eines Autors zur Moderne – und ein andrer gehört dann auch dazu – Aehnlichkeiten festschreibt, die doch gar nicht bestehen. Also wenn das nun nicht die in der Lit.geschichte verankerten Marken Schmidt und Beckett wären, die, wie man historisch weiss, eindeutig miteinander – auch in Ablehnung – verbunden sind, käme wohl niemand auf die Idee, da einen Vergleich anzustellen.[79]

[The most striking difference, then, between Schmidt and Beckett is visible in the quotations. You treat them as commensurable. If you see the excerpts from the one chap confronted with those from the other one, you can only grasp your head and ask yourself if texts can really be so far apart from each other. I really think that this affiliation of an author to modernism – and then there's another one who also falls into that category – fixes similarities that in reality don't exist. Well, if this weren't the trademarks Schmidt and Beckett, both embedded in literary history and, as we historically know, definitely connected – if in refusal – with each other, surely nobody would come up with the idea to venture a comparison.]

This leads Laederach to complain about the dilemma contemporary authors (himself included) have to face when writing in full consciousness of the works of Beckett and Joyce:

---

[78]     Jürg Laederach, Letter to Friedhelm Rathjen, 11 January 1989.

[79]     Laederach, Letter to Friedhelm Rathjen, 26 November 1990. The book in question is Friedhelm Rathjen, *Reziproke Radien: Arno Schmidt und Samuel* Beckett (Munich: edition text + kritik 1990).

Mich macht die Grundästhetik sowieso wahnsinnig: der eine, Schoiss oder wie er heisst, Schoissel also schreibt literarisch perfekt 'über alles schlechthin'. Der nächste, dieser Bäckert, schreibt literarisch ebenso perfekt 'über nichts, vielleicht noch weniger'. Welche Positionen bleiben den Nachgeborenen noch übrig? Man muss sich in die Liffi stürzen in Döbling.[80]

[The fundamental aesthetics drives me mad anyway: the first one, Choyce or whatever he's called, Choycel then writes with literary perfection 'about everything in general.' The next one, that Bakert, writes with equal literary perfection 'about nothing, perhaps even less.' What positions are left over to the posthumous at all? You have to drown yourself in the Liffie in Döbling.]

This point was also stressed by Laederach during a public discussion with his colleague Matthias Politycki and myself in September 1989, when he complained about modernism being perceived in a distorted shape by the public and invariably linked to just a few canonical names: "Die Moderne [...] ist in ungenügendler Weise selbstverständlich geworden; dadurch hat sie sozusagen nur einen Fuß in die Tür reingebracht. [...] Dann läßt sich an jedem Text, der eine sogenannte avantgardistische Auffälligkeit besitzt, ein Ahnvater herleiten, und es ist immer eine dieser fünf Zehen. [Modernism [...] has become self-evident in an insufficient way; so that it has managed to get just one foot through the door. [...] And now for each and every text showing a so-called avandgardist peculiarity a forefather can be named, and it's always one of these five toes]".[81] Among the "toes" Laederach names here are both Joyce and Beckett.

Being a part-time translator himself, Laederach occasionally comments upon the quality of Beckett translations into German. On 12 June 1989, he bemoaned Christian Enzensberger's recently published German version of Beckett's *More Pricks than Kicks*: "Ich finde die Übers. von "Prügel + Flügel" entsätzlich! Kann es fast nicht lesen, Heil Tophoven [I find the trans. of *Pricks + Kicks* horrible! Nearly can't read it, hail Tophoven]." The name "Tophoven" here refers to Elmar but apparently not to Erika Tophoven, as Laederach's remarks in a letter of 6 November 1989, after having checked her German version of *Worstward Ho*, indicates:

Wichtig: die Uebersetzung der Frau Tophofer [sic] ist unselig schlecht. Es ist eine andere Schlechtigkeit als die Ch.Enzensbergersche, of course, aber ich war entsätzt, wiesehr sich der gloriose Bäckerett unter ihren Händen verformt hat, da war der selige Elmar besser, vor allem würdiger. Puckett braucht stilistischen Glanz, sonst ist alles verloren. Ich mich bewerben?

---

[80] Laederach, Letter to Friedhelm Rathjen, 26 November 1990.

[81] Friedhelm Rathjen, "Politach und Laederycki in Bückeburg: Mit einem Auftritt des gasförmigen Wirbeltiers," *Der Ernst des Lesens: Beinharte Forschung zu Arno Schmidt & Consorten* (Scheeßel: Edition ReJoyce, 2006), pp. 15-26, p. 21. This is not a faithful report but rather a heavily fictionalised version of our public discussion; all statements by Jürg Laederach and Matthias Politycki included in the text, however, are reproduced here *verbatim*.

[Important: the translation of this Frau Tophofer [sic] is wretchedly bad. It is quite another badness than the Ch.Enzensbergerian, of course, but I was horrified how much glorious Bakerett was deformed under her hands, blessed Elmar was definitely better, and in particular more worthy. Puckett needs stylistic brilliancy, otherwise everything is lost. I myself apply?]

Laederach never officially 'applied' for the post of Beckett's German translator, but he did indeed translate one of his works. In a letter written to me on 12 July 1995 he stated: "Ich sattelte zwischendurch kurz den Gaul und übersetzte im Sololauf Becketts frühestes Stück 'Eleutheria' (postum), leider hatte der Verlag schon mit einem anderen Uebersetzer ausgemacht, sodass die Mühe [...] vergebens war. [Meanwhile I briefly saddled my horse and in solo run translated Beckett's earliest play *Eleutheria* (posthumous), unfortunately the publisher had already arranged with another translator, so that the effort [...] was in vain]". Unfortunately this translation of *Eleutheria* by Laederach has remained unpublished to date.[82] But at least some of its qualities may be deducted from a question Laederach formulates in expectation of Simon Werle's official German version of *Eleutheria*:

> Die Frage wird sein, ob er so'n knappes, sehr gut konstruiertes Deutsch wählt, den 'edlen Satz', oder eher nen Stil, der sowas wie Geschwätzigkeit transportiert. Ich tat eher das zweite, es ist ja je nachdem, ob du Eleutheria als eine Ausgeburt von Weisheit oder von Palaver siehst, d.h. ob du das Stück pur Auge-auf-Text liest oder immer Grand Sam dahinter ehrst.[83]

> [The question will be if he choses a concise, very well constructed kind of German, the 'noble sentence,' or rather a style which transports something like loquaciousness. I more or less did the latter, of course it depends on whether you take Eleutheria as a product of wisdom or of palaver, i.e., whether you read the play purely eye-upon-text or always venerate Grand Sam behind.]

Laederach's review of *Eleutheria* ('Salonkomödie und Säurebad') was written before Werle's German version became available and therefore does not address questions of translation.

The fact that Jürg Laederach – without being commissioned to do so – decided to translate one of Beckett's most voluminous works reveals the degree of admiration involved here. Another fact is, perhaps, even more telling. In early 1989, after I had sent him a photocopy of Beckett's *Stirrings Still* as printed in a British newspaper (*The Guardian*), Laederach undertook the task to typewrite the complete text on his computer in order to have a neat printout, which he then returned to me with the comment that the text is "ganz großartig, von den kürzeren einer der besten [absolutely brilliant, one of the best of the shorter ones]." Full of admiration, he adds: "Die Technik, Sprache,

---

82    A copy of the typescript donated by Friedhelm Rathjen to James Knowlson is archived by the Beckett International Foundation, University of Reading, as UoR MS 4801.

83    Laederach, Letter to Friedhelm Rathjen, 17 December 1995.

Wörter abzufeilen, bis sie alle gleich klingen, ist ungeheuer. Manchmal scheint es, als gäbs ein ostinato, dabei erzählt er munter vom Erzählen weiter [The technique to file off language, words, until they all sound alike, is monstrous. Sometimes it seems like there will be an ostinato, but jauntily he goes on narrating of narration]."[84] Apparently, this is what Laederach cherishes most in Beckett's *oeuvre*: the ability to achieve virtuosity by way of impoverishment. For on yet another occasion, he called Beckett's prose "dichter, dichter [denser, denser]."[85]

It should be noted, however, that what Laederach seems to admire most in Beckett is not what he practices himself in his prose; Beckett is admired but not aped. Laederach's own artistic virtuosity is never achieved by means of impoverishment: it always relies on the density of a verbally rich and linguistically polymorphic texture. In a speech held in honour of being awarded the Italo Svevo Prize in 2005, Laederach (without openly referring to Beckett) briefly stated what differentiated him from his admired colleague: "Ich bin kein Reduktionist, außer man, das heißt die formalen Umständen zwingen mich. Ich erzähle auch keine Geschichten, außer man findet dies; von diesem Finden bin ich abhängig [I am not a reductionist, unless I'm forced to be one – which means: forced by the formal circumstances. Neither do I narrate stories, unless it is decided that I do; I am dependent on this decision]."[86] This sounds something like a reformulation of what Laederach had already written to me on 12 February 1990, after I had missed a certain textual tightness in his hefty novel *Emanuel*: "Dass ein 500-Seiter halt was von Strategie an sich hat, kann ich nicht ändern. Idealiter würde man einen komplett durchgearbeiteten 25-Seiter veröffentlichen. Oder, wie Sam, 7 Seiten, eher still als stirring. Aber dazu muss ich erst 75 sein [That a 500-pager really has something of a strategy, I cannot prevent. Ideally one would publish a thoroughly and completely worked through 25-pager. Or, like Sam, 7 pages, rather still than stirring. But in order to do so I'll have to turn 75 first]." Now, 17 years later, it seems that Laederach (who, meanwhile, has not turned 75 but at least entered his seventh decade) has followed the example of Beckett's attempts to approach silence in a much more rigid manner than he may have previously expected: Laederach has more or less given up publishing. Which is a pity – after all, in his most productive years, Laederach was one of the strongest writers attempting to face the overwhelming influence of both Joyce and Beckett, and to nevertheless avoid epigonism. Laederach, even though writing more in the Joycean than in the Beckettian tradition, knew quite well that as one of the most creative writers of the twentieth century, Beckett was both on a par with Joyce and a counter figure to him – and that everyone else had to find his or her place somewhere in between.

---

[84]   Ibid., 19 March 1989.
[85]   Ibid., 25 January 1992.
[86]   Jürg Laederach, "Du hast. Du haast. Du Hase: Ansprache eines Gehetzten – über Sumo-Ringer, Wiener Schnitzel und den großen Schriftsteller Italo Svevo," *Die Zeit* 17 (21 April 2005), available at: <http://www.zeit.de/2005/17/Svevo-Rede>.

James Joyce in der
# ƎDITION ReJOYCE

Als limitierte Ausgaben sind noch erhältlich:

James Joyce:
*Winnegans Fake. Aus dem Spätwerk.*
Herausgegeben und übersetzt
von Friedhelm Rathjen.
ISBN 978-3-00-037359-6,
302 Seiten, € 50,-.

Passagen aus *Finnegans Wake* und zwei
kleinere Texte im Stil des *Wake*,
präsentiert im Original und in
deutscher Übersetzung. Die Ausgabe
ist limitiert auf 111 numerierte und
vom Übersetzer signierte Exemplare.

James Joyce:
*Irland auf der Anklagebank. Reportagen
aus der irischen Wirklichkeit.*
Herausgegeben und übersetzt
von Friedhelm Rathjen.
ISBN 978-3-00-042744-2,
160 Seiten, € 35,-.

Reportagen zur Kultur, Literatur und
Politik Irlands aus der Zeitung *Il
Piccolo della Sera*, präsentiert im italie-
nischen Original und in deutscher
Übersetzung. Die Ausgabe ist limitiert
auf 111 numerierte und vom Übersetzer signierte Exemplare.

Details im Internet: http://tinyurl.com/22fybo — Bestellungen und Anfragen an: rejoyce@gmx.de

James Joyce in der
# ƎDITION ReJOYCE

Als limitierte Ausgaben sind noch erhältlich:

James Joyce:
*Mamalujo.*
Drei Fassungen eines Kapitels
aus *Finnegans Wake.*
Herausgegeben und übersetzt
von Friedhelm Rathjen.
ISBN 978-3-00-047620-4,
156 Seiten, € 35,-.

Alle Fassungen des ersten Kapitels
aus *Finnegans Wake*, das Joyce schrieb,
präsentiert im Original und in deutscher Übersetzung. Die Ausgabe ist
limitiert auf 111 numerierte und vom
Übersetzer signierte Exemplare.

James Joyce:
*Earwicker.*
Fünf Fassungen eines Kapitels
aus *Finnegans Wake.*
Herausgegeben und übersetzt
von Friedhelm Rathjen.
ISBN 978-3-00-049245-7,
156 Seiten, € 35,-.

Alle Fassungen jenes Kapitels aus
*Finnegans Wake*, mit dem Joyce seinen
Helden fand, präsentiert im Original
und in deutscher Übersetzung. Die
Ausgabe ist limitiert auf 111 nume-
rierte und vom Übersetzer signierte
Exemplare.